whose Goals whose Aspirations?

LEARNING TO TEACH UNDERPREPARED WRITERS ACROSS THE CURRICULUM

Stephen M. Fishman
Lucille McCarthy

UTAH STATE UNIVERSITY PRESS
Logan, Utah

Utah State University Press
Logan, Utah 84322-7800

Manufactured in the United States of America.
Cover design and typography by The Visual Pair LLC.

An earlier version of Chapter 2 appeared in *Written Communication, 18.2*, 180–228.

Library of Congress Cataloging-in-Publication Data

Fishman, Stephen M.
   Whose goals? Whose aspirations? : learning to teach underprepared
writers across the curriculum / Stephen M. Fishman, Lucille McCarthy.
      p. cm.
Includes bibliographical references and index.
   ISBN 0-87421-447-5 (alk. paper)
   1. English language—Rhetoric—Study and teaching—United States.
2. Report writing—Study and teaching (Higher)—United States.
3. Interdisciplinary approach in education—United States.
4. Minorities—Education (Higher)—United States. 5. Multicultural
education—United States. 6. Language and culture—United States.
7. Remedial teaching—United States. 8. Education—Aims and objectives.
I. McCarthy, Lucille Parkinson, 1944– II. Title.
  PE1405.U6 F57 2002
  808'.0071'1073—dc21
                           2002007110

WE DEDICATE THIS BOOK TO OUR PARENTS

BIRDIE AND IRVING FISHMAN

AMY AND ROBERT PARKINSON

WHOSE LOVE FOR THEIR CHILDREN KNEW NO BOUNDS.

Contents

Acknowledgments

Teachers of underprepared college writers are a special breed, a committed and caring group whose work often takes place at the margins of the university yet carries out one of its central missions. We wish to thank a number of these teachers who have taken time from their busy schedules to share their expertise. We are grateful to Linda Adler-Kassner, Russel Durst, Peter Elbow, Keith Gilyard, Eli Goldblatt, Joseph Harris, Eleanor Kutz, Min-Zhan Lu, Deborah Mutnick, Marilyn Sternglass, and Patricia Stock for generative conversations about our project and the field of basic writing. We also thank Vivian Zamel and Ruth Spack for their enthusiastic invitation to study ESL students. It was their push in this direction that led us to write the second chapter of this book. In addition, for their help with theorizing our study, we are indebted to George Demetrion, David Russell, and Ira Shor who guided our entry into the worlds of Freire, Gramsci, and Whiteness studies. And special thanks go to Chris Anson, Gregory Glau, Donald McCrary, Ira Shor, Marilyn Sternglass, and Kathleen Weiler who read drafts of our manuscript at various points and gave us valuable feedback. In an environment that is often highly competitive, each of these colleagues has set a high standard for generosity, strengthening our faith in what is best about the academic community.

We are also indebted to generous colleagues at our home institutions. At the University of North Carolina Charlotte, Steve Fishman thanks his chair, William Gay, and his dean, Schley Lyons, for supporting his request for a semester's leave to write portions of this book. In addition, Steve acknowledges his longtime colleague in the philosophy department, Michael Eldridge, for his part in their ongoing, productive dialogue about John Dewey. At the University of Maryland Baltimore County, Lucille McCarthy's department chairs, Kenneth Baldwin and James McKusick, have gone out of their way on numerous occasions to facilitate her participation in this project. For their encouragement and support, she is most grateful.

Finally, we thank Michael Spooner and his staff at Utah State University Press for their thoughtful assistance throughout the publication process.

SURRENDER OF WHAT IS POSSESSED, disowning of what supports one in secure ease, is involved in all inquiry and discovery; the latter implicate an individual still to make, with all the risks implied therein. For to arrive at new truth and vision is to alter. The old self is put off and the new self is only forming, and the form it finally takes will depend upon the unforeseeable result of an adventure.

John Dewey (1925/1989, p. 201)

CHAPTER ONE

Introduction: A Kaleidoscope of Conflict

Although the immediate focus of this book is learning to teach underprepared writers in college classes, it raises and explores two of the major questions facing public education as we begin the 21st century: Whose goals should schools pursue? Whose aspirations should they honor? These questions go back at least as far as Horace Mann's defense of the "common school" in the mid-19th century, but they have drawn increasing attention during the last 45 years as our pupil population has grown more diverse. The myriad answers that have historically been given to these questions are sortable into four general categories of goals: student career preparation, exploration of cultural knowledge, promotion of social reform, and student personal growth (see Bowles & Gintis, 1976; Dewey, 1916/1967; Kliebard, 1995; Spring, 1996).

This book narrates the struggles of a college philosophy teacher— Steve Fishman, one of the co-authors—to respond to our title questions as he encounters underprepared writers who challenge his normal teaching practices. As we will see, these questions about appropriate school aims do not lead Fishman to simple, either/or responses. Rather, Steve must decide to what extent he should support students' careerist aspirations and to what extent he should maintain his own differing goals. That is, Steve's pupils, by and large, see school as vocational preparation and their degrees as tools for professional advancement. By contrast, his own aims and aspirations as a philosophy teacher emphasize, first and foremost, exploration of the Western cultural heritage and then, in lesser degrees, promotion of social reform, student personal growth, and student career preparation. This disjunction between Fishman's and his students' educational goals frequently leads to clashes that impede pupil learning and force Steve to consider ways he can modify his classroom objectives without surrendering what he considers his central mission as an instructor of philosophy.

The decisions Fishman makes, as we will show, are not always in line with what his students want. Nor do they always please his co-author, Lucille McCarthy, a composition researcher and longtime observer of his classroom. However, as we will also show, since answers to our basic questions are not either/or, Steve and his students sometimes discover that their complex aspirations overlap. On such occasions, they are able to sufficiently soften their differences to fashion some shared objectives and participate in a community of collaborative inquiry.

Because the perspectives of teacher, students, and outside researcher sometimes coincide but often clash, the report we present is indeterminate. That is, rather than privileging one point of view while silencing others, we make space for competing perspectives: for example, student's careerism as well as Fishman's disciplinary commitments, McCarthy's Freirian radicalism as well as Fishman's Deweyan gradualism. In trying to understand and position these diverse viewpoints, we are led to interrogate the ways that Steve Fishman's identity as a White, Euroamerican, middle-class teacher affects his classroom goals, featured literacies, and relations with students. Our study of a teacher and his novice writers, thus, brings us face to face with broader issues of multiculturalism, race cognizance, and social class.

THE AUDIENCE FOR THIS BOOK

This book is intended for all teachers who, like Fishman, find that because of changing student demographics they no longer can assume that their pupils think and speak just like they do. That is, they cannot assume their students' answers to the basic questions we have raised about the function of public schools match their own. Thus, we believe our account of Fishman's efforts to bridge the gap between himself and his pupils—a gap that Freire (1970/1997) famously calls the teacher-student contradiction—is potentially useful for teachers in a wide variety of settings.

An important subset of our teacher audience is composition specialists. A number of scholars in the composition field have called for studies like the present one of underprepared writers' experiences in courses across the curriculum (see Belcher & Braine, 1995; Gilyard, 1997; Guerra, 1997; Hirvela, 1999; Leki, 1992; Royster & Taylor, 1997; Spack, 1997; Sternglass, 1997; Zamel, 1995). They make this request for two reasons. First, writing teachers need information about what goes on in discipline-based courses if they are to prepare their composition students for subsequent academic writing.

Second, such studies help compositionists better advise, consult, and workshop with discipline-based teachers like Fishman. Compositionists' ability to help instructors in the disciplines is important because it is widely agreed that if underprepared students are to develop academic literacy, they must write across their college years. And, given recent proposals from both the political left and right for jettisoning remedial writing classes at the university—and some schools, like the City University of New York actually doing it—increased numbers of inexperienced writers are likely to appear in discipline-based classrooms (see Gleason, 2000; Greenberg, 1993, 1997; Shor, 1997; Soliday, 1996, 1999; Stygall, 1999; Wiener, 1998.)

One specific way our study can help compositionists more fruitfully advise professors across the curriculum is that it informs them about the context in which discipline-based instructors encounter underprepared writers: a setting very different from remedial and first-year composition courses. For example, in Fishman's philosophy classes, like many in the disciplines, students must engage with difficult texts, a challenge that can be especially daunting for underprepared writers. In addition, students come to Fishman's class without label or pretesting. This makes it quite likely that when he approaches underprepared writers regarding the quality of their work, he brings unwanted, unpleasant, and highly charged news. Finally, novice writers are, in his philosophy classes, few in number. Sometimes there may be only one in a class of 25, at other times, three or four, but never more than a small percentage. This, plus the fact that he must teach his philosophy curriculum, makes it difficult to require the sort of helpful class-wide assignments—for example, comparison of oral and written discourse, study of students' different home and community languages, instruction in writing mechanics —which can be major foci of composition instruction (see Campbell, 1997; Dean, 1986/1999; Kutz, Groden, & Zamel, 1993; Zamel, 1995). Therefore Fishman, like most teachers in the disciplines, must figure out how to bridge the gap between himself and underprepared writers while still offering a course that is faithful to his discipline's historic texts and literacy practices. As we will report, sometimes Fishman succeeds in bridging this gap in whole class activities, and at other times he and his students make progress in one-on-one tutorials.

In short, underprepared writers' progress depends upon their writing in courses beyond the composition classroom, and their success in subsequent courses in the academic disciplines depends upon content-area instructors providing appropriate support. With information of the sort our book presents, compositionists will be better able to recommend to these instructors potentially useful teaching techniques. Our fear is that in the absence of such advice, professors in the disciplines may find it all too easy to dismiss their novice writers as incompetent or unmotivated.

HOW THIS STUDY BEGAN

This study began with an arresting classroom event. Fishman's fall 1998 Introduction to Philosophy class presented him with several students whose writing was so far from what he saw as the norm that he found himself at a loss about how to respond to them. Given his longstanding commitment to employ writing as a tool for learning in his classes, his initial confusion about how to relate these students' literacies to the discourse of philosophy caused him to reflect upon his experiences in his university's writing across the curriculum (WAC) program.

When Fishman thought back on the dozen or more WAC workshops he had attended since 1983, he realized that there had been no discussion of underprepared writers. Further, when he asked people at conferences of English teachers (e.g., NCTE) and educational researchers (e.g., AERA), they were unable to point to research that might help instructors in the disciplines deal with novice writers. Although the experts Fishman talked to had little advice for him, they were quick to admit that he was not alone. For example, the director of the writing lab at Fishman's own school—UNC Charlotte—told him that many teachers across the disciplines were "pulling their hair out" about the inexperienced writers in their classes. Unable to get help from colleagues, Fishman asked McCarthy to join him in studying his own classroom. This book is the result.

DEFINING "UNDERPREPARED WRITER"

In composition studies, underprepared writers are defined as those students who, as a result of their initial placement tests, are typically assigned to remedial and ESL composition classes. However, since students in Fishman's philosophy courses appear without designation, he uses the term in a different way: to single out, in his own mind, pupils whose lack of experience reading and writing in the so-called standard code puts them at a disadvantage in his classroom. Although he is the sole person making the judgment—one based on early-in-the-semester homework papers—he believes it is not an arbitrary one. He makes this judgment when, because of numerous rhetorical and mechanical mismanagements, he cannot figure out what students are trying to say. That is, he cannot understand their contentions or the ways they are attempting to support them.

But why bother characterizing pupils in a philosophy class as novice writers at all, especially since Fishman never mentions it to the students themselves? He answers that the designation is helpful because it places underprepared writers in the context of 35 years of research by compositionists into basic writing. Fishman has in mind, for example, Shaughnessy's (1977) finding that many underprepared students "resent and resist" their vulnerability as in-school writers (p. 10). He also has in mind Grego and Thompson's (1996) generalization: "Without language to express their struggles as part of the intellectual scene of the academy, students express these struggles often as isolated feelings and emotions: anger, frustration, the desire for success" (p. 71). Using these sorts of generalizations to contextualize novice writers and their compositions makes them and their work seem less mysterious to Fishman and suggests a wider repertoire of teacherly strategies than would otherwise be available to him.

Although these observations about novice writers increase Fishman's ability to bridge to these students, he quickly adds that he is conscious of the dangers of essentializing inexperienced writers, and he agrees with those researchers who point out that novice writers defy simple classification in terms of other characteristics (Cross, 1971; Delpit, 1995; Greenberg, 1997; Lazere, 1992; Royster & Williams, 1999; Stygall, 1999). That is, his experience confirms the heterogeneity of underprepared writers. He has found that they are returning students as well as typical college age, native speakers as well as non-native speakers of English, transfers from community college as well as straight from high school, and first generation college students as well as pupils whose parents have advanced degrees.

OUR RESEARCH APPROACH

Our research approach is rooted in the teacher-research tradition (Anderson & Herr, 1999; Cochran-Smith & Lytle, 1993; MacLean & Mohr, 1999; see also Fishman & McCarthy, 2000). More specifically, we collaborate to provide a detailed account of Fishman's classroom, combining systematic data collection with teacher narrative in order to develop what Stenhouse (1985) calls an "illuminative" account (p. 26). That is, as readers step into the classroom and tutorial situations we describe, our intent is that they will determine what is transferable to their own pedagogical contexts and compare our judgments with theirs.

To this end, we try to collect enough sorts of data, over a long enough period, to convince our readers that our findings are trustworthy. We want them to believe that our accounts are not just our idiosyncratic constructions but are faithful to our informants' interpretations. The present study, however, complexifies this quasi-positivist approach by assuming that researchers can never fully transcend their situatedness and, furthermore, that they have a responsibility to focus on injustices in the classroom being explored. That is, we assume that researchers should use the information they collect to ameliorate the inequities they find and work on behalf of the oppressed (see Lincoln, 1990).

Although both of us accept this responsibility, there were times, as we relate in subsequent chapters, that we could not fully resolve our conflicting views about what constituted justice in Fishman's classroom. Put differently, we disagreed about how best to answer our title questions—Whose educational goals should be pursued, and whose aspirations honored? As a result, our research report is indeterminate, as we have noted, and reflects the mixed nature of our objectives: our desire, on the one hand, to be faithful to our informants' perspectives and, on the other, to acknowledge the particularity of our own standpoints, including our differing views about the proper function of public schooling. (See appendix A for a complete record of our data collection and analysis.)

Research Questions

This research was driven from the beginning by Fishman's sense that he was as underprepared to teach novice writers as they were underprepared to read and compose in his philosophy class. When the study began, in fall 1998, our primary question was, How can Fishman help his novice writers compose in Standard American English? But as we reviewed the data we were collecting, we saw repeated examples of novice writers misunderstanding the texts they were reading. That is, we started to realize that part of these students' problem was rhetorical: they did not have a clear idea of what they wanted to write because they did not have a satisfactory grasp of the reading they had been asked to discuss. Thus, we widened our inquiry to include scrutiny of novice writers' reading and its significance for their writing. In other words, the question was no longer just, How might Fishman help these students write about philosophy better? It became, How might he help them improve their reading of philosophy so as to write about it better?

Our concern with connecting underprepared students' reading and writing was further strengthened by our study of the education and composition literature. The consensus of researchers is that teachers of non-mainstream students should put more stress on the content and writing strategies of their students' papers and less on grammatical correctness (see Ball, 1999; Banks, 1968; Bartholomae & Petrosky, 1986; Benesch, 1991; Cummins, 1986; Elbow, 1999; Leki, 1990, 1992; Mutnick, 1996; Rose, 1989; Spack, 1997; Sternglass, 1997; Zamel, 1995). This led us to investigate the instructional supports that help students produce rhetorically successful work.

Our refocusing on the content and writing strategies of novice composers' texts rather than on their surface mechanics was, however, only one outcome of our reading of the literature. Because teaching the dominant code and the European intellectual tradition has become a lightning rod for discussions about the politics of schooling—in particular, the role of education in perpetuating unjust power structures—we were led to consider a number of other issues as well. We thus began to collect data about the ways in which Fishman's being White and middle-class affected his pedagogy and relations with students of different ethnic and class backgrounds. These data revealed the conflicting goals and aspirations we noted above. In subsequent chapters we report our findings about how Fishman and his students negotiated these differences and how, at least on occasion, they found enough common ground to work cooperatively toward both shared and individual goals.

Research Setting and Participants

Our two-year study took place on the Charlotte campus of the University of North Carolina, a branch serving some 14,000 students. In this report, we spotlight five participants: Fishman, the teacher-researcher, three of his pupils, and McCarthy, the outside observer. In addition, numerous other informants provided data that contextualize our study. These include eight classmates of our three focus students, Fishman's student assistant, and four other discipline-based UNCC professors who later taught our focus pupils.

Focus Students

The three pupils we spotlight in this study are Neha Shah, a 23-year-old recent immigrant from India, a non-native speaker of English and senior math major who enrolled in Fishman's Introduction to Philosophy course; Neha's classmate, Ellen Williams, a 36-year-old African American, a community college transfer and junior criminal justice major; and Andre Steadman, a 21-year-old African American transfer student and junior computer science major in Fishman's advanced Philosophy of Education class. Although Fishman judged each of these pupils to be underprepared for the reading and writing in his course, they all made what we considered significant progress, achieving both some of Fishman's objectives as well as some of their own. What makes their stories interesting, especially in juxtaposition, is that each of these students' achievements depended upon quite different instructional supports. Because they brought disparate histories and attitudes to Fishman's philosophy class—not only diverse goals and aspirations but also different cultural, academic, social, and economic "capital" (Bourdieu, 1982)—each drew upon different pedagogical techniques to take advantage of his or her particular competencies.

The Researchers: Teacher-Insider and Compositionist-Outsider

In an effort to give our readers a sense of our situatedness, the histories and points of view that we, as researchers, bring to this study, we outline something of our ethnic, family, and educational backgrounds. Steve Fishman, the teacher-researcher insider, is a long-tenured, full professor of philosophy who was 60 years old at the time this study began. The outside composition researcher, Lucille McCarthy, is a full professor of English who was 54. Both are Euroamerican and native speakers of English. At first glance, the two of us may seem to stand on the opposite side of the race, class, and school-success divide from many of the novice writers Fishman meets in his classroom. But this is too simple. It masks serious differences between the two of us as well as important sites of identification between us and the underprepared writers we studied.

In some obvious ways, the two of us both belong to the dominant culture. We are both White and middle-aged with roughly equal academic, economic, and cultural capital. McCarthy did her under-graduate work at Stanford, her masters degree at the University of Chicago, and her Ph.D. at the University of Pennsylvania. Fishman did his three degrees at Columbia University in New York City. In addition, we are similar in that Fishman's mother and both of McCarthy's parents were secondary school teachers. Thus, the two of us were introduced at a very early age to the need to succeed in school, if for no other reason than to please our parents. Put differently, we both imbibed the cultural and academic capital required for school success—the language and values of the classroom—at our mothers' breasts.

However, despite these similarities, we are, in crucial aspects of our social capital, quite different. McCarthy's great-grandparents were Scandinavian and English immigrants who settled on farm-lands in Iowa and South Dakota in the decades after the Civil War. As the descendent of Anglo-Scandinavian immigrants, she is located in a very different sector of the 19th century immigration tide than Fishman. Growing up in Sioux Falls and Des Moines, and, as a teenager, in a suburb of Los Angeles, McCarthy lived in homogeneous communities in which her Protestant Christianity and her blonde hair and fair skin registered in the very center of the American paradigm. When she opened her Dick and Jane reader, the charac-ters' skin color and facial features were identical to those she saw when she looked in her own mirror. McCarthy's religion, appear-ance, and background—her social capital—gave her a high-level passport into the most powerful strata of America's dominant class.

By contrast, Fishman's inherited social capital is far less impres-sive. Although America often prides itself on being a nation of immigrants, it has actually not been hospitable to most of them (Higham, 1963). Whereas McCarthy's great-grandparents got free land in the West, Fishman's Jewish grandparents, when they arrived from Eastern Europe in the 1880s, got living space in the basements of New York tenements and jobs in garment-district sweatshops to pay for them. And, unlike McCarthy, when Fishman looked in the mirror, he saw a foreign face, one whose swarthy complexion and Semitic features bore no resemblance to Dick or Jane. In contrast to the characters in his basal reader, none of Fishman's friends had paper routes, porches, or leaves to rake. His feelings of being an outsider were exacerbated by growing up during World War II and hearing stories of the holocaust. In fact, he developed the kind of self-loathing which often accompanies the identity formation of American minorities (see Baldwin, 1963/1988; Mura, 1988; Tatum, 1992). And he carries evidence of this self-consciousness, like pockmarks on his skin, to this day. Even casual comments about his Semitic features or about Jewish cleverness at business remind him that, although he is a second-generation American, he is here by the suffrance of the dominant class and will never fully belong. In sum, Fishman belongs to an ethnic group that has, at times, been characterized by Whites as racially other for the purposes of exclusion and/or extermination (See Dyer, 1997; Miles, 1993).

This history suggests why Fishman is someone who has often been forced to question his own identity, someone whose self-reflections have frequently uncovered feelings of alienation from the dominant culture, the academic world, and, at times, even from his own ethnic group. This is not to say that his minority experiences as a Jew are the same as those of all other minorities. In fact, his status as the grandson of voluntary immigrants to America is very different, as Ogbu (1988) points out, from the situation of descendents of involuntary immigrants. Neither do we want to claim that Fishman's sense of not belonging makes him an especially good teacher of inexperienced writers whose identities may also have been shaped by feelings of discomfort in mainstream culture. What we do claim, however, is that Fishman's own history as an ethnic minority accounts in part for his desire to overcome the contradictions between himself and his novice writers and increase their chances for academic success.

McCarthy shares Fishman's desire to help novice writers succeed in college, but her conviction has a different source. Rather than originating in a sense of being an outsider to the dominant culture, McCarthy's commitment grows out of her experiences as a teacher and researcher. Across twenty years of classroom studies her data collection has involved many conversations with novice writers, and she has seen close up the negative effects of teachers' failure to draw upon the linguistic and cultural knowledge of other-literate students.

Watching these pupils' struggles and frequent defeats in such settings, she has found herself increasingly taking their part. Thus, she has, over time, come to support more radical approaches in the classroom, ones like those proposed by critical and borderland pedagogists (eg. Freire, 1970/1997; Giroux, 1992; Horner & Lu, 1999; Ladson-Billings, 1994; Shor, 1992).

Theorizing Our Data

To help us analyze the data we collected about competing ethnic discourses and perspectives in Fishman's classroom, we drew upon the work of Critical Race Theorists (eg. Bell, 1992; Delgado, 1995b; Williams, 1991) and Whiteness studies scholars (eg. Dyer, 1999; Frankenberg, 1993; Roediger, 1991, 2002). To make further sense of the politics and pedagogy in Fishman's class, we employed the theories of three 20th century educational philosophers—Dewey, Gramsci, and Freire—ultimately relying most heavily on Dewey and Freire. Since these latter two theorists wrote a great deal during long careers, and since the positions both adopt are richly complicated, we offer a preliminary word about our reading of their work.

Interpreting Dewey and Freire

In the chapters that follow, we characterize Dewey as a gradualist reformer of society, a philosopher who places primary emphasis on expanding the democratic tendencies within capitalism. By contrast, we characterize Freire as a radical transformer of society, a theorist who stresses the proletarian struggle to unmask and unseat the oppressor class. However, once we identify them this way, we recognize that our labeling may be oversimple since there are aspects of Dewey's approach that are radical and there are times when Freire sounds gradualist. For example, Dewey's (1935/1991) radicalism can be heard in his deep unhappiness with certain aspects of American capitalism (p. 45), his (1934/1986a) warnings about the power of "capitalist psychology" to "sabotage" workers' interests (p. 104), and his repeated focus on the inequities between what he calls the "leisure" and "labor" classes (1916/1967, pp. 136, 252, 323). Displaying similar complexity, Freire (Shor and Freire, 1987), despite frequent references to himself as a "revolutionary" (pp. 69, 71, 89, 167), often engaged in activities that suggest a more gradualist stance. We have in mind his work between 1989 and 1991 as Secretary of Education for Sao Paulo's public schools and his role as one of the founders, in 1979, of the Brazilian Workers' Party, a group that sponsors candidates in popular elections (see Torres, 1993, p. 136). Freire also suggests a gradualist rather than radical stance when he cautions liberatory teachers about engaging in resistance that might result in professional "suicide," urging them instead to proceed prudently by developing an "ideological map" of friends and foes in their particular educational situations (Shor and Freire, 1987, p. 61. For further comparison of Dewey's and Freire's ideology, see Shor, 1999).

Despite the complexities of Dewey's and Freire's politics, there are three reasons we hold to our characterizations of Dewey as gradualist reformer and Freire as radical transformer. First, we believe that our readings are true to the fundamental ideological roots of their seminal and most widely read works on education: *Democracy and Education* (1916/1967) in the case of Dewey and *Pedagogy of the Oppressed* (1970/1997) in the case of Freire. Second, our emphasis on the political differences between Dewey and Freire, rather than on their similarities, helps us make clear the range of political orientations available to teachers of underprepared writers. Finally, our interpretations of Dewey and Freire help the two of us explore our own differences about the politics Fishman brings to his courses. Specifically, McCarthy seizes upon the more radical aspects of Freire's position to reveal what she sees as shortcomings in Fishman's classroom. Conversely, to defend his approach, Steve often appeals to the gradualist aspects of Dewey's work, ones that promote collaborative inquiry and social reconciliation over class conflict. (For more on Dewey's gradualism, see Demetrion, 1997, 2001.)

In line with our reading of Dewey and Freire as occupying different places on the political spectrum, we see them as promoting different pedagogies. That is, we view Dewey, the political gradualist, as trying to balance assimilation with critique and, as a result, emphasizing exploration of cultural knowledge and the development in students of a spirit of social service alongside personal growth. By contrast, we characterize Freire, the radical social transformer, as working to make explicit the political nature of education, and, as a result, promoting a social change pedagogy that focuses on unveiling the myths foisted on proletarian students by the dominant elite.

Once again, however, as in their approaches to politics, Dewey's and Freire's pedagogies are richly complicated. As we explain in chapters 2 and 4, there are times when Dewey and Freire recommend classroom practices that seem much the same. In fact, people who knew Freire tell us that he felt very much indebted to Dewey's work and wished he had studied it more extensively (Shor, personal communication, 2000; Torres, personal communication, 2001; see also Feinberg & Torres, 2001, p. 28; Freire, 1967/1973, p. 57; Mackie, 1980/1981, pp. 95–96).

Of course, using the theories of Dewey and Freire to analyze a North American college teacher's work with underprepared writers involves considerable extrapolation. Dewey rarely says anything about college instruction, and, although Freire taught at the college level for many years (beginning in 1980), he was probably not thinking of a first-world, university classroom or tutoring situation when he analyzed teacher-student relations in *Pedagogy of the Oppressed*. In other words, neither Freire nor Dewey offers "recipes" or specific instructional techniques for situations like Fishman's. In fact, Freire, in conversation with Macedo, says that he could not tell first-world teachers what to do even if he wanted to because he does not "know the contexts and material conditions" in which they work (Freire & Macedo, 1987, p. 134). Similarly, Dewey (1904/1964b, 1929/1988b) declines to provide pedagogical "tool kits" for teachers at any level, arguing instead that instructors need to develop judgment so they can evaluate and reshape their own teaching practices.

However, despite Dewey's and Freire's unwillingness to spell out particular applications of their educational principles, both believe their theories are widely useful. For example, Freire, in his "Letter to North American Teachers," gives his readers what he views as a universal classroom axiom. He argues that instruction is *always* a political practice, and, therefore, teachers will always "either serve whoever is in power or present options to those in power" (Freire, 1987, p. 212). Dewey (1902/1990c) enunciates a principal he considers equally universal when he suggests that teachers in *all* situations need to connect school curriculum with their students' interests. Thus, as we employ Dewey's and Freire's educational theories to analyze Fishman's teaching, we believe we are doing what both would likely expect and approve.

ORGANIZATION OF THIS BOOK

Following this introductory chapter, Fishman, in chapter 2, offers his own answers to our title questions—Whose goals? Whose aspirations?—responses he roots in the educational theories of Dewey, Gramsci, and Freire. We then focus on his student, Neha Shah, the 23-year-old, recent arrival from India who enrolled in Fishman's Introduction to Philosophy class in fall 1998 to fulfill a graduation requirement. Neha came to Steve's course reluctantly, having been forced to take it to fulfill a "writing intensive" requirement for graduation. After describing the clash between Neha's aims and Fishman's, we outline what Steve viewed as Neha's progress in philosophy and the instructional supports she said helped her. At the end of the chapter, in a coda, we reveal a second set of conflicts about goals and aspirations, those that existed between Fishman and McCarthy. These involved McCarthy's claim that Fishman was hegemonic in refusing to expand his notion of what counts as appropriate reading and writing in his discipline and insensitive to the literacies that Neha brought to his classroom.

In chapter 3, our focus student is a classmate of Neha Shah: 36-year-old Ellen Williams who, like Neha, came to Intro to Philosophy reluctantly, soley to fulfill a graduation requirement. Although Ellen's resistance to Fishman's goals, as well as her underpreparedness for his course, were rooted in a very different personal and educational history, she, like Neha, managed to make progress in philosophy. We describe the instructional supports that helped Ellen Williams, ones that differed from those upon which Neha Shah drew. In this chapter, we use Critical Race Theory and Whiteness studies as lenses through which to view the gaps that separated Fishman and Ellen Williams as well as to understand their efforts to overcome them. We close chapter 3, like chapter 2, with a coda in which we offer an account of our own disagreements regarding Fishman's teaching of this underprepared writer. These revolved around McCarthy's claim that when Fishman evaluated Ellen's work, both his focus and method were inappropriate.

In our fourth chapter, we tell the story of our final featured student, 21-year-old Andre Steadman, an African American computer science major who took Fishman's advanced philosophy course the semester after Steve taught Neha and Ellen. This time, the critical lenses we apply to Fishman's pedagogy are Freirian and neo-Marxian. Specifically, we analyze the effectiveness of Fishman's Deweyan orientation in overcoming Freire's "teacher-student contradiction" between working-class pupils and their middle-class teachers. Although Andre Steadman resembled Neha Shah and Ellen Williams in being, in Fishman's estimate, an underprepared writer, Andre differed from them by coming to philosophy voluntarily, encouraged by a friend who had taken Fishman's course the previous semester. Andre's positive attitude toward the class, combined with Fishman's growing understanding of novice writers, made a dramatic difference in the relationship that Steve and Andre could establish, and they quickly developed what we call a cooperative Deweyan community. This success notwithstanding, McCarthy argues in the coda at the end of this chapter that Fishman could have done more to help Andre become a political change agent, an activist in the service of a less hierarchical, exploitive, and class-stratified culture.

In our concluding chapter, we look back on our contrasting answers to our title questions: Whose goals? Whose aspirations? After reviewing the instructional supports we agree helped our three focus students, we summarize our pedagogical conflicts and the ideological differences that fueled them. Steve then offers his final reflections on his successes and failures with underprepared students and concludes the book by giving advice to discipline-based teachers about how they might help such students in their courses. He recommends particular teaching techniques as well as what he sees as desirable sorts of teacher-student and student-student relations.

CHAPTER TWO

An ESL Writer and Her Discipline-based Professor: Making Progress Even When Goals Don't Match

To affirm that men and women are persons and as persons
should be free, and yet to do nothing tangible to make this
affirmation a reality, is a farce.
                                    Paulo Freire (1970/1997, p. 32)

In this chapter, we present the story of Neha Shah, a 23-year-old
senior math major and recent immigrant from India. As we describe
Neha's experiences in a writing intensive Introduction to Philosophy
class, we attend not only to her reading and writing but also to her
goals for the course. Given that Neha's goals diverge in significant
ways from those of her teacher, Steve Fishman, we also explore the
relationship that develops between this ESL student and her teacher.
Although researchers are well aware that the quality of interpersonal
relationships between non-mainstream students and their teachers
is crucial to these pupils' success (see Cummins, 1986; Gonsalves,
2002; McLeod, 1997), this affective dimension of learning has been
little studied at the college level, perhaps because attention to relationships is viewed at the university as women's work (Grego &
Thompson, 1996; Rodby, 1996). As we attend to the interactions
between Neha Shah and Steve Fishman, we take seriously the idea
that if student and teacher are unable to develop common objectives
and, as a result, work at cross-purposes, the student's performance
often suffers (see Durst, 1999; Nelson, 1990; Smith, 1997).

As we investigate Neha Shah's efforts to acquire philosophic literacy, and as we describe the contradictions between her goals and

Fishman's, we also explore Steve's pedagogy: a dialogic approach rooted in the educational philosophies of Dewey (1916/1967), Gramsci (1971), and Freire (1970/1997). This approach encourages students to be active, to alternate teacher and learner roles, and to develop solidarity through cooperative, problem-posing inquiry. We found that despite Neha Shah's and Steve Fishman's lack of common purpose, and despite what Fishman took to be this ESL student's underpreparedness for his course, his approach facilitated her progress in Intro to Philosophy.

By "progress in Intro to Philosophy," we mean Neha Shah's ability to achieve at least some of her professor's objectives for his students. These included, as Fishman explains in more detail below, the ability to effectively read and write Standard American English within the context of philosophy. Of course we realize that the notion of progress in the classroom has been the subject of considerable debate (see Cummins, 1986; Dean, 1986/1999; Horner & Lu, 1999; Leki, 1992; Nieto, 1996; Villanueva, 1993). We also realize that Fishman's teacher-centered definition—his emphasis on exploring what he considers "cultural knowledge"—exposes him to the charge that Neha was driven toward assimilation in his class, that his course created unnecessary tensions for her between her loyalties to her home and adopted cultures. Although we ourselves, as co-researchers, clashed at times about this issue, McCarthy, in this chapter, sets aside her own viewpoint until the coda as she works to capture her teacher-informant's perspective.

We divide this chapter into three sections. In the first, Steve Fishman relates his classroom goals to the educational theories of Dewey, Gramsci, and Freire. He also presents his initial response to this novice writer. In the second part, Lucille McCarthy reports our collaborative study of Fishman's classroom, describing the experiences and texts of our ESL focus student, Neha Shah, as well as the instructional supports Neha found most helpful. In the final section of this chapter, the coda, we engage in a dialogue in which we reveal McCarthy's concerns about Fishman's pedagogical approach to Neha Shah.

Part One

A Discipline-based Professor's Overall Classroom Goal: Exploring Cultural Knowledge

STEVE FISHMAN

When I consider the four categories of school goals that we name in our introductory chapter—student career preparation, exploration of cultural knowledge, promotion of social reform, and student personal growth—I take the second of these, exploration of cultural knowledge, as my primary classroom objective. As an instructor of philosophy, I aspire, above all else, to promote cooperative student consideration of canonic texts, discussion of ethical, social, and epistemological issues, and practice of philosophic ways of thinking. However, I do not see my primary classroom goal as incompatible with the other three educational aims we have described as historically significant. This is because I urge my students to find connections between my course subject matter and their non-school concerns: professional, social, and personal. This compatibility of my main classroom objective—exploration of cultural knowledge— with other school goals—student career preparation, promotion of social reform, and student personal growth—is important to me because it widens my chance of finding mutual ground or overlap between my own educational aims and the aspirations of my students.

BEING SPECIFIC ABOUT OBJECTIVES FOR UNDERGRADUATE PHILOSOPHIC THINKING AND WRITING

My overall goal of developing a classroom in which students cooperatively explore cultural knowledge undergirds the five more specific objectives I have for student writing and thinking. I now list these, relating them to alternate typologies proposed by several composition and feminist researchers. In class discussion and student writing, I expect to see the following:

1. *Argument Extraction.* The ability to read a philosophic article and demonstrate an understanding of it. By this I mean recognizing the major points of an author's argument and how the author defends them. Argument extraction also requires that students use at least some of their own language to show that they have made the author's argument their own. This sort of reading and writing is related to Sternglass's (1993, 1997) notion of writing-to-recall-facts, Rose's (1989) summarizing, Smitherman's (1977) summarizing and explaining, and Belenky and her colleagues' (1986) notions of received and connected knowing. Argument extraction, as I see it, not only facilitates the exploration of cultural ideas, it can also forward students' career preparation by helping them read critically.

2. *Argument Evaluation.* The ability to listen and read carefully in order to evaluate an argument or position. Such evaluation may include not only appraising an argument in and of itself but comparing it to other positions as well. This sort of thinking and writing recalls Sternglass's (1993, 1997) writing-to-analyze, Shaughnessy's (1977) comparing and interpreting, Rose's (1989) classifying and analyzing, and Belenky and her co-researchers' (1986) notion of critical or separate knowing. My stress on argument evaluation forwards exploration of cultural ideas and may also promote social reform by increasing students' ability to critique the status quo.

3. *Intellectual Reconstruction and Contextualization of One's Own Position.* The ability to see that behind alternative positions on ethical issues, and behind certain key terms (like freedom, knowledge, and morality), lie differing assumptions about the constitution of the good life, the physical world, and human nature. I want students to be able to step into various positions—and step back from their own—in order to reconstruct the fundamental assumptions undergirding these positions. This sort of thinking and writing is related to Smitherman's (1977) questioning and

answering and Shaughnessy's (1977) hypothesizing and contextualizing. It is also an amalgam of what Belenky and her co-researchers (1986) call connected and critical knowing. This third objective is important not only for exploration of cultural knowledge but also for personal growth as students learn more about the sources of their own beliefs.

4. *Application of Philosophy for the Purpose of Critique.* The ability to find connections between one's own life and course subject matter. In other words, I want students to apply philosophic concepts and methods to personal experience in order to organize and challenge that experience in new ways. In turn, I want them to honor their own experiences by using them to critique both the positions presented by class texts, the teacher, and their classmates as well as the social structures in which they live. This sort of work resembles Sternglass's (1993, 1997) writing-to-create-new-knowledge and Belenky and her colleagues' (1986) constructed knowing. These transactions between philosophy and students' understanding of their life trajectories can facilitate exploration of cultural knowledge, social reform, and personal growth.

5. *Coherence in Student Texts.* The ability to develop and organize one's paper around a central theme or thesis. In other words, I want students to be able to write coherently. By this I mean sticking to the topic, being deliberate about arguments, explaining key terms, and offering appropriate transitions so that readers can follow a student author's line of thinking. My desire echoes Larson's (1991) finding that faculty across the curriculum want student writing to have a clear subject, make a specific point about that subject, and exhibit logical organization (p. 145). I also want students to write in Standard American English. Coherent pupil writing and increased mastery of the dominant code are, as I see it, important for all four historically significant school goals.

With regard to Neha Shah, it was the lack of coherence and clarity in her early homework papers that first led me to doubt her preparedness for my course. However, before providing details about my initial response to Neha's early written assignments, I further explicate my pedagogical goals and aspirations by relating them to the theories of three influential philosophers of education.

USING DEWEY, GRAMSCI, AND FREIRE TO EXPLICATE THE ROOTS OF MY CLASSROOM GOALS AND ASPIRATIONS

In explicating the roots of my classroom goals and aspirations, the work of three well-known educational theorists, Dewey (1916/1967), Gramsci (1971), and Freire (1970/1997), is helpful, although their influences on me are in unequal proportions. Because of my commitments to student exploration of cultural knowledge, social reform, and student personal growth, Deweyan pedagogical principles predominate over those of Gramsci and Freire. This is because Dewey's educational goals—ones which are shaped by his political stance as a gradualist reformer—seem closer to mine than Gramsci's or Freire's. For example, whereas Dewey (1916/1967) asks progressive teachers to focus on the quality of student experience, cooperative pupil projects, and transmission of society's ideas and practices, Freire's (1994) political radicalism leads him to see the task of liberatory teachers in more explicitly class-conscious terms. He tells teachers that regardless of their subject matter their goals should include raising student consciousness about bourgeois-worker conflict. Specifically, humanizing teachers should help their students unveil the realities behind the distortions perpetrated by the dominant class so that they may, one day, change the social order (p. 78).

Dewey's Politics and Pedagogy As Closer To My Own Than Gramsci's or Freire's

Regarding the politics behind their pedagogies, I read Dewey and Freire as wanting the same social end: the further extension of democracy into economic and civic spheres. However, I view Dewey's means to this end as contrasting with Freire's since Dewey

(1935/1991), unlike Freire, vigorously denies that the key to achieving this political goal rests with proletarian victory (pp. 54–55). Dewey doubts that such a victory is possible, and even if it were, he argues, we would be no better off unless we changed the way we think about our social problems. Rather, Dewey wants us to apply to the social world the step-by-step, experimental, and gradualist methods of science that have been so successfully applied to the natural world. He (1930/1988c) writes, "The general adoption of the scientific attitude in human affairs would mean nothing less than a revolutionary change in morals, religion, politics, and industry" (p. 115; see also Dewey 1921/1983, pp. 433–435).

Because Dewey (1935/1991) so respects the scientific method, or what he calls "organized intelligence" (p. 61), and because this method has arisen within capitalism, Dewey views capitalism in less negative ways than Freire (1994, pp. 94–96). Dewey (1930/1988c) believes, for example, that it would be "in accord with the spirit of American life" for a council of capitalist owners, labor representatives, and public officials to coordinate and plan the regulation of US industrial activity (p. 98). He (1939/1988d) also advocates that economic reforms be designed by members of "freely functioning occupational groups" like medical professionals. However, no matter the source of proposals for reform, the bottom line for Dewey is always that these proposals be judged by their ability to increase "free choice . . . on the part of individuals" (p. 96, 94). That is, while acknowledging serious problems with the way wealth gets distributed within capitalism, Dewey argues that this system does have positive features, most notably its liberal tradition, which emphasizes the individuality and liberty that allow for collaborative, experimental inquiry to flourish. It is the further development of this sort of collaborative inquiry—not the victory of the working class—that Dewey claims will lead to more equitable social arrangements. (For a similar reading of Dewey's aims as radical and his means as non-radical, see Westbrook, 1991, p. 179. For an alternative view, see Hook, 1939/1995, chapter 8.)

These progressive features of capitalism are what Dewey urges teachers to build upon in their classrooms. He (1935/1991) believes that educators need to encourage students to develop their

individuality while, at the same time, engaging in the sort of cooperative inquiry "which has won triumphs . . . in the field of physical
nature" (p. 51). His hope is that pupils will, ultimately, use the
collaborative methods they have practiced in the classroom to
reform repressive institutional relations and personal attitudes
outside of school.

Not only is Dewey's reformist approach closer to my own than the
more radical ones of Freire and Gramsci, Dewey is also more
optimistic than either Freire or Gramsci about the possibility of
actually being a progressive teacher within the school establishment.
For instance, whereas Dewey (1916/1967) believes schools are our
"chief agency" for establishing a "better" future society (p. 20,
316–319), Freire (Shor & Freire, 1987) doubts that schools can play
more than a limited role in social reform since they are under capitalist control. In fact, he tells us, liberatory teachers are always swim-
ming against the current and can expect "constantly to be punished"
(p. 37; see also Freire, 1976, p. 70).

It is hardly surprising that I would find Dewey's pedagogy and
politics more useful than Gramsci's and Freire's given the fact that
Dewey developed his philosophy under classroom and social conditions more closely resembling my own. Whereas the pedagogies of
Gramsci and Freire are significantly influenced by their work with
urban poor and rural peasants in informal instructional settings,
Dewey generated many of his insights by studying middle-class
children at the University of Chicago Laboratory School. With
regard to his politics, Dewey had many more spaces than Gramsci or
Freire in which he could democratically oppose the status quo. Put
differently, the class distinctions that Gramsci witnessed in Sardinia
and Freire observed in Northeast Brazil were more pervasive, socially
oppressive, and dangerous to oppose than anything Dewey encountered in Burlington VT, Chicago, or New York. (For more on the different contexts in which Dewey and Freire worked, see Betz, 1992.)

Dewey's influence on my classroom practice is most noticeable in
the way I try to establish the conditions for collaborative student
inquiry into cultural knowledge. Specifically, I organize my classroom around Dewey's (1916/1967) idea of desirable social groups

and their modes of communication. This means I seek to increase exchanges among class members so that we may engage in open give and take about philosophic subject matter and our different points of view. My intention is to develop common purpose around commitment to our mutual learning, to an exploration of ideas which is honest and genuine enough that, at least at times, we forget who is teacher and who is student. My hope is that this expanded communication will not only generate collaborative cultural inquiry but will also lead to a type of social reform. That is, following Dewey (1916/1967), I hope this reconstruction of the usual teacher-pupil relationship will democratize the classroom by breaking down some of the racial, class, and cultural barriers which often separate students from one another and from their teacher (p. 87, 160, 289; see also 1927/1988a).

In addition to exploration of cultural knowledge and promotion of social reform, Dewey helps me encourage student personal growth as I try to follow his advice to integrate pupil interests and my course subject matter. Put in Deweyan (1902/1990a) terms, I want pupils to connect to philosophy by using their own objectives (or "for-whats") to determine which aspects of my subject-matter deserve their primary attention (their "to-whats"). I also want pupils to use what they already know as bridges (or "with-whichs") to explore that which they find unfamiliar in my curriculum (pp. 272–76).

As I have said, in striving for student exploration of philosophy, social reform, and personal growth through a Deweyan form of cooperative inquiry, my approach does not fully coincide with the more class conscious orientations of Freire and Gramsci. Unlike Freire (1970/1997), I neither see my classroom as divided between the oppressive banking teacher and oppressed student vessels, nor do I see my principal objective as preparing my students to struggle against and disempower the dominant elite (pp. 38, 55–58, 124–25). Unlike Gramsci (1971), I do not view my course as part of the "formative," "disinterested" education of the underclass, one designed to develop the "organic intellectuals," the "permanent persuaders," needed to create the cultural climate for a worker/ peasant revolution (pp. 27, 6, 10).

Gramsci's and Freire's Impact on My Pedagogy

The fact that I do not put unveiling class antagonism at the top of my agenda does not mean I am indifferent to students' complacency about the negative consequences of American economic inequalities, racism, and sexism. That is, Dewey's strong influence on me does not reduce my appreciation of important aspects of Freire's and Gramsci's approaches to education. For instance, these latter two theorists, like Dewey, want students to be active, to teach as well as learn in the classroom (Dewey, 1916/1967, p. 160; Freire 1970/1997, pp. 53, 61; 1970/2000, p. 27; Gramsci, 1971, p. 350). In addition, it is Freire (1970/1997), not Dewey, who shows me the difficulty of achieving this sort of democratized space. Freire underlines the chasms separating instructors and pupils when he warns about the supposed "generosity" of members of the middle-class, alerting me that instructors who seek to be "helpful" to the oppressed, to move to solidarity with the exploited, may "bring with them the marks of their origin: their prejudices and their deformations" (p. 42).

I also learn from both Freire and Gramsci about the difficulty of getting students to use philosophy to reconstruct their own experiences and the dominant class's values and practices. That is, although Dewey wants students to be critical and aware of social inequities, Freire and Gramsci teach me how hard it is to get a critical angle on the exploitive relations in capitalism that have become so familiar as to be almost invisible. In particular, I profit from Gramsci's (1971, pp. 12–13) discussion of hegemony. Gramsci, a leader of the Italian communist party in the 1920s, rejects the classical Marxist idea that analysis of the forces of production can, by itself, enable us to predict the social future. Instead, Gramsci moves beyond this positivistic Marxism to recognize the role of civil society and personal experience in the development of hegemony (pp. 184, 410–412). He explains that the controlling industrial class governs by assent, successfully shaping the national culture and, thereby, tacitly influencing the thinking of the proletariat so that it aligns itself with the goals and aspirations of the bourgeoisie (see also Freire, 1970/1997, p. 59; 1970/2000, p. 25; 1994, p. 56).

Although Gramsci emphasizes the difficulty of examining our fundamental presuppositions, he does share with Dewey (1925/1989, p. 35) the hope that philosophy can be helpful in this regard. According to Gramsci (1971), one way of deconstructing the bourgeois grip on national culture is through philosophic reflection. He praises philosophers for their ability to "inventory" their thoughts, to understand and make explicit the ways in which their ideas have been shaped by various intellectual currents and systems. Such self-consciousness, Gramsci says, leads to lives that are less the result of a "fragmentary collection of ideas and opinions" and more the product of a consciously chosen and coherent direction. Philosophy, he concludes, helps people order "in a systematic, coherent and critical fashion, [their] own intuitions of life and the world" (pp. 324, 327; see also Dewey, 1916/1967, p. 161).

Freire (1970/2000), although primarily concerned with literacy programs for agrarian peasants as opposed to Gramsci's cultural programs for industrial workers, faces a similar challenge: how to develop critical understanding, specifically, how to help peasants "problematize" their social and political situation (p. 27). Getting his adult students to "objectify" the dominator's practices is not an easy task, as Freire points out, since they have "internalized" the oppressor's views (1970/2000, p. 24; 1970/1997, pp. 29–30). He writes, "The dominated consciousness does not have sufficient distance from reality to objectify it in order to know it in a critical way" (1970/2000, p. 48). This explains why Freire's literacy programs are designed to teach language not as politically neutral but as a potent shaper of behavior and social structure. His use of slides or pictures, what he calls "codifications," is intended to bring about the sort of objectification he describes, helping peasants to "problem-pose," to critically examine the oppressor ideology by viewing their work, family, and living situations from new angles (1970/2000, p. 27).

My own classroom efforts to achieve the ideological self-consciousness that Gramsci and Freire rightly describe as elusive rests, as I have said, on collaborative inquiry. My faith is that, as students work together, they will hear other points of view that force them to critically examine and clarify their own. I also try to make the familiar seem unfamiliar by using what I hope will be provocative readings: selections from political activists like Fanon (1965/1995), Carmichael—later called Kwame Toure—(1966/1995), and Russell (1929/1970) as well as from feminists like Daly (1973/1995), Starhawk (1979/1995), and hooks (1981/1995). My intention is to use these texts to help us view from fresh perspectives the language and values of such familiar, and often exploitive, institutions and practices as the patriarchal family, personal and cultural racism, private property, and capitalist competition and acquisitiveness.

I now turn from the theory that underlies my teaching goals to describe my efforts to enact it in my classroom practice. I begin McCarthy's and my report on Neha Shah's experiences in my Intro to Philosophy course by describing my responses to her early home-work papers and class participation.

MY CLASSROOM GOALS AND ASPIRATIONS AND AN ESL WRITER

On the first day of my writing intensive Introduction to Philosophy class in fall 1998, I asked students to freewrite about their home cultures and the values they took from them. My 25 students and I sat in a circle, and, after ten minutes, I looked up and asked everyone to read over what they had written or, if they had not finished, to move their work toward closure. After I made a few changes on my own three paragraphs, I put down my pencil and scanned the class-room, wondering which student to call on to get us started. As I have already explained, to promote exploration of cultural knowledge and the practice of philosophic ways of thinking, I want open give and take as we explore different points of view. On that first day, Neha Shah, the 23-year-old senior math major and focus of this chapter, was sitting immediately to my right. I called on her first, thinking she might say something about her home culture which would challenge my students' (and my own) values and beliefs. By giving a prominent place in our first discussion to a woman of color, I also intended to show that I favor an inclusive class community, one in which minority or unorthodox positions are valued and explicated with care.

Although Neha spoke very quietly in accented English, I could follow her responses to my questions about her freewrite. That is, her contribution during that first class period raised no warning flags in me. However, what did get my attention were her first homework assignments (for course assignments, see appendices B and C). They totally defied my expectations for student writing since they were so different from papers I had typically received during my 31 years of teaching. Although I gave Neha passing grades on these early papers—not wanting to discourage her and hoping she would somehow improve—concern was building for me in three areas.

First, Neha's surface errors and mismanagements were serious and frequent. For example, on her homework response to an essay by Lin Yutang (1937/1995), she wrote, "On the day of his mother funeral, he felt himself by selfish. This defines his not arrogant. And by Confucian colleague experienced, he felt like he cut off his tie with Christianity. Like this, he calling by himself a 'pagan'."

Although in the above example, I could figure out what Neha wanted to say, there were times I could not. So my second area of worry was one Shaughnessy (1977, p. 121) noted long ago. Discipline-based teachers, Shaughnessy rightly observes, are generally more interested in *what* students say than *how* they say it, and thus they ignore errors when they can. I typically do that. However, when Neha's writing mismanagements made it impossible for me to follow her thinking, I started to realize she presented me with an unusual problem. In other words, the level of Neha's papers seemed significantly below that of most of the other 24 students in my Intro class, all of whom were native speakers. For instance, I was mystified when, in her homework response to hooks's (1981/1995) claim that women are unaware of the extent to which their psyches have been warped by racism and classism, Neha wrote, "I agree with her because I am a girl. I know how is woman's nature. Woman has a jealous characteristic than man." I was equally confused when Neha attempted, two assignments later, to summarize Holmes's (1929/1973) arguments for immortality. She concluded, "Therefore, for believing in immortality or for being ready to believe in immortality, is the primarily interesting fact that there is no reason for not believing in immortality." (For more on faculty perceptions of ESL students' errors, see Johns, 2001; Leki, 1991, 1992, 1995; Santos, 1988. See also Harrington & Adler-Kassner, 1998.).

My third concern about Neha's writing focused on those occasions when I realized she did not understand the assigned text. That is, I began to suspect Neha not only had a writing problem but a reading one as well. For example, in response to an essay by Carmichael (1966/1995), she wrote:

> On the behalf of nonviolence and integration, Carmichael used political and economic power term. . . . In this article, he gave one example and compare to the real life. When he was a boy, he used to see movie of Tarzan. He saw in movies, White Tarzan used to beat up the black natives because they were black in skin. By this he explained that White Tarzan beat black native in movies, same way it happens in real life that White people hate and ignore black people, not because black are ignorant, or not because they are stupid, only because they are black.

Regarding Neha's first sentence, it seemed to me that she had misunderstood Carmichael's point. Whereas she describes Carmichael as working on "behalf" of nonviolence and integration, in fact he argues against it. Regarding her response to Carmichael's example, she again seems to miss his point. He is less concerned with the fact that Tarzan is beating up Black natives than he is with the fact that he, as a young African American, was rooting for Tarzan.

In pointing out my concerns about Neha's writing—my worries about her surface errors, her inability at times to make herself clear, and her misunderstanding of assigned texts—I do not mean that I blamed Neha. Nor did I take these writing problems as a sign she was not highly intelligent, diligent in her work, and serious about her education. However, as sympathetic as I was to Neha's situation, I could not just ignore her reading and writing difficulties. To the contrary, very much in my mind was the fact that my class was designated "writing intensive" and it was my job to certify that students who passed it were reading and writing Standard American English at the college level. I simply had no idea how, in a matter of 14 weeks, I could bring Neha's reading and writing in English up to the level of her better prepared classmates. As a discipline-based teacher with only one ESL student, I felt I could not adopt the sort of pedagogy recommended for ESL and "basic" composition classes in which students devote much of the semester to studying, celebrating, and building upon their home languages and cultures (see, for example, Campbell, 1997; Dean, 1986/1999; Kutz, Groden, & Zamel, 1995). That is, I did not think it was appropriate for me to simply jettison my philosophic curriculum, a diverse and fairly challenging set of texts and issues that I believed it was my responsibility to teach and for which the majority of my students were prepared.

In sum, as I reflected on Neha's early papers, I felt handcuffed. If Neha was unprepared for my course, I, as a teacher, was equally unprepared for her.

The Ghost of Louis Heller: Whose Errors? Whose Expectations?

In being taken aback by Neha's writing, I believe my reactions may have resembled those of Louis G. Heller, the CCNY classics professor alarmed by the way CUNY implemented its open-admissions policy in the fall of 1970 (Heller, 1973; Lu, 1992/1999a; Traub, 1994). Although my university situation nearly three decades later was far, far different from Heller's, my knee-jerk response to Neha was the same as his to the new CUNY students: I viewed her as not belonging in my classroom. My first thought was, "Golly, her work wouldn't get a passing grade from my old high school English teacher, Mrs. Wachs." My second thought was, "With everything else the university is asking me to do, teaching this student to read and write is a particularly difficult burden to add."

However, I could not dismiss Neha, as I have said, because of her underpreparedness, nor, in contrast to Heller (1973) and many of his CUNY colleagues, could I blame outside militants and misguided politicians for her presence in my classroom (chapters 3, 14, 19). Thus, I was, I have to admit, a little embarrassed by my reactions to Neha's work. Obviously, it was people at my own university who had decided that she belonged in my Intro course. So I began to doubt myself. Perhaps the important errors were not on Neha's pages but in my responses to her. Perhaps the unreasonable expectations were not hers but mine. This admission put me in a painful moral vise, trying to honestly evaluate Neha's writing while, at the same time, being sensitive to her special situation. On the one hand, her work deserved low grades because it reflected not only poor command of Standard American English but also limited understanding of the assigned philosophic texts. On the other hand, I knew Neha faced unusual hardships, ones which might justify more lenient or atypical evaluation. But this did not seem right either because I suspected my other students also shouldered hardships, ones that were just less apparent. If this were true, how in the world could I construct a fair evaluation system which would take into account all the apparently relevant factors?

Further compounding my dilemma was Neha's unhappiness—as McCarthy describes below—with my responses to her writing. My saying anything negative about her work seemed to open a wound, as if I were a customs official turning her away at the Ellis Island gate. Her passing grade in freshman composition at my own university was a passport I was now questioning. When I first spoke with Neha about her writing, she seemed surprised and offended. She told me that her instructor in composition the previous summer had given her an "A" because, as Neha put it, "she understood I have been in your country only a short time." I do not know exactly what I expected, but I thought, "Even if Neha cannot be grateful to me for pointing out her writing difficulties—for not lowering my standards—I wish she would at least acknowledge the importance of improved writing for her future."

Counterbalancing these early, negative conversations with myself about Neha, my sense she was out of place in my Intro classroom, were recollections which I could not put aside of my grandfather, Moishe Gluck. Had this unschooled Hungarian peasant come to America to improve his life so his privileged grandson could, two generations later, prevent other immigrants from improving theirs? If I knew nothing else, I was sure he was not dreaming that dream as he headed steerage toward the lamp beside Lazarus's golden door.

These were my initial thoughts and concerns about Neha. In the sections which follow, Lucille McCarthy offers Neha Shah's perspective as the only non-native speaker among my 25 philosophy students. Lucille will describe Neha's goals and aspirations for the course and further detail the ways they differed from mine. She will also try to account for the fact that despite the mismatch of Neha's and my aims, and despite our mutual unpreparedness for one another, Neha was able, in significant ways, to reach some of my course goals.

∾

Part Two
Student-Teacher Relations: a Mismatch of Goals and Expectations
LUCILLE McCARTHY

Neha Shah's goals in Introduction to Philosophy bore little resemblance to those Steve Fishman has outlined above. Whereas Steve wants exploration of cultural knowledge and attention to philosophic ways of making meaning, Neha simply wanted to pass the course so she could graduate at the end of the semester. She could, then, she told me, get back on track with her life plans, a trajectory that had been seriously disrupted by her immigration to the U.S. two years earlier. That students' and teachers' goals and aspirations may differ significantly is, of course, well known. For example, Durst (1999), in his book-length study, *Collision Course: Conflict, Negotiation, and Learning in College Composition*, describes the conflicts between a "critical literacy teacher" at the University of Cincinnati and her "pragmatic" students. Whereas the instructor wanted students to engage in self-reflection, understanding the ideologies or masked values behind various uses of language, her pupils wanted only to learn writing skills that would enhance their workplace success. At UCLA, Smith (1997) describes a similar incongruity between teachers' humanist, social change agendas and the careerist goals of their composition students (see also Shor & Freire, 1994, p. 69).

Like the students Durst and Smith describe, Fishman's pupils are also marketplace-oriented. Although Fishman is well aware that virtually none of his pupils will major in philosophy or become a professional philosopher, he nevertheless sees exploration of cultural knowledge as practical for them. That is, he believes his course is relevant no matter what his students' career objectives. Whether they become engineers, scientists, or accountants, they need to be intellectually and socially aware, attending to the connections between their professional lives and the philosophic and moral issues they encounter in his class. These issues—for example, race, class, and gender discrimination—will provide the context for their work lives. As Dewey (1897/1964a, pp. 118–119) tells us, advanced math students, for example, should know the "business realities," and the social relationships behind the realities, in which their skills will be used (see also Du Bois, 1930/1973, pp. 72–82). Intellectually and socially aware accountants, thus, focus not only on math. They also ask about the purpose of their work: whom is it serving, and what are its consequences?

Stepping into the Student's Shoes: Impediments to Achieving Common Goals

Throughout the semester, Steve Fishman and Neha Shah retained their divergent goals. Steve never succeeded in showing Neha the possible significance of philosophy for her professional and personal concerns, and Neha never succeeded in convincing Steve that the workload he imposed on her was unreasonable. Although limited English proficiency partially explains Neha's alienation from Steve's course, two other factors also played a powerful role. These impediments to her wholehearted participation were, first, that she believed she had been unfairly required to take the class. Second, she found its curriculum irrelevant. Both of these impediments were based on the particular sort of "bicultural ambivalence" that Neha experienced in this setting, her particular conflicts as a recent immigrant to this country (Cummins, 1986, p. 22).

An Unexpected Detour through "Unfair" Requirements

Neha believed from the start that it was "unfair" she had to take Intro to Philosophy. In my first interview with her, in mid-September, Neha described a distressing interruption in her schooling, one that challenged the self-image of this serious and ambitious student. Neha and her parents, both professionals, had come to the U.S. two years earlier because they knew it was an "advanced country" where they could learn about "new technologies [that were] invented day by day." Before arriving, she had completed her BS degree in mathematics at a university in India and thus came to the U.S. at age 21 seeing herself as already "educated," that is, fully trained in math at the undergraduate level and ready to begin her graduate work. Starting her masters degree immediately was important, she explained, because this was the "traditional" path in her family and culture. Young people complete the masters degree right after the bachelors and are, then, able to secure a good job and get married.

However, to Neha's understandable consternation, this timetable for achieving her aspirations was disrupted when, as she put it, "the American system did not accept the value of my degree." That is, before granting her a BA degree from the University of North Carolina Charlotte (UNCC), the dean required another year of general distribution courses: humanities and social sciences classes, a composition course, and one course designated "writing intensive." (Two of the latter are generally required for graduation at UNCC.) This was painful for Neha. Not only were American educational authorities contradicting Indian ones who said she was already "educated," the Americans were also putting her in a difficult situation personally. It was embarrassing, Neha told me, to be 23 years old and still living at home, her marriage yet unarranged. However, despite being "mad" at the dean for this setback—one Neha viewed as a kind of insult—she knew she needed the U.S. degree and had little choice but to comply with his requirements. Neha described her distress, as well as her uncertainty about which educational authorities to trust, in her end-of-semester, multi-draft essay which she titled "Confuse to choose the best way for a good life." She explains that the disruption in her plans caused by this conflict between American and Indian systems made her feel "sad and sorry" for herself. "[I am like] a traveler [who] does not know which way is correct road to get his or her place."

A Course Serving Only One Instrumental Goal: Getting a Degree

Neha Shah was, then, in the unenviable position of being a successful student in her home country who is, nevertheless, deemed "uneducated," as she put it, by the university system in her adopted homeland. Yet the sting of the dean's insult might have wounded Neha less had she been able to view these extra required courses as serving some functions for her. Although Neha ultimately admitted to having benefitted from taking philosophy, she was never able to develop personally meaningful objectives or "for-whats," to borrow Dewey's term (1902/1990a, pp. 272–74). And Fishman was unable to help her in this regard. This distressed him because he knows, again following Dewey, that when teachers cannot help students develop their own reasons for doing course work—reasons other than just getting a passing grade—pupils have trouble finding foci of interest ("to-whats") and building bridges ("with-whichs") to connect prior and new knowedge (1902/1990a, pp. 272–76). Such students often remain passive, their class participation perfunctory.

Writing Improvement Was Not a Goal. A "for-what" or goal that students in Fishman's "writing intensive" course frequently identify for themselves is writing improvement. Although they may care little about cultural knowledge, and be little inclined to self-reflection, most acknowledge that, because they need to know how to write, Steve's "writing intensive" philosophy course can be vocationally useful. Neha, by contrast, believed that, for a mathematician, she already wrote well enough. Mathematicians don't need to write much anyway, she told me, because "they work with numbers, not [like philosophers who] ask what's that mean." Given Neha's sense that Fishman's course would not help her career preparation, and given the fact she did not enjoy composing even in her native language (Gujarati), it is hardly surprising that she was upset about the amount and difficulty of the writing in philosophy. At the end of the course, in her Class Reflection Log (CRL), a non-graded journal in which Fishman asks students to reflect on their learning, Neha complained,

> The homework assignments for this class is really hard and consume too much time to do it (especially if you don't have typing skills). And philosophy is totally new for me, a subject I never learned.

Although she worked diligently on Fishman's assignments, ultimately improving her writing, as I will show, writing betterment was not a "for-what" that Neha believed worth the many hours she spent on it.

And, in fact, she may have been right. When Neha and I spoke a year and a half after Fishman's course concluded, she told me she was now only a semester away from her masters degree at UNCC and had taught two sections of undergraduate algebra as a teaching assistant. In all this time she had no need to write anything except her course syllabi and a few notes on student papers. However, that would change, she said. The following semester she had to write a masters thesis.

Learning Philosophic Curriculum Was Not a Goal. A second "for-what" or instrumental end that Steve's students may identify—often at the end rather than the beginning of the semester—is course subject matter. In this regard, Neha, as a recent immigrant, was at a serious disadvantage because Steve designs his course with American students in mind. That is, he selects readings that deal with issues he assumes American college students will find provocative: for example, racism, sexual morality, patriarchy and the role of women, and the existence of God. Even resistant students often connect to course content because they find these issues relevant to their lives and a source of personal growth.

By contrast, Neha, as a "traveler" between two cultures, a newcomer to this one, entered Steve's class with different interests and background knowledge—different cultural capital—than her American classmates (Bourdieu, 1982). As a result, she found herself, once again, experiencing bicultural tension, saying that course content was confusing to her, sometimes even upsetting. For example, she was puzzled about her classmates' emotional involvement in discussions of racism after they read Fanon (1965/1995), Carmichael (1966/1995), and hooks (1981/1995). She had been unaware, she said, that Blacks and Whites in America were in conflict. Trying to bridge to her new world, she found a "with-which" in her own culture that helped her relate to the American racial situation: the Indian caste system. But then, as if unwilling to bring her two cultures together, reluctant, perhaps, to objectify or critique her home culture, Neha dismissed the connection. "But castes were 200 years ago," she said. "Now everything is okay."

Similarly, several weeks later, when the class discussed Bertrand Russell's *Marriage and Morals* (1929/1970), Fishman once again failed to get Neha's goals and his to coincide. He missed a chance to show that his course could promote her personal growth when he was unable to help her see the relevance of Russell's critique of patriarchy and its underlying assumptions about sexual morality and women and children as property. Neha told me that during class discussion, she just laughed inside, so far was this topic from any-thing that would be discussed among Indians. In her Class Reflection Log she elaborated, focusing on the very different conventions in the two cultures regarding open discussion of sex:

> In class I learned about sex education, which is general topic and most common in this country. I was shocked when I became aware of the fact that sex education is taught in American high school.

In a mid-October interview, Neha again found a parallel in her own culture with Russell's analysis of the oppression of women. Her marriage, she told me, would be arranged by her father with no input from her. However, after making this connection, she said no more, unable or unwilling to push the analysis further.

Whatever the causes of Neha's unwillingness or inability to think critically about patriarchy—for example, arranged marriages and lack of sex education in her home culture—Neha's reluctance illus-trates Gramsci's (1971) point about the difficulty of gaining critical perspective on the conventions or values of the dominant class. Neha mentions the ways oppression works in her culture, and she herself is, as a woman, oppressed—or so it seems from the outside. Yet these conventions seem "natural" to Neha, non-challengeable ways of living life. Her reactions not only reinforce Gramsci's claim that hegemonic ideologies are hard to see but also that oppressor and oppressed alike espouse them as the way of the world. That is why, Gramsci argues, philosophy is important for helping people contextualize—and thus render visible—their most fundamental beliefs.

By semester's end, however, and to Neha's great credit, she was able and willing to try this sort of philosophic work, to engage, in her final exam, in some limited "objectification," to use Freire's term (1970/2000, p. 24), and contextualization of her situation. As I will show, she was able by December to extract Bertrand Russell's argument and apply philosophy, offering an analysis of the "pluses and minusues" [sic] of patriarchal structures in her own life. Given the place Neha started, it was, in Steve Fishman's view, a significant achievement.

Stepping Into the Student's Shoes: Neha Shah's Expectations

In examining the mismatch between Neha and Steve, I found not only divergent goals but also divergent expectations about the nature and amount of writing that would be required. This sort of mismatch between ESL students and their discipline-based teachers is not unusual and has been noted by other researchers (see Johns, 2001). Neha initially expected, she told me, that Intro to Philosophy would be "really easy, and I would pass with an A." She apparently also believed she could do this without expending much effort because, in addition to taking two other courses, she was working 45 hours a week at two jobs. When I asked Neha in early October why she expected Intro to Philosophy to be easy, she mentioned her composition course the previous summer. She received an A in that class, she explained, writing three papers about personal experience and one about an interview with a family member. She assumed philosophy would be the same. She told me,

I thought I would just write something on the paper and turn it in.

In composition, I could write whatever I wanted. When I was writing about my family story, I know how to do that. I just tell what I watch. And I can make up things.

By contrast, in philosophy, Neha now realized,

Dr. Fishman wants us to understand the reading . . . . But philosophers use big words, different words. I'm looking in the dictionary all the time. And it is totally new for me, a subject that I never learned. . . . I have to work very hard.

Neha's experience in her composition course, then, led her to expect she would write personal essays in philosophy. It also caused her to undervalue the importance in the academy of error-free prose. Steve, as he has already noted, is like many teachers in the disciplines who are willing to overlook a certain number of surface errors. However, when it comes to major mechanical mismanagements, ones that present time-consuming obstacles to his deciphering the student's meaning, his tolerance is limited. By contrast, Neha's composition teacher was, apparently, more forgiving. Neha told me, "She was sympathetic. . . . She understood I was new in this country and said grammar wasn't important. She cared about my content." (For a possible explanation of this teacher's emphasis on substance to the exclusion of form, see Mutnick, 2000, pp. 77–78).

Neha's expectation that Steve would value content over form was, as I have indicated, not altogether wrong. But there were limits. Moreover, the content required in philosophy papers was, as Neha quickly recognized, less familiar to her than that in composition and, therefore, more demanding. That is, instead of multi-draft personal essays drawing on her narrative skills, Fishman asked students to write about assigned readings: frequent, single-draft pieces analyzing and evaluating primary source material. Thus, not only was the content of Neha's philosophy writing not what she expected, but the frequent, shorter assignments also meant she had little time to visit the University Writing Center, something that had helped her with drafts of her essays for composition. The tutors at the Writing Center, Neha told me, "changed my papers and gave me suggestions."

In sum, Neha's expectations for writing in philosophy were unrealistic because they were, in large part, based on her experiences in a composition course that did not require writing about sophisticated texts. Neha realized this and became alarmed, she said, when, three weeks into the course, Fishman wrote on her homework paper: "Fail. It is a struggle for me to follow your writing. I cannot understand what you are trying to say. Please get help at the Writing Center."

When Steve wrote this note in early September, he was, he told me, as alarmed as Neha. He was trying to be honest, he said, warning her that, in terms of his expectations, her writing was below what he considered "college level." In this situation, neither student nor teacher could relate to one another very well. That is, neither could get into the other's shoes and begin the community building that Dewey finds (1916/1967) essential for learning (pp. 4, 20–21, 80–84; see also 1929/1988b, pp. 148–50). For Steve's part, he had little idea about how to respond to Neha, as he has said. Given what he saw as her underpreparedness, he was not sure how to provoke her interest in his curriculum or engage her in philosophic exploration. Neither did he know how to respond to a student's writing that, in addition to displaying significant surface errors, indicated she was having trouble understanding the reading.

For Neha's part, she was a frightened outsider for whom the rules had "unfairly" changed, a confused pupil in a do-or-die situation, having to do labor which was not of her choosing. Yet when she received Steve's "Fail," she decided, after speaking with her advisor, that she would remain in the class. "I have to graduate in December," she told me. "So I have to pass this course. I have no choice."

AN ESL WRITER'S PROGRESS: ACHIEVING SOME OF HER PROFESSOR'S OBJECTIVES

Steve Fishman and Neha Shah were, thus, poles apart both in terms of their goals for the course and their expectations concerning student preparation and effort. To show the consequences of this mismatch, I begin my analysis of Neha's writing in philosophy with her fourth homework assignment, the piece that Steve failed. What characterizes the writing in this paper? What led Steve to fail it? By contrast, what caused Neha to believe it was perfectly acceptable— perhaps even A—work? Following my examination of this early-September homework paper, I jump to the end of the semester, to Neha's final exam, to show the way she was able to achieve some of Fishman's objectives despite his and her mismatch.

An Early Piece: Clashing Expectations Made Manifest

Across the semester Fishman asks his Intro students to respond to their reading in 20, short, written homework assignments in various genres. He also requires a multi-draft, end-of-semester essay. In addition to these assignments, which he responds to and grades, Fishman also requires frequent, informal writing, both in and outside class, that he does not grade. (Graded assignments are listed in appendix B, ungraded Class Reflection Log assignments in appendix C.)

The fourth homework assignment was due September 8th and took the form of a letter to a fellow student, one of four such assignments in which students actually correspond with a randomly paired classmate. Fishman assigned two Platonic dialogues (1993), the *Apology* and *Crito*, and asked students to describe their questions or confusions about these texts in a letter to their partner that solicits his or her help. The class period following students' exchange of these letters, they bring in their responses to one another, letters attempting to answer the questions their partners have posed.

In this assignment, Steve is offering students an opportunity to write to each other about unfamiliar texts in a genre that is known to all. In addressing questions to their classmates, philosophic novices like themselves, instead of to the teacher, he is inviting students to use ordinary language and to display their uncertainties, admitting what they do not understand in ways they seldom do when writing for him. Although pupils realize Fishman will read a copy of their letter and grade it, they generally see their paired classmate as their primary audience. And this peer audience is a powerful one, Fishman has found, providing pupils with a motivation, or "for-what," for completing the work. Students tell him that although they may consider skipping homework written solely for him, they are reluctant to do that with the letter assignment because it would leave their partner in the lurch. (For more on the letter exchange technique, see Fishman & McCarthy, 1998, chapter 9).

The assignment sheet that Fishman handed out for the fourth homework paper reads as follows:

Assignment #4 - Letter Exchange

All homework is to be typed. Hand-written letters are not acceptable. Two copies of your letter are required. One copy is to be given to me and the other copy is to be exchanged with your letter-partner at the start of class on Tuesday, September 8.

Reflect on your reading of Plato's *Apology* and *Crito*, and then write a 200-300 word letter to your partner in which you describe some aspect of the dialogues that you are having trouble understanding—a specific area you are having difficulty interpreting or fully comprehending.

You should make distinctions where you can—that is, describe what you understand and what you do not understand. You should refer to one or more particular passages in the dialogues where you are experiencing difficulty. Don't just say, "I don't understand the passage beginning at line 10 of page 64." In other words, you should provide a context for what you do not understand so your reader can see your difficulties and thereby give you some assistance.

I hope this assignment will help you clarify your thinking about the *Apology* and *Crito* dialogues as well as describe a particular problem or problems to a classmate that you really want to know more about.

Teacher Expectations Clarified

In conversations with me as we prepared this chapter, Steve articulated his expectations for this assignment. First, he assumes that students will have little trouble reading Plato's account of Socrates' trial and Crito's discussion with Socrates following the trial. The text is, as Fishman sees it, a narrative with several vivid conflicts and lots of details. So when he asks students to explain their questions about it to a classmate, he expects they will focus on substantive issues, for example, challenging Socrates' line of thinking or asking for clarification. Put differently, Fishman wants argument extraction and argument evaluation, the first two on his list of five goals for student thinking and writing.

And generally students are able to do this. For example, although they do not use these terms, pupils often spotlight moral conflicts in these dialogues between responsibility to family versus responsibility to one's principles, between living according to one's beliefs versus living expediently, between valuing material existence versus valuing spiritual life. Typical student questions are of the following sort: Wouldn't Socrates be better off escaping from prison rather than accepting the death verdict? (This way he could both care for his family—he has two young sons—and continue to fight for his principles.) Why was Socrates contentious during his trial rather than apologetic? Who is the oracle of Delphi, and why did Socrates take him so seriously?

When Steve read Neha's paper, his expectations were severely undercut. In her letter to her partner, Robert Bullerdick, a 30-year-old, Euroamerican student, Neha asked Robert not about substantive issues but about the meaning of words. It was, Fishman recalls, a complete surprise. He had never before had a student ask lexical questions. Although Neha was obviously comfortable with the letter genre—she adopts an appropriately informal tone with Robert, by whom she sometimes sat—her questions confirmed for Fishman something he had begun to suspect: Neha was not comprehending the reading. Apparently she understood so little of Socrates' argument that she was neither able to summarize nor evaluate it but was, rather, limited to word-level concerns. Neha writes:

> Dear Robert,
>   Hi, how are you? I didn't get your letter for long time and not even talk by phone. I know you are busy with study and work. I have same situation here; school give me lot of work. In this semester I am taking three classes and going to graduate in December. I am so happy, how about you? How many semesters you left for graduate?
>   Here, I need your help in my philosophy class. I know you are real good and excellent in philosophy. . . . Last night I read "The last day of Socrates" book written by Plato. In this book I read the Apology and Crito's conversation with Socrates.

In the Apology I understand everything. In the Crito's I understand pretty much, except Crito's arguments and believe that Socrates should escape.

. . . In the first argument [Crito] said Socrates should escape, because he is endangering the good reputation of his friends and he need not worry about and risks these friends may be running. . . . Actually, I do not understand what endangering mean. So, could you please explain me what Crito trying to say?

. . . At the last, Socrates said, he only wish that ordinary people had an unlimited capacity for doing harm and power for doing well. In this sentence I do not understand what kind of unlimited capacity he was talking about. Because he said only ordinary people has unlimited capacity. I am wondering what about other people.

I hope you can understand my question. Please explain me in brief, So I can go straight. I am really waiting for your explanation letter about my question.

I know it will make you busy, but you are my friend so please help me out. Take a time and write me back.

Your friend,

Neha shah [sic]

In retrospect, Steve recalls that "what put [him] under" was Neha's having trouble with a word like "endangered." This indicated to him that she was even less prepared to do the work in his course than her early papers had led him to believe. He explained,

> Although I did not see Neha's reading and writing problems as her fault, I do expect students to come with a certain proficiency. Furthermore, I knew the Plato text was simple compared to what was coming, and I wanted to alert her to this sooner rather than later.

That Neha was extremely upset by Fishman's grade of "fail"—she cried as she told me about it—is understandable. Her previous three grades in philosophy—a "pass" and two "low passes"—apparently had not signalled the seriousness of her situation. And, as I have shown, nothing in her composition course prepared Neha to expect either the sorts of assignments or the sorts of difficulties she was now encountering. Neither had her other courses at UNCC helped her anticipate these challenges. In her English as a Foreign Language course the previous semester, as in Composition, she received an A, and her courses in religion and theatre were "easy," she said. No writing was required in either, only multiple choice tests, and she made Bs in both. However, in Intro to Sociology, a 100-level course she also took the previous semester, her experience was different. Required to write essay exams about extensive reading, she received a D. Despite this possible warning flag, Neha was as unprepared as Fishman for the distress both were feeling in early September.

A Late Piece: Visible Successes by Semester's End

Despite the distress generated by failing the first letter assignment, Neha, as I have noted, decided to stick with philosophy because of her strong desire to graduate in December. Although this grade did nothing to change her goals for the course, it did transform her expectations. No longer did she believe Intro to Philosophy was an "easy A." In fact, she said, she realized that she would have to "work hard" just to pass. To this end, by mid-September, she had cut back her job hours on Monday and Wednesday so she could devote these days to preparing for philosophy's Tuesday-Thursday class sessions. On these preparation days, she spent as much as six hours reading and writing, and, in addition, she visited the Writing Center for an hour once a week.

Neha's effort paid off, according to both student and teacher. By the end of the semester, Steve observed, Neha had succeeded in doing two of the five sorts of thinking and writing he expects. Although he deemed the quality of Neha's papers still far below that of his other students, and below college writing in general, he believed she had learned something about "reading tough texts." He also believed she was more realistic about her skills and what college writing may sometimes require.

When Neha and I spoke in December, she agreed. "I improved my writing skills, and I learned new philosophical words." In addition, she had been exposed to American culture, she said, discussing "new topics such as racism, sexism, feminism, family values, and moral values." And now, at semester's end, she found the teacher and class more "friendly." When I questioned her about why this was, she said, "Because now I think I will pass."

Neha's improved ability to read and write in philosophy can be seen in her final exam when she focuses on Bertrand Russell's *Marriage and Morals* (1929/1970). In comparing her writing on an exam to that in her letter to a classmate three months earlier, I realize I am studying genres that differ in form, audience, and writer persona. However, because both require argument extraction and evaluation or critique, and because students had the exam questions in advance, as I explain below, these assignments serve my comparative purposes.

Marriage and Morals is a book, as I have indicated, that the class read, discussed, and wrote about (in another letter-exchange) in mid-October. Now, in this early December exam, Neha shows she can do, in limited ways, what she could or would not do two months earlier. She summarizes some of Russell's points and applies them to her own life (numbers 1 and 4 on Fishman's list of five specific goals). Because I want to avoid painting an overly rosy picture of Neha's progress, I note that Neha's discussion of Russell is, in Fishman's view, the best part of her exam. Her other responses are less coherent and accurate, perhaps because they focus on more difficult (less narrative) texts by Daly (1973/1995), Mill (1843/1973), and hooks (1981/1995). In what follows, then, I present the strongest section of Neha's exam. The test question about *Marriage and Morals* reads,

> a) What are some of the events and beliefs that Bertrand Russell says provided the foundation for our patriarchal society?
> b) In your opinion, what are the pluses and minuses of patriarchy?

Neha responds,

> a) 'Marriage and Morals' by Russel is viewed as a great and famous book. In this book he talked about different cultural, traditions, society and marriages. He mainly talked about patriarchal society, which means the male is the head of the family and female always considered below than male. About his talked it seems to me like all

civilized modern societies are based upon the patriachal family, and the whole conception based of female virtue which has been built up in order to make the partriarchal family. I believe that in patriarchal society mother and father have different expression and behaviour for their child. The relation of father and son in a patrilineal society is more closer then any relation between male which is exist in other society, and man inherits from his father. I also believe this society is one kind of "primitive" society. Because in this society a father (man) has everything means power, property, affection and the patriarchal family is more closely. The main provided thing for patriarchal system is that man came to desire virginity in their brides. Men has strongly feelings for this virginity. A father has strong power over his children and wife, child could not marry without their father's consent, and it was usual for the father to decide whom they should marry. In sort, a woman has not period in her life for any independent existence because being above situation first to her father and then to her husband. At last, patriarchal society provided as the DOMINION of the father.

b) About my opinion, our society is patrirachal society. Woman always consider below than man that means male is head of the family. About my family my mom and dad are modern (new generation) but we still have to follow our society. I think there are all points and which is all minuse. Woman and man both have to have equal rights, power and oppertunity. If father is head in the family why should mother not? The main minuse point is about marriage. Why only father decide to whom child should marry. If men desire for virginity then what about woman. All this should be subtract (minuses) in patriarchy. There is only one pluse in it, and it is about respect. Means woman has to give a respect to her mother-in-law, father-in-law and her husband, and stay with her husband with all equal oppertunity. These all are the pluses and minsues points about my opinion.

When Fishman reread Neha's exam a year and a half later as we prepared this chapter, he worried that someone might accuse him, in awarding Neha a C- on this test and a C in the course, of lowering his standards. Recalling the work of Delpit (1995) and Ladson-Billings (1994), he worried he might be accused of doing this student a disservice, of "winking" at her underpreparedness and passing her in a social promotion rather than taking her writing problems seriously and holding her back. He mused,

I'd be embarrassed if someone saw Neha's writing without knowing the context—if they thought I'd certified this student as a competent college writer without confronting her. It is obvious that she doesn't understand many of the issues, and her application of Russell's concepts is somewhat garbled. Yet I believe she does step back and think about things a little differently, and that pleases me. . . . As I see it, the University accepted Neha, and it put her in my barrier class. What good would it have done for me to prevent her getting a college degree? She really tried, and she made modest progress, so I let the barrier down. In the end, I was proud of her.

INSTRUCTIONAL SUPPORTS THAT HELP AN ESL STUDENT: COMBINING WRITING-TO-LEARN WITH DIALOGIC PEDAGOGY

Although Neha Shah and her teacher had very different goals and aspirations, she nevertheless made progress in his eyes. In fact, Fishman says that in the end he was proud of her. How did this come about? Answering calls for pedagogies that help ESL students in mainstream courses, I describe those aspects of Steve's teaching which facilitated Neha's development (see Belcher & Braine, 1995; Hirvela, 1999; Leki, 1992; Zamel, 1995).

The instructional supports Neha mentioned as being particularly helpful all reflect key principles of Steve's three core theorists: Dewey, Freire, and Gramsci. That is, these instructional supports require (1) that students be active, (2) that they switch roles, alternately playing teacher and student to one another, and (3) that they enter into "dialogue" with one another, to use Freire's (1970/1997) term, or engage in "cooperative inquiry," to use Dewey's (1916/1967). Her interactions with classmates led Neha, at some moments at least, to experience what Freire terms "solidarity [through] communication" (p. 58), thus giving her a social motive or "for-what" for doing course assignments.

In Neha's comments about the instructional supports that most helped her, it is clear that writing-to-learn was not as effective for her when done by itself as it was when combined with peer interaction. And this is understandable for an ESL student who was less comfortable writing English than speaking it with her classmates. In a December interview, Neha remarked that being required to write about every assigned text was good for her because it made her read actively: "not just like normal... [but] deeply so I understand everything." However, she quickly added that despite spending as much as six hours on her assignments, she still frequently came to class unclear about the text's meaning. But once there, she said, she knew she would get help. That is, she would get to talk about her own homework and hear her classmates describe theirs, and this was key to her understanding. In Neha's description of Steve's pedagogy, there are echoes of Freire's (1970/1997) dialogic, problem-posing approach. She explained,

> We had already done the assignment, right, and after assignment he will talk what the assignment about. Then, [in pairs or small groups or class discussion], I hear what my ideas are and what other people's ideas are, and I finally understand the material better. My mind clicks on... and I clear up some of my confusions.

I turn now to three types of assignment that Neha identified as most helpful to her: first, the letter exchanges with classmates; second, student-generated exams; and, finally, student-generated questions for class discussion.

The Letter Exchange: Helping Students Teach One Another

I have already analyzed Neha's early-September letter to Robert Bullerdick about two Platonic dialogues, the first of four such exchanges across the semester. Three months later, in December, Neha and I spoke about her fourth letter, one focusing on a chapter in Dewey's (1920/1962) *Reconstruction in Philosophy*. Neha was paired with 36-year-old Ellen Williams, a classmate whom she knew and liked from their prior classroom interactions, and for whom, Neha told me, she had tried hard to write clearly so Ellen could respond. When I mentioned that I had just spoken to Ellen, another of my research informants and a student I will report on in the next chapter, Neha asked, "Did she understand my question?" (Ellen and

I had not discussed this.) The fact that Neha felt responsible to a classmate, not just the teacher, invested the assignment with social meaning and provided her, in addition to her usual worry about her grade, with an additional "for-what." Neha genuinely wanted to communicate with Ellen. However, in order to achieve this goal, Neha had to adopt one of Fishman's. She had to engage with Ellen in collaborative exploration of cultural knowledge, precisely the outcome Steve hoped for from this assignment.

In addition, these two students were teaching and learning from one another, and, in the process, they were developing the sort of solidarity that Dewey, Freire, and Gramsci all want. That is, Neha identified with and cared about Ellen, and she was committed to working with Ellen in ways she was not with Steve. Neha described her letter writing process:

> I have to read [Dewey's chapter] twice because when I read first time I don't understand. I'm lost. After the second time my mind is clearer. I highlight, and I put in the margin what I'm going to ask Ellen. . . . My question is I'm not sure if [Dewey] believe in science or he just believe in philosophy. . . . I mean does he believe philosophy is related to science or not? Because I'm not sure. At first he said philosophy's just imagination, but later he said philosophy is a science experience, and then he says philosophy is also like a social tradition. I was lost, so I just asked her what Dewey believes. . . .

Steve was pleased at what he saw as Neha's progress since asking Robert Bullerdick three months earlier what "endangering" means. Instead of being limited to word-level concerns, she was now doing textual interpretation, trying to extract Dewey's argument and shape a good question for Ellen. In her letter, she describes what she understands of Dewey's argument before asking, "Does Dewey believe philosophy is relevant with science and the practical experience?" Here, Neha is playing both student and teacher, the sort of role-changing that Freire, Gramsci, and Dewey recommend. As a student, Neha is confused, she tells Ellen, and really needs help. However, to make it possible for Ellen to mentor her, Neha must put herself in the teacher's position. In order to ask intelligible questions, teachers must make clear to students where they are coming from. Put differently, teachers must provide their students with a context for their questions. Neha strove to do this and was eager, she told me, to read Ellen's response at the next class meeting. She also knew that Steve would provide an opportunity to discuss these letters, calling on pairs in class to report on their exchanges and what they had learned from one another as they corresponded about the Dewey text.

Student Generated Exams: Promoting Dialogue and Cooperative Inquiry

In addition to the letter exchanges, Neha named a second instructional support as particularly helpful: Steve's student generated exams. He structures both mid-term and final in ways that invite students to study together and, more than that, to feel ownership of the test itself. To achieve this he asks students to generate the actual questions that will appear on the test. Allowing them to set the agenda in this way is reminiscent of Freire's (1970/2000) insistence that his adult literacy students choose their own "codifications" or objects of study (p. 27). That is, in order for his adult learners to be able to objectify and critically examine their situation, Freire argues, they have to participate in choosing the images upon which they will focus. Similarly, by writing the test questions, students are involved in shaping the foci of their concentration as they prepare for and write the exams.

In this pedagogy, Fishman is, once again, asking students to engage in active intellectual exploration as they become teachers to one another. He assigns each of them a text that might be covered on the exam and requires, for a homework assignment, that they construct a possible test question about that reading. Students hand these in, and Fishman chooses six, which he gives to students a week before the test. From these six questions he chooses three on exam day that students must write about. As they study for and write the test, then, pupils are focusing on questions posed not by Fishman but by themselves and their classmates.

In addition to wanting students to feel ownership of the test, to be involved in shaping their own codifications, Fishman also intends to promote collaborative inquiry outside class. Since pupils have the exam questions in advance, he encourages them to exchange phone numbers in hopes that they will get together outside class hours. In fact, this often happens. Some students tell me they arrange to go to dinner together or to meet in groups on campus to jointly construct answers. Others tell me they converse on the phone. This assignment thus provides additional opportunities for students to practice philosophic exploration and break down social barriers, to build upon their individual strengths as they contribute to group projects (see Dewey 1916/1967, p. 84).

The exam structure worked well for Neha. She was on her own during the exams, of course, but she indicated that these tests were less frightening and isolating for her than the typical exam. Although she did not plan to meet with other students to prepare for the test, she did discuss the questions in a chance encounter with a classmate. Neha ran into Tonya McInnis, a 30-year-old African American pre-nursing student, in the cafeteria about three hours before the exam. Neha told me that she asked Tonya about the test question with which she was having most difficulty, and, after moving to a nearby student lounge, Tonya explained her interpretation of it. Neha remarked that she was grateful to Tonya for her kindness that morning, and she believed their conversation helped her.

Student Generated Questions for Class Discussion: Integrating Individual and Group

A final effective instructional support Neha identified involved, once again, dialogue among students which Steve orchestrated but in which he did not directly participate. Four times during the semester he asks students to bring in a question about an assigned reading that might serve as the basis for small group discussion. Once again, Fishman avoids the banking model by asking students to pose their own problems, to join together in cooperative exploration of ideas and become "critical co-investigators" (Freire, 1970/1997, p. 62).

When students arrive in class with their questions, Fishman puts them in groups of four or five. Here, they discuss their questions about the reading and choose the one they think is best, the one most clearly about a key issue or passage. They then pass it to a neighboring group for an answer. This second group discusses it, and, in order to insure that all students stay active and no one pupil becomes too dominant, Fishman has all members of that group write the answer that they have constructed together. Fishman's concern about one student dominating the others echoes Freire's (1970/1997) worry about hierarchies within any human association (chapter 4). It also echoes Dewey's (1916/1967) warning against "machine-like" relations among people working on common projects, that is, relations in which powerful members of the group use less powerful ones "without reference to the emotional and intellectual disposition and consent of those used" (p. 5).

When the small group members have agreed upon their common answer and each student has recorded it, Fishman calls the class back together. But instead of playing teacher, he takes the role of student, asking real-information questions, that is, queries to which he does not have answers. He wants to hear from each group about the question it received and the answer it constructed. After each group reports its answer, Fishman turns to the group in which that question originated and asks those students to evaluate the answer. Thus, working collaboratively and speaking for their groups, students inform Fishman and their classmates about their interpretations of the text and their evaluations of each others' questions and answers. In addition, throughout this activity students comment on their group's interactions, describing their dialogue, their conflicts and compromises, and their decision-making processes.

How did these small group conversations serve Neha? First, she told me, she had been excited when, on one occasion in early November, her group chose her question as its best. "I told everybody [in the next group,] 'That's my question.' I was proud." Her satisfaction is understandable. She had been able to join with her classmates in conjoint activity, and she had understood the requirements for group participation well enough that her question had been judged the best. In a course where she felt very much at risk as a student, Neha had been picked by her group to represent it, to play teacher, in essence, to pupils in the adjoining group. Her pleasure at having her question chosen corroborates Dewey's (1897/1964a) contention that students have a desire "to give out . . . and serve" (p. 119).

Not surprisingly, this social "for what" or goal of contributing to collaborative exploration worked better for Neha in the small group interactions than in whole-class discussions. In the small groups, she said, she could forget about her grade and just converse with her classmates, whereas in the whole group she remained "nervous" about speaking. It also helped her in these small groups, she commented, when she realized that other students also struggled at times to understand the assigned texts.

In sum, then, Steve Fishman's dialogic pedagogy facilitated Neha Shah's reading and writing progress in Intro to Philosophy. It gave her an opportunity to practice philosophic exploration, often by becoming teacher or student to her peers, and this helped her understand course material. Equally important, Steve's dialogic pedagogy gave Neha a new social goal or "for-what" for doing the work. At moments when she contributed to joint inquiry and became part of the group, she told me, the hours she spent on her homework seemed more worthwhile.

FREIRIAN, GRAMSCIAN, AND DEWEYAN EVALUATIONS

At the end of the semester, as I have noted, Steve said he was proud of Neha's effort, satisfied that she had a good experience in his class. In particular, he mentioned Neha's hard work, which he clearly respected, and the fact that she left his class knowing what it is to wrestle with challenging reading and writing. Put differently, she had met, at least in some measure, two of his five expectations for philosophy students: argument extraction (objective 1) and application of philosophy for the purpose of critique (objective 4). As for Neha herself, as I have also noted, she felt her writing skills and vocabulary had improved and she had been exposed to tensions in American culture about which she had previously been unaware.

To extend my evaluation of Neha's experience in Steve's class, I also ask, What would the three theorists at the heart of Fishman's pedagogy say? How would Freire, Gramsci, and Dewey evaluate Neha's learning? How would they evaluate Steve's teaching?

Freirian Evaluation

Freire, I believe, would be disappointed in some ways and pleased in others. On the one hand, Neha and Steve do not achieve the dialogic, problem-posing ideal he proposes. Teacher and student never shape questions and goals together, as Freire wants, nor do they trade ideas in ways that help Neha (re)name the world. In fact, Fishman remembers his and Neha's exchanges in class as being very limited. When he called on her, he told me, she would offer her viewpoint, but she generally avoided eye contact, apparently hoping he would pass her over, and when she did contribute, she spoke so quietly it was difficult to hear her. During some class periods, he recalls, she even sat outside the class circle. On the other hand, as I have shown, Neha experienced something of the "solidarity" Freire (1970/1997, p. 58) hopes for in small group interactions, contributing her opinion as readily as other students to conjoint inquiry.

Steve's classroom is, thus, far from Freire's educational nightmare: an oppressive lecture-banking situation in which students are totally silenced. Nevertheless, Neha hardly became the person, as Freire (Shor & Freire, 1987) wants, whose "critical consciousness" had been raised about the work she was going to perform as a mathematician/computer scientist and the class-divided society in which she would carry out her vocation (p. 69). Freire (1970/2000) might well argue that this was Steve's fault. The "codifications," the texts, that Steve presented Neha, Freire might say, were inappropriate for Neha and thus mitigated against her successfully "problematizing" her social and political situation (p. 27).

Gramscian Evaluation

In a Gramscian evaluation, Neha and Steve fare somewhat better. By contrast with Freire, Gramsci (1971) would commend Steve on his assignments because it is important, in Gramsci's view, to expose students to the history of ideas, to show them something about how systems of thought develop. This provides a context for students' own ideas and helps them articulate and reflect on their views, a practice that is crucial if they are to align their beliefs with their actions in responsible ways. Thus, Gramsci would be less concerned than Freire that Steve imposed texts on Neha in which she had little interest. For Gramsci, being challenged by difficult and unfamiliar subject matter (such as Greek and Latin) helps students learn self-discipline, and he would applaud the work habits Neha employed in Steve's class. Her ability to sit at her desk for hours on end and her strong desire for academic credentials were useful forces of academic production she brought with her from India. Although Gramsci's ultimate objective for students—critiquing the values and practices of their own culture in light of those of others—was elusive for Neha, she did open the door a crack to such thinking by semester's end, as I have shown. Neha's consideration of patriarchy and the roles of women did not result in reconstruction of her views during Steve's course, but it may one day provide a basis for thinking more deeply about these issues.

Deweyan Evaluation

Finally, an evaluation of Neha's experience through Deweyan lenses also provides a mixed report. On the negative side, Dewey would notice that Neha achieved little of one of his primary goals for students: personal growth or expanded interests. For the most part, she did not see her beliefs in new ways, nor did she leave Fishman's class wanting to read or write more philosophy. This failure is rooted, Dewey (1902/1990c) would say, in Steve's inability to help Neha achieve another of his ideals: student-curriculum integration. Agreeing with Gramsci, Dewey would find the assigned texts appropriate, but he would lament that despite Neha's occasionally connecting with philosophic subject matter, she seemed more often to keep it at bay. Put differently, Steve failed to help Neha see learning philosophy as a personally meaningful "for-what," and she developed no additional objectives of her own, although, as I have shown, Steve's pedagogy at times provided her with a social motive for doing the work. Instead, the one goal Neha started with—passing the course—kept her almost always focused on grades, her labor alienated, her work commodified for its exchange value rather than its intrinsic value. Neha's concern for grades is an understandable "to-what" given her fear of failing, but it is one Dewey would abhor. This focus, along with other conditions I have described, meant that Neha seldom, if ever, experienced the sort of "wholeheartedness" Dewey (1916/1967) values, the "intellectual integrity" which allows students to see their school work as reflecting their genuine interests and self-expressions (pp. 173–79; see also 1933/1960, pp. 30–33).

However negatively Dewey might evaluate Neha's experience, he would also find things to celebrate. This is because Dewey (1938/1963a, chapter 2) insists that student progress must be measured not against across-the-board standards but according to an individual's particular trajectory. That is, teachers must compare the place where the pupil began with the place where he or she finishes. In this regard, Dewey would find Neha's story praiseworthy. This is because she developed as a reader and writer, as I have shown, and because, in the process, she had an experience that challenged her in ways unique among her college courses. Most important, she joined in cooperative inquiry with her classmates—and appreciated the benefits of doing so—in ways Dewey would certainly applaud.

Finally, for Dewey, a significant test of an educative experience is the residue students carry forward to future experiences. In terms of this test as well, Dewey would have some grounds for optimism. In an interview a year and a half after the course concluded, Neha told me that her work in philosophy had been sufficiently valuable to cause her to recommend the course to her sister, now a freshman at UNCC.

Conclusion
STEVE FISHMAN AND LUCILLE McCARTHY

What do we learn from this account of an ESL writer and her discipline-based professor, their mismatch of goals and aspirations, their struggles and eventual satisfaction?

This study shows the importance of giving ESL students in discipline-based courses frequent opportunities, and various types of opportunities, to engage with classmates, sharing and discussing their work. As Neha Shah explained, her difficulties reading philosophic texts and her difficulties writing about them meant that even after six hours on a homework assignment, she was still confused. But given the way Steve structured his classroom—offering students chances to explore ideas with one another, share their questions about assigned texts, and read each other's homework—Neha said that in class, frequently, things "clicked." We believe this is significant because it shows that writing-to-learn by itself may not be enough for students whose English reading and writing skills are weak. However, when set in the context of student give and take with peers, writing-to-learn pays off.

Although we cannot generalize from a single case, we believe our study is illuminative since Neha's so-called "instrumental" approach to her philosophy class is fairly typical of undergraduates. Further, her unhappiness at having to take the course in the first place and her expectations that it would require no time yet be an "easy A" meant that she and her instructor shared few goals and experienced little likemindedness. In this way, Neha presented a difficult challenge for Steve's pedagogy. Yet despite having very different aspirations from those of her teacher, Neha achieved two of Fishman's specific classroom objectives and made progress toward a third. She was able to do argument extraction as she read and wrote about philosophic texts, and she was able to apply philosophy to her own life, critiquing, if only in modest ways, the power structures in which she lives. She also developed increased sensitivity to some of the tensions within American culture, sowing seeds that may, one day, help her contextualize the social dilemmas she encounters in her newly adopted country.

Coda

The Researchers Continue to Converse

STEVE FISHMAN AND LUCILLE McCARTHY

We choose in this coda to complexify our research story, to reveal some of the conflicts between the two of us that are not evident in the report we have just presented. Although we have necessarily neatened our report for the sake of clarity and the development of a narrative line, in this section we describe some of the rough-edged disagreements that actually punctuated our conversations as we conducted this study.

Whereas both of us thought Neha made progress and found aspects of Fishman's pedagogy helpful, in the end McCarthy believed that Fishman had not done enough for Neha. Reflecting McCarthy's familiarity with the research on ESL and "basic" writing, she believed that it was Fishman's failure to draw upon and celebrate Neha's home language and culture that was a key factor in Neha's troubles. As Cummins (1986) says, students like Neha will not realize their potential unless they are helped to feel good about their own language and perspectives as well as those of the dominant group. In addition, McCarthy thought that despite Fishman's apparent recognition, on the first day of class, of the value of Neha's borderland perspective, he still missed numerous opportunities to learn from her.

For example, whereas Fishman gave Neha an F on her letter to a classmate about Plato's *Apology* and *Crito*, McCarthy believed he should have seen it as one of the most valuable papers he got. She argued that both its rhetorical style and content could be interpreted as challenging the Eurocentric, male, academic tradition, especially that tradition's overemphasis on rationality and mind. With regard to the form of Neha's writing, McCarthy thought that if Fishman had been more sympathetic, he might have seen Neha's unconventional style as a protest against the sterility of academic discourse. He might have recognized in her unique locutions a resistance that should be celebrated rather than criticized, her innovations echoing those of writers like Gloria Anzaldua (1987), Theodore Dreiser (1981), and Gertrude Stein (1933). (See Lu, 1994/1999b; Leki, 1992.) With regard to Neha's content, McCarthy thought that, in asking about the word "endangered," Neha was, perhaps, just following Fishman's and Socrates' lead in making a fetish of clarity about particular words and concepts. And later, when Neha focused on Socrates's argument about ordinary people's limited capacity to harm his most important part, his soul, McCarthy thought Neha may have been questioning western philosophy's elevation of mind over body.

In McCarthy's conversations with Fishman across the semester, she chided him not only for failing to excavate ideas that may have been beneath the surface of Neha's writing but also for giving up on her too easily in class. Apart from the first day, he called on her only six times during the semester, on one occasion asking her to describe her own Hindu views of the afterlife, an experience she recalled proudly a year and a half after the course concluded. Had Fishman moved more actively into Neha's culture, McCarthy argued, rather than expecting her to do all the moving into his, Neha could have built upon the cultural capital she brought with her rather than having to leave it at his classroom door. In short, McCarthy believed that Fishman missed chances to do what Cummins (1986) advises, namely be Neha's advocate rather than her assessor and gatekeeper.

Behind McCarthy's unhappiness with Fishman's response to Neha was not just her familiarity with ESL and composition research. McCarthy's disagreements with him were also the result of ideological differences, her commitment to Freirian (1970/1997) and Gramscian (1971) principles of social transformation that she believed Fishman underappreciated. In his failure to let Neha develop her own codifications or alterations of his curriculum, and in his failure to listen carefully to Neha or to engage in authentic dialogue with her, McCarthy thought him deaf to Freire's call to teachers to truly learn from their students and renounce their class identity to develop solidarity with them. This meant for McCarthy, to borrow Freirian language, that Fishman overlooked valuable chances to help Neha transform herself from an "object" of dehumanizing oppression in his classroom into a "subject" who was becoming humanized and liberated (1970/1997, chapters 1, 2). These were the same negligences, according to McCarthy, that prevented Fishman from being the sort of "organic intellectual" to Neha that Gramsci would have wanted. In the end, McCarthy felt that Fishman was too much influenced by Dewey's assimilationist pedagogy, an approach she sees as serving the interests of the professional middle class, one that ignores the negative effects of mainstream teachers upon students who differ in culture, race, and gender (see also Delpit, 1995; Ladson-Billings, 1994).

Fishman, for his part, replied that he found it difficult to see ways to modify his pedagogy to take advantage of Neha's unique cultural knowledge, and he invoked some of the same theorists to defend his approach that McCarthy used to criticize it. He kept insisting that to adopt McCarthy's stance, to read into Neha's writing ideas that he thought were not there, was to hinder the balance he was trying to achieve between what Dewey (1930/1990b) calls "construction and criticism." That is, he thought such a stance would tip his classroom discourse too much toward student expression and not enough toward student taking in. He feared it might be an example of what Gramsci (1971) terms an exaggeration of "libertarian" ideology in education (p. 32), an overemphasis on students' self-assertion to the neglect of students' critical thinking.

In addition, Fishman kept invoking Gramsci's idea that to effectively resist the dominant culture, students must also master it. They have to understand its history, command its language, and learn its logic. Although he admired the determination and self-discipline Neha displayed after he warned her she might fail his course—in fact, he often wished outloud that more of his students would come to his class with the sort of academic capital or know-how Neha possessed—he continued to lament that because he could not help her find the relevance of his curriculum to her personal growth and career preparation she acquired only a minimal understanding of philosophy.

Thus, the many suggestions that McCarthy presented to Fishman from the composition research—for example, ideas about having students audiotape narratives in order to compare oral and written forms of expression, assignments in which students might compare home and school languages or dominant and minority cultures—did not strike a responsive chord in Fishman. For example, he worried that to go along with McCarthy and present Neha's Plato letter to his philosophy class as a superior paper, one that could be seen as challenging the Western tradition and its emphasis on what Habermas (1972) labels "technical rationality," would support an "anything goes" attitude, what Gramsci (1971) might call a relaxation of standards (pp. 37–38). Put differently, Fishman feared that to follow McCarthy's interpretations would be to lead his students down a path of radical relativism where all responses to a written work are seen as equally valuable, with no way to distinguish ones that are more responsible to the text and coherent from those that are less.

Despite Fishman's unwillingness to adopt McCarthy's suggestions, he remained conflicted. Referring to the Freirian epigraph with which we began this chapter, he had to admit that it was precisely students like Neha for whom he wanted to provide "tangible" help, and he feared McCarthy was correct when she said he was narrowminded in the ways he approached the issues and opportunities Neha's appearance in his classroom presented. He was particularly stung when, at one point, McCarthy—referring to a well known account of a Mexican American's assimilation—accused him of having "Rodriguezed" Neha (see Rodriguez, 1982). Still, Fishman continued to try to justify his stance to McCarthy. He was stuck with the idea that, although it was important for his students to be innovative and to critique his discipline's practices, they needed to get to know something of the philosophic tradition in order to intelligently challenge it. He could not give up the thought that it was self-defeating to encourage his students to resist the authors and the works he selected for his syllabus before they had a reasonable grasp of what these authors had to say.

CHAPTER THREE

Conflicting Discourses: Teacher and Student Making Progress in a Racialized Space

The starting-point of critical elaboration is . . . "knowing thyself" as a product of the historical process . . . which has deposited in you an infinity of traces, without leaving an inventory.

Antonio Gramsci (1971, p. 324)

In the previous chapter, we reported Fishman's success in helping a recent immigrant, Neha Shah, make progress toward his goals for undergraduate thinking and writing. In this chapter, we describe Steve's success with another underprepared writer, a pupil with a very different history: 36-year-old, African American, returning student, Ellen Williams. Although Ellen's improvement with regard to the surface features of her writing was, like Neha's, modest, the change in her attitude toward philosophy and her ability to use it in personally meaningful ways was quite dramatic.

OUR CENTRAL FINDING: STORYTELLING IS NOT ENOUGH

Our main finding in chapter 2 was that writing-to-learn was not enough for Neha Shah, that she also needed small group discussion of her writing-to-learn homework exercises in order to succeed in Fishman's course. Our central finding in this chapter echoes that one. We found that, for Ellen Williams, storytelling was important but that, by itself, it was not enough. Ellen's stories and accounts of personal experience were productive for her only when Fishman could help her contextualize them—that is, help her see them as reflective of broader philosophic issues. Thus, just as writing-to-learn was important for Neha but required connection to small group work, so, in similar ways, storytelling was important for Ellen but required opportunities for reflection and questioning.

Unfortunately, Fishman was not always successful in orchestrating such opportunities. As McCarthy will show, when he could not help Ellen examine her stories from new angles, her accounts of personal experience were unproductive, actually erecting or strengthening barriers between her and her classmates and teacher. By contrast, when he did provide philosophic background for Ellen's stories, she came to see her views less as transcendent truths and more as social constructions. She could, thus, step back to explore and appraise them in ways both she and Steve deemed productive.

Fishman's effort to provide philosophic background for student stories and opinions reflects his commitment to Gramsci (1971) and Dewey (Dewey & Bentley, 1949). Following Gramsci, Fishman believes that for students to know themselves they have to investigate the intellectual movements that, as Gramsci puts it, have deposited their "traces" in pupils' ideas but have left no "inventory" (p. 324). That is, Fishman sees contextualizing stories as a way of enabling students to label their beliefs, to make explicit their ideas' histories and the ways these histories carry with them implicit worldviews and assumptions about power. In Deweyan terms, setting student accounts in philosophic and historical context is important because it encourages students to see their experiences as transactions between their interpretive frameworks and their material conditions. It helps them recognize the ways in which their own perspectives shape their experiences and the meanings they take from them.

When Fishman succeeded in helping Ellen do what Gramsci and Dewey wish—put her ideas in historical and philosophic context—we found there were two consequences for her. First, she could gain critical distance on her narratives and, thus, achieve one of Steve's overall goals for students: an appreciation of the value of exploring cultural knowledge and its usefulness for developing a better understanding of oneself and one's world. Second, it helped her realize another of Fishman's general goals—social reform—as it gave her, as well as other students who contributed to joint inquiry in class discussion, a sense of a democratized and transformed social space. More specifically, it enabled Ellen and her classmates to become more sensitive to the effects of their actions upon others, to develop the social intelligence Dewey sees as the hallmark of democratic living (1916/1967, pp. 87, 121–122). This feeling of mutual concern and trust among classmates that Ellen experienced in this space was something that not only Dewey treasures but Gramsci and Freire as well.

In sum, we agree with Critical Race Theorists and feminists who argue that storytelling is essential to giving minorites and women a voice (eg. Bambara, 1984; Bell, 1992; Christian, 1987; Delgado, 1989, 1990, 1989/1995a, 1995b; Grumet, 1988; Ladson-Billings, 1998; Russell, 1983; Schniedewind, 1985; Shrewsbury, 1993; Williams, 1991). However, we also agree with hooks (1989, p. 110) and Giroux (1991, p. 254; 1992, p. 80) who warn that storytelling and personal opinion are not enough if students are to achieve powerful and influential voices. To do this, hooks and Giroux claim, students must also forge connections between their narratives and cultural, historical, and political themes. Our study of this particular under-prepared writer corroborates their claim.

Following our organizational pattern in chapter 2, we offer a three-part account. In the first, Steve Fishman describes what he sees as Ellen Williams's progress toward his goals by contrasting her early and late semester papers. In Part Two, Lucille McCarthy outlines the instructional supports that Ellen indicated were significant in her progress. Finally, at the end of this chapter, as at the close of the previous one, we provide a coda in which we explore our unresolved differences: our disagreements about appropriate course requirements and grading criteria for Ellen Williams. Throughout this three-part chapter, in order to gain a critical edge on Fishman's pedagogy, we employ, in addition to the theories of Dewey, Gramsci, and Freire, the work of the Critical Race Theorists we have just mentioned as well as scholars engaged in Whiteness studies (eg. Dyer, 1997; Frankenberg, 1993; Marshall & Ryden, 2000; Miles, 1993;

Prendergast, 1998; Roediger, 1991, 2002; Thompson, 1998).

We begin our account of Ellen Williams's experiences in Intro to Philosophy by contrasting her with Neha Shah.

TWO UNDERPREPARED STUDENTS: SIMILAR INSTRUMENTALIST GOALS, DIFFERENT HISTORICAL AND MATERIAL CONDITIONS

Ellen Williams, a junior transfer student who had completed an associate of arts degree 12 years earlier, came to Steve's course, like Neha Shah, with little preparation for the sort of reading and writing he assigns. And, like Neha, Ellen's goal for taking the course was solely to fulfill a graduation requirement. She had no interest in philosophy and believed, more generally, that undergraduate education is without intrinsic value. But Ellen needed "that piece of paper," as she referred to the bachelor's degree, because, without it, she could not advance in her job as a prison guard working the night shift in a minimum security facility. Thus, she sounded much like Neha Shah when she told Lucille that, for her, UNC Charlotte was a useless and time-consuming stepping stone to her real objective. Alternatively put, Ellen, like Neha, approached her work in philosophy as alienated labor.

Although Neha and Ellen were both female members of minority groups, uninterested in and new to the reading and writing Fishman required, and although both had full-time jobs when the semester began, this is where their similarities ended. The historical and material conditions within which they labored were very different. Whereas Neha lived with her family and could afford to reduce her out-of-school work hours, Ellen could not.[1] She was a single mother supporting two sons, ages 9 and 11, housing a 25-year-old nephew who had moved to Charlotte from New York to live with her, and caring for her ill mother. And whereas Neha saw Steve's philosophy class as unnecessary because she already had a degree from a university in her home country, Ellen's alienation was differently rooted. Her grievance about having to take Intro to Philosophy was not directed, as it was for Neha, against a particular university administrator. Rather, Ellen's alienation was from the entire culture of the university, and its origin lay in the very racial tensions and prejudices in America which came as a surprise to Neha and which are at the center of Critical Race Theorists' concerns.

More specifically, Ellen's aversion to taking philosophy was rooted in two fundamental beliefs. First, it was Ellen's tacit sense that the university is a racialized space, one designed to maintain the economic and cultural dominance of Whites, or, as Critical Race Theorists put it, to maintain Whiteness as a valuable property (Bell, 1987; Harris, 1993; Ladson-Billings & Tate, 1995). That is, UNC Charlotte represented for Ellen a public school system that has historically excluded African Americans, an institution that has used admission requirements and writing placement exams to conceal its role in the perpetuation of deep-seated social injustices. Second, Ellen's alienation from the university was rooted in the related belief, one she frequently articulated to Lucille, that book learning is of little value in comparison to life experience. This valuing of wisdom gained from life experience above that gained in school is, according to educational researchers, common among Black reentry women (see Luttrell, 1989; Weis, 1985, 1992).

Thus, Ellen's and Neha's resistances to Fishman's course sprang from their histories as members of different minority groups. Whereas Neha is a member of a high-status minority, a product of voluntary immigration in pursuit of increased economic opportunity, Ellen is a member of what Ogbu (1988) calls an involuntary immigrant group, one that has had to battle centuries of negative attributions and exclusions by the dominant Euroamerican class (see Cummins, 1986; Suarez-Orozco, 2001). That is, Ellen, unlike Neha, grew up in a society that deprecates her home culture, its language and practices. These differences between Neha Shah and Ellen Williams meant that, although they both were instrumentalists and approached their work in philosophy as alienated labor, the material, political, and social conditions under which they labored were quite different. In particular, there were significant disparities between these students in the amount of time they could afford to devote to Intro to Philosophy, the forces of academic production they could bring to their reading and writing, and the family supports they could draw upon.

Different Forces of Production: Time, Habits, Skills

As we have explained, Neha Shah had been a good student in her native India and came from a financially successful and professionally oriented family. When Neha had to revise her expectations about the amount and difficulty of the work in Steve's course, she had well established academic study habits she could bring into play. The fact that Neha could spend as much as six hours preparing for philosophy class separates her not only from Ellen but from the majority of Steve's students. Neha's previous schooling had given her one of the skills Gramsci (1971) believes a pre-university education should provide: the self-discipline to focus for long hours on intellectual tasks (p. 37). In addition, Neha told McCarthy, she received considerable help at home, her older cousin and younger sister acting as respondents and editors for her philosophic writing.

The forces of production that Ellen Williams brought to philosophy stand in sharp contrast to Neha's. By the time Ellen arrived in Steve's course in fall 1998, she had been trying for 12 years to move beyond the associate's degree she had received from a community college. On three occasions, in 1990 at the University of Connecticut at Storrs and in 1993 and 1995 at UNC Charlotte, she had enrolled in a baccalaureate program only to fail or withdraw. So not only did Ellen have heavy family and financial responsibilities that were absent from Neha's life, Ellen's discontinuous education and uneven record of school success meant she had less experience with the rhythms and routines of academic labor which Neha found so familiar. (For more on the challenges facing working class reentry women, see Lewis, 1988; Zwerling & London, 1992. For discussion of the correlation of college success and numbers of hours worked at an outside job, see Brint & Karabel, 1989; Soliday, 1999.)

Ellen's situation is, however, more complex than we have presented so far. Although she did not have the same financial resources and academic work habits as Neha, she brought other types of capital to

Fishman's course, strengths and motivations which were considerable. Alongside Ellen's instrumentalist approach to "that piece of paper," and alongside her sense that universities are racialized spaces, were more positive feelings about higher education. She told both of us about her aspiration to set an example for her young sons, to show them that college was within their grasp. She also told us that she wanted to follow in her mother's footsteps, a woman who, while raising six children, managed to go back to school and earn an associate's degree so she could become a practical nurse. In addition to motives arising from family relationships, Ellen brought important English oral skills, or linguistic capital, which Neha simply did not possess. For example, Ellen was an engaging storyteller and courageous about expressing her views even when the majority or those in authority opposed her.

Achieving Different Successes

Because Neha Shah and Ellen Williams brought different sorts of capital to Fishman's course, it is not surprising that they also achieved diverse successes. Whereas Neha achieved two of the five specific objectives for student thinking and writing that Fishman outlined in chapter 2, we found that by the end of the semester Ellen had achieved four: (1) argument extraction, (2) argument evaluation, (3) contextualization of one's own opinion, and (4) application of philosophy. Most striking, as we will show, was Ellen's achievement of goal 4. She came to understand, in ways Neha never did, the value of applying philosophic issues and methods to her own life. In so doing, she practiced the sort of Socratic inquiry—the critical examination of alternative perspectives—that characterizes philosophic thinking. As she told Lucille in a follow-up interview 5 months after the course concluded,

> That class really made me open my mind. I question things now—like religion—that I never even knew you could question. . . . At first, I didn't want to; I just did not have time or interest. But then I heard people putting all sorts of ideas on the table, and I thought, Why not think about these things? The seed was planted, and me being me,

even if I did not want to think about these ideas, I was going to. At 11:00 at night—when I went to work—that class was still on my mind.

By the close of the semester, then, Ellen saw philosophy in less instrumentalist terms than when she began the course. That is, unlike Neha, Ellen came to see her work in philosophy as personally valuable and growth-producing, intrinsically worthwhile instead of just a forgettable means to her degree. Her academic labors came to have, to employ Marxian language, *use* value as well as *exchange* value (Marx, 1867/1967, pp. 47–93).

In Part One that follows, Fishman begins by analyzing Ellen's first homework assignment, one that manifests her resistance to his book knowledge, her relative unpreparedness to write in the dominant code, and her perspective on American racism. He then skips to the end of the semester to describe Ellen's final essay which, he argues, represents significant growth in terms of his specific class objectives.

༄

Part One

An Early-Semester Homework Paper: White Teacher, Black Student, and Their Conflicting Discourses

STEVE FISHMAN

As was the case with Neha Shah, I was dismayed by Ellen's early papers, compositions that, once again, made me feel that this student was underprepared for my "writing intensive" philosophy course and that I, in turn, was underprepared for her. As an example of Ellen's early work, I reproduce her first paper of the semester, a homework response to a five-page excerpt from Stokely Carmichael's essay, "What We Want" (1966/1995). The Carmichael piece was the second of three readings in my opening unit, a section dealing with racism that featured the work of Fanon (1965/1995), Carmichael (1966/1995), and hooks (1981/1995). I began the course with this topic in an effort to get my students' attention, to let them know that we were going to be dealing with important social issues and that the readings in the class were intended to challenge beliefs which may be so deeply held that, as Gramsci (1971) tells us, they are invisible.

For homework, I asked students after they read Carmichael's essay—a critique of integration as a subterfuge for maintaining White supremacy—to respond to the following prompt:

> Please type a brief summary of Carmichael's argument against racial integration of White and Black in America. Conclude your summary with a question about Carmichael's position which you would be willing to present to the class as discussion leader.

In this prompt, I was asking, first, that students summarize Carmichael's argument (objective 1) and, second, that they question or evaluate it (objective 2).

Ellen's response to this assignment, which I reproduce below just as she typed it, is satisfactory because she accurately summarizes Carmichael's argument about the negative consequences of desegregation. I was pleased that she was strongly engaged with the topic, apparently really wanting me to know what she believed. However, as I explain below, there are two aspects of Ellen's homework— the unusual number of surface errors and a style of argumentation characterized by numerous non sequiturs—which drew my critical attention. Ellen writes,

Stokely Carmichael's

Carmichael believes that black America has two problems. First they are poor and second they are black.This country does not function by morality ,love or non violence, but by power and black people have no power. Name ten black millionaires

He believed that integration speaks only to the problem of blackness. Integration means the man who becomes successful and makes it leaving his black brother behind in the ghetto. It says in order to have a decent house or education blacks must move in to a white neighborhood or go to a white school, and this only reinforces among black and white that white is better and black is inferior.It just allows the nation to focus on only a handful. This situation will not change until black people have power to control their own schools, and communities,when Negroes will become equal. That is when integration ceases to be a one way street. It means white people moving into black communities. White people joining groups such as NAACP that is when integration becomes relevant. A lot of people like my mother will tell you that we as a people have came a long way ,she will also tell you how she remembers being ordered to get to the back of the bus .Now a days many black people that ride the bus every day may not have ever sat in the back of the bus. I look for the times when blacks and whites will come together as a people ,but I really donot belive it would happen at least not in my life time.

The laws are not grovern for the black people Who made the laws the white man You can only get as far as someone lets you, especially if you are poor. If you are a poor black man and in the wrong place at the wrong time you can kiss your freedom good bye for a while.

That semester I was using an evaluation scheme of "high pass," "pass," "low pass," and "fail," and I gave Ellen a "pass" on this assignment because of her satisfactory summary of Carmichael's main point. At the top of Ellen's paper, however, I made no comment about the content of her homework. Instead, I suggested, "Please try to get help with your writing at the Writing Center," a remark that reflected my uncertainty, once again, as with Neha, about how to respond to this sort of work. At a loss about what else to do, I circled or marked 38 errors or mismanagements—punctuation, sentence boundary problems, and misspellings—and, in the margin just above the final paragraph, I queried, "transition?" At the time, I told McCarthy,

> Ellen's writing is shaky but passable when she is following Carmichael's text, but when she gets to her own comments, her mechanical errors and non sequiturs make it tough for me to follow her thinking. I'm keeping my fingers crossed that pointing out her surface problems will be of help to her.

The one substantive comment I did write on Ellen's paper was a marginal note in response to her command at the end of her first paragraph to name 10 Black millionaires. Although she implies that this is an impossible task, in my comment I disagree. I say there are many Black millionaires today but that Carmichael's conclusion still holds, namely, that integration means that many of these people leave the ghetto to join upper class American life, thus depleting the resources available to those who remain behind. To prove my point, I list 10 Black millionaires, all of them professional athletes, all of them living among Whites.

As I discussed my marginal note with Lucille at the time, I worried about directly disagreeing with a student. This is something I try to avoid, both in class and in my comments on student writing, because it makes me a combatant in the discussion rather than a questioner or a facilitator, the roles I prefer to play. In fact, on Ellen's first day in class (the third meeting of the semester), I had succeeded in backing away from this very argument with her when she contradicted my claim that things have gotten worse in the ghetto since the 1960s when Carmichael wrote. When she took issue with me, saying "No, things have always been as bad as they are today," I replied, "Well, Ellen, you may be right. I'm only quoting from some books I read" (Gibbs, 1988; Wilson, 1996).

However, when I responded to Ellen's homework, I found myself unable to hold my tongue in face of the absolute certainty of her tone. I told Lucille, "Ellen's voice in this piece seems so loud and angry that she makes me nervous." I was concerned because I knew from past experience that students who believe they have the truth and seem uninterested in questioning can make class discussion— the careful philosophic exploration of alternative positions I try to orchestrate—very difficult. My taking Ellen up on her challenge to name 10 Black millionaires, I told Lucille, was my way of trying to slow her down. I wanted Ellen to see that things were more complicated than she made them out to be.

A White Professor's Blindness to White Privilege

Looking back at my response to Ellen's first homework from the distance of 2 1/2 years, I see things differently. I now believe there are those who could legitimately charge me with being "color and power evasive," that is, with being blind to the racialized nature of American society, my university, and my own classroom (Frankenberg, 1993, p. 14; see also Barnett, 2000; Dyer, 1997; Fordham, 1988, 1997; Gilyard, 1999; Ladson-Billings, 1998; Omi & Winant, 1994). These race cognizant critics would likely dismiss my justifications for my responses to Ellen—my claim that I was acting to promote improved writing and a philosophic exploration of alternatives—as simply a self-deceptive effort to remain blind to my White privilege.

Evidence of my blindness can be found, these race-cognizant commentators might continue, in my failure to openly acknowledge and dignify the anger Ellen vents when she asks her reader to name 10 Black millionaires. In this rhetorical imperative, Ellen is, of course, not really asking for 10 names. Rather, she is virtually shouting her frustration at the fact that, although some of the details of the canvas of American race relations have changed in the last 50 years, most of the larger picture has not.

Not only can evidence of my blindness to White privilege be found in my sidestepping Ellen's real point but also in my failure to suggest ways she (and the class) might explore the roots of her anger. Such exploration might have focused on articulating the many advantages that Whiteness confers on America's dominant class, advantages that are invisible to most Whites and often left out of conversations about racism. In fact, even Ellen herself, in the final section of her Carmichael paper, attends only to the negative side of racism for Blacks, not mentioning the positive consequences for Whites. Specifically, she notes America's insensitivity to the history of discrimination against Blacks ("Now a days [sic] many black people that ride the bus every day. . ."), the absence of African Americans in lawmaking bodies ("The laws are not grovern [sic] for the black people. . ."), and the injustice of racial profiling by law enforcement agencies ("If you are a poor black man and in the wrong place at the wrong time you can kiss your freedom good bye for a while.") To summarize, my critics might say I committed a grievous mistake, one made by many White educators (as well as some non-White), by analyzing the essays of Fanon, Carmichael, and hooks for what the authors say about different sorts of racism and their negative effects on America's minorities while failing to explore their points about racism's favorable consequences for America's Whites (see Fine, Weis, & Powell, 1997).

Now, 2 $1/2$ years later, I see the wisdom of these potential charges against me by Critical Race Theorists and Whiteness studies scholars. Although I am embarrassed by my shortsightedness—the missed opportunities to decenter Whiteness—at the time I read Ellen's first homework paper, a number of other concerns were at the center of my attention. For better or worse, I was focusing on Ellen's writing mechanics and her rhetorical strategies. Not only did I want to help move her papers closer to the dominant code, I also wanted to assist her with the way in which she argued. I believed she needed to balance her strong feelings and opinions with a more critical, detached way of knowing. Thus, what could be seen as small mindedness and blindness to White privilege on my part—my naming 10 Black athlete millionaires—was, as I saw it then, my attempt to say to Ellen, in effect, "Philosophers back up what they say. Please don't shoot from the hip so much." After all, the discourse that is most important to the history of Western philosophy, as I have noted, is careful Socratic questioning and argumentation, an effort to explore as many sides of an issue as one can bring forward. In short, Ellen's paper showed me she could meet the first of my specific objectives for students, summarizing an author's argument with substantial accuracy. But I wondered about her ability to ever meet my second and fifth goals, argument evaluation and coherent writing in Standard American English.

Another way to look at Ellen's situation in my course is that the cultural and linguistic capital she brought to my classroom worked for her both as an advantage and a liability. As Lucille will show, the force and conviction behind Ellen's oral contributions ultimately had a positive effect on class discussion. However, in this early piece of writing, her tone—her certainty that her interpretations were correct and her apparent unwillingness to allow any room for doubt or alternative positions—was, in my view, a disadvantage, so far off was it from the careful, openminded inquiry I value. Although at the time Ellen's voice seemed "loud" and irrational to me, I now see her confrontational and narrative stance as resembling that of Alice Walker's (1983) "womanist," Black feminist (p. xi). Such a woman is "audacious," "courageous," and inquisitive, according to Walker, adopting a combative style that researchers argue is common among African American students in general and reentry Black women in particular. These researchers also note that this discourse may, in the school situation, lead to misunderstanding between Blacks and Whites (see Ball, 1992; Fordham, 1988, 1997; Johnson-Bailey & Cervero, 1996; Kochman, 1981; Laden & Turner, 1995; McCrary, 2001; Thompson, 1998).

Although the academic discourse I value has its roots in a very different culture, that of White European males, it is, nevertheless, the way of speaking and writing of many minorities, as well. The readings I assign—including those by Black men and women like Fanon, Carmichael, and hooks—all display this careful, step-by-step effort at persuasion. This style of composing and argumentation might not have been the most comfortable for Ellen, but I felt that it was my responsibility to encourage her to give it a chance and to practice it. Although I was not sure initially that Ellen would be open to such practice, it turned out that there were enough instructional supports in place in my class—and Ellen open enough to them—to allow her to make noteworthy strides in this direction.

For evidence of what I consider to be Ellen's progress in achieving my objectives for student thinking and writing in philosophy, I now turn to her final paper of the semester.

A LATE-SEMESTER PAPER: VISIBLE SUCCESS IN ACHIEVING SOME OF THE PROFESSOR'S OBJECTIVES

Ellen Williams's final piece of the semester was the multi-draft essay I require of all my Intro students. I ask them to write about a moral dilemma they face and to consider the philosophic assumptions behind alternative solutions to their dilemma. I respond to their initial drafts by talking aloud into an audiotape cassette for 5 to 10 minutes, giving no grade evaluation. In these tapes I offer students my reactions to their drafts and make suggestions about how they might complexify, enrich, and/or better organize their essays.

In Ellen's final paper, which I reproduce below, she makes progress toward achieving four of my five class goals: argument extraction, argument evaluation, intellectual reconstruction, and application of philosophy. In particular, her essay illustrates what was, as I have said, Ellen's most striking achievement in the course: her ability to apply philosophy to her own concerns (objective 4), in this case, to bridge between my subject matter and her professional life. Ellen's paper is, as I see it, her effort to take what she has learned about the historic philosophic discussion of freedom and responsibility and relate it to her own and others' views of capital punishment.

A second feature of Ellen's paper that stands out for me is her willingness to adopt a Socratic, questioning stance, the very discourse I feared at the beginning of the semester she might never attempt. As she presents her reader with the results of interviews she conducted with her mother and Carolyn, an inmate at the prison where she works, Ellen is offering points of view with which she totally disagrees. And not only does she try to be philosophic by looking at capital punishment from a variety of perspectives, she also engages in the difficult work of intellectual reconstruction (objective 3). That is, Ellen tries to reconstruct the assumptions about human nature and the world which lie behind her own pro-capital punishment position as well as those behind her mother's and Carolyn's rejection of the death penalty.

In praising Ellen's essay for its achievement of some of my objectives for student thinking and writing, I am also pleased to note that this piece retains many of the features of Ellen's discourse that initially made me nervous and wary. For example, in this essay, I hear again Ellen's strong voice, her use of rhetorical questions, and her commitment to personal experience. In addition, there is in this last piece, like her first, an undeniable earnestness about the importance of the social issue she is discussing.

I now reproduce the final draft of Ellen's term essay just as she typed it.

The Death Penalty

The crime rate has tripled within the last five years and more and more people are being murder. It is not just adults that are committing these crimes, we have children as young as ten committing hideous crimes. We have a problem when you have more prisons then you do schools. We have a problem when someone that was released from prison with in one year has committed another hideous crime after serving twenty years of prison time. What message are we sending? You have police officers being gunned down for no reason.

I have worked in the prisons for over twelve years and it is just another world inside of a world. Often it is inmates killing inmates. There is nothing that you really can not get if you want it bad enough. Society says that this is your punishment. Some people live better in prison then they do when they are free. I have had a man tell me that he comes to prison every winter so he can have free rent, food, cable television, and heat.

(not to mention the other luxuries)

I often hear the people saying we send people to prison to get rehabilitated. I am here to tell you that if someone does not want to be rehabilitiated then they will not no matter what you try to do.

Prisons have became a holding cell with a revolving door which is often used, because many people often come back.

These are just some of the serious problems that we are facing.

Something must be done, or it will only get worst.

Section II

Here are some alternative views towards the capital punishment Made by different people.

1. Against the death penalty?

Women named Carolyn whose mother was murdered for no possible reason asked me these questions.

When does murder constitute justice?

Did the Ten commandments say thou shall not kill?

Why does a legal system that doesn't condone murder try to use it as a mechanism of punishment?

Carolyn stated to me that God gave life and only god can take it away. She stated that she does not wish for him to receive the death penalty basically because of this fact.

My mother states that two wrongs just do not make a right. Could he just be put into prisons and be rehabilitated?

2. In favor of the Death Penalty whenever some one kills another. The old saying an eye for an eye and a tooth for a tooth.

Section III

My position of why I believe that the death penalty is Superior to the maximum life sentence.

Prisons are just a world inside of another world anything an inmate wants they can get. Some prisons are made better than some inmate's place of residence. Some people do not care about any thing or anybody and therefore start killing more innocent people in the prisons. What do you do with this person? Do you add more time to there one hundred and thirty-year sentence?

Where is the punishment?

Where is the deterrent?

What about the children that think killing makes you a man.

So many children have watched people get killed and often see the person that has committed the crime walking freely. People say that I will go to prison that is not a problem, they can not hold me forever.

Assumptions people often believe.

People are given many assumptions about prisons. A lot of people assume that if you go to prison then you can be rehabilitiated and can come out a change person. That is not true especially if the person does not want to be rehabilitiated, you can be in prison for twenty years and never change if you choose. That person could come back out the same way that he came in I have personally Witnessed this. Another assumption is that inmates are treated badly and are often feed the worst food. That is another misconception some times inmates may have steak, the are feed very well, some times better than the man that makes minnum wages.

I gave Ellen a C+ for this paper, and, ultimately, a C for the course, but I confess that, despite the strengths I noted above, as I review this essay from a substantial distance in time I am still dismayed by its surface errors, lack of transitions, and absence of topic sentences. In other words, as with Neha's work, I believe that an outside evaluator, reading Ellen's paper out of context, might accuse me of having lowered my academic standards and done Ellen a disservice by passing her, especially in a class that is one of two capstone writing courses. Although I continued throughout the semester to mark her surface errors and transition problems, when I saw little improvement by mid-October, I began to focus more on the positive changes that were occurring in the content of Ellen's papers: their increasingly openminded tone and serious attempt at philosophic argumentation. Thus, given what I saw as Ellen's efforts to practice philosophic ways of knowledge construction, and understanding how far she had come in this regard, I believe the grade is justifed. That is, given where the two of us started—the clash between our goals and discourses, between her cultural, linguistic, and academic capital and my own—I see this paper as a triumph.

For Ellen's part, she too was pleased with her essay, expressing satisfaction at having experimented with new ways of thinking and inquiring. She told McCarthy a few days after she completed the paper that as she questioned her mother and Carolyn, she heard herself "sounding like Dr. Fisherman [*sic*]:"

> I was doing what he does in class: listening to people and then ask-ing Why? Why do you believe that? Why do you think that? It took me a while to learn to question, to be tactful like Dr. Fisherman, but I now do it a lot. . . . I've learned it's good to hear what other people think—even if you do think their ideas are strange. You never know what you can learn.

In fact, Ellen said, she now models a questioning form of inquiry with her sons, asking them such questions as "Why do you think you did that?" or "Why do you think people behave that way?"

In my view, then, despite significant remaining mechanical and rhetorical writing problems, Ellen made substantial progress toward my classroom goals. What were the instructional supports that facilitated her positive experience? That is, what happened during the many contacts between Ellen and me and among Ellen and her classmates that made her feel safe enough to risk trying new ways of thinking and writing? Lucille McCarthy will now address these ques-tions. In doing so, she draws upon data we collected during the semester that Ellen took my Intro course as well as data she collected as she followed Ellen in the three subsequent semesters leading to her graduation.

Part Two

Instructional Supports That Helped: Class Discussions,
Ungraded Writing, and Audiotaped Teacher
Responses to Essay Drafts

LUCILLE McCARTHY

My first reaction to the two papers that Steve Fishman has just discussed is to side with Critical Race Theorists and Whiteness studies scholars and agree that Steve was blind to White privilege. The consequence of this blindness that stands out for me is not only that he failed to help Ellen and her classmates properly explore Ellen's anger but also that he unwittingly robbed Ellen of her voice by insisting she speak in a way that put her at an enormous disadvantage relative to him and most of her peers. When I first interviewed Ellen in early September, her alienation from Fishman's discourse was obvious. She explained,

> It's like the teacher in that class is from another planet. He looks different from other professors, you know: his hair everywhere, his hand motions. . . . I'm not saying he is bad looking, just unusual. . . . And when he talks, I can't understand a word he's saying.

Just as Ellen Williams was mystified by her professor's looks and language, so she was equally puzzled by his syllabus. When I asked her why she thought Fishman assigned the texts he did, she responded,

> A philosopher is someone who goes any way the wind blows. Maybe it was something he read the night before. I don't know. His ways and my ways are not the same.

I originally took Ellen's comments about how foreign Steve's class felt as further evidence that he was trying to silence her, resisting what Critical Race Theorists might view as her efforts to transform his White, hegemonic language. That is, at first it seemed to me that both in Ellen's papers and class discussion Fishman was discouraging her from using the genre and tone she knows best—personal storytelling with a strong confrontational feel. However, when I reviewed the class videotapes and other data from across the semester, I found this was not the whole story. To the contrary, Fishman actually provided Ellen and her classmates with many opportunities to articulate their personal experiences in their own ways. Furthermore, he established a safe discursive space for students to do this in part by offering his own personal disclosures, stories that were often funny and self-mocking, reflective of a long history of Jewish humor. The opportunities Fishman offered students for narrative and personal disclosure underlay all three of the instructional supports Ellen named as most helpful. I now describe the first of these.

Instructional Support #1: Class Discussion

The class videotapes show numerous occasions on which Steve did a better job of acknowledging the import of Ellen's stories and helping her explore their broader meaning than he did when responding to her Carmichael paper. However, before turning to these positive class discussions, pivotal moments in which Ellen developed sufficient trust to try out some philosophic exploration, I describe an early class discussion in which Ellen's and her classmates' stories were not productive. This is because competing student stories were left unconnected and decontextualized and, thus, led not to collaborative inquiry but to a hardening of positions and a maintenance of the barriers that separated Steve and his pupils along race, class, and gender lines.

Ellen was one of four African Americans in Fishman's Intro class of 25 students in fall 1998, and on the first two days she attended (days 3 and 4 of the semester), she said a number of things that seemed to draw a line in the sand indicating she was different from her White classmates. She told them that they would never get to know who she really was, and, further, she told Steve, she would leave his class unaffected by the work he would ask her to do.

*An Unproductive Class Discussion: Competing Stories
Left Unconnected*

On Ellen's second day in class, September 3rd, as students discussed an article by hooks (1981/1995) and the current status of racism in America, a White student, 19-year-old, sophomore business major, Kathy Curtis, raised her hand. "Things have gotten better between the races," Kathy volunteered. "In my high school we had a whole month devoted to Black history." Sitting directly across the circle from Kathy, Ellen glared at her and snapped,

> I'm supposed to be grateful?!! I don't care how many Black history months you have, you'll always see me first and foremost as a Black woman. And if a Black man comes toward you at night, you'll clutch your pocketbook and walk faster. . . . And if you're right that things are so much better, why are there so few Black judges, lawyers, and doctors?

Ellen then added an afterthought that made the class titter. Her body turned sideways in her chair, her face indicating disgust, Ellen launched her final salvo at Kathy: "You and I are different. You wash your hair every day; I don't."

With these comments Ellen succeeded in silencing Kathy Curtis. However, Keith Falls, a 21-year-old, White, senior psychology major, sitting four seats to Ellen's left, was not so easily vanquished. He leaned forward and turned to face Ellen. "You gotta stop this 'us and them' talk!!" he advised her in a loud tone. "If you really want to end racism, you gotta stop being so divisive."

How did Fishman handle this exchange among Kathy, Ellen, and Keith? Apparently unsure what to do with these students' emotionally charged and conflicting stories, he retreated. Instead of picking up on their comments, he directed the class back to what he saw as the main purpose of hooks's article: distinguishing between personal and institutional racism. He asked if anyone could name examples of institutional racism, but no one could, and students continued to talk about racism as it exists on a personal level. Class ended with Tonya McInnis—the 30-year-old, African American, pre-nursing student who later that semester would befriend Neha Shah—telling a story about the overt bigotry she experienced in San Francisco as a young child. Tonya then offered her own assessment of the progress that has been made regarding discrimination in the 35 years since Carmichael wrote his text: "It is no better than it was in 1960s," she said. "It's just better hidden."

As I analyze the three-way exchange among Kathy Curtis, Ellen Williams, and Keith Falls from a Critical Race Theory and Whiteness studies perspective, I get disappointing results. I conclude that these students were, at the end of their conversation, as far apart as they started. None appeared to have learned from it; none appeared to see his or her position regarding race in new light. Both Kathy Curtis and Keith Falls seemed to be feeling positive about their positions and were trying to explain to Ellen that they are not prejudiced or racist. In fact, however, both invoked what Critical Race Theorists and Whiteness studies experts would say is the color and power evasive tale that many contemporary Americans tell (see Frankenberg, 1993). This tale is that there once was a time when Whites thought themselves superior to people of color and made rules to exclude them from economic, political, and cultural power, but that time is past. Because of the Civil Rights movement, Jim Crow laws are no longer on the books, and good Americans are now color-blind, treating everyone the same regardless of race, creed, or ethnic origins. Put another way, Kathy and Keith were implying, "You've got it wrong. Times have changed. Whites no longer think Blacks are inferior. Everyone is being treated equally." Kathy went a step further when she invoked multiculturalism, suggesting that Whites, by sponsoring Black History Month, are now not only tolerant of but also interested in minority cultures.

Kathy's and Keith's statements corroborate Frankenberg's (1993) contention that discussions about race in America occur in the shadow of the view held by our country's forefathers and dominant until the early 20th century. Races, it was believed, are biologically and genealogically distinct and located on a hierarchy with Whites at the top. However, Kathy and Keith appear to feel that since they no longer believe in such a hierarchy, they are off the hook. They imply that racism in America would end if only everyone would take the color-blind view they have adopted and devote at least token attention to minority cultures. What Kathy and Keith fail to understand —that Ellen apparently does understand—is that color-blindness and multiculturalism are doing little to upset the balance of power that remains so overwhelmingly in favor of Whites and that Kathy and Keith are the beneficiaries of several centuries of racial discrimination. Ellen's rhetorical question to Kathy about Black History Month—"I'm supposed to be grateful?!!"—thus represents her felt sense that, given the pervasive social segregation of our society, Kathy's and Keith's White privilege is, in Frankenberg's (1993) terms, "a lived but not seen aspect of [their] white experience" (p. 135).

When I analyze this same exchange among Kathy, Ellen, and Keith from a social class rather than race perspective, I get equally negative results: a disappointing maintenance of unarticulated class barriers. Freire might categorize the comments by Kathy and Keith as acts of naive *noblesse oblige*, offerings that only serve to keep the bourgeoisie in power. That is, Kathy and Keith, despite their good intentions, may not really be in solidarity with Ellen at all. Rather, they appear to remain sequestered in their own middle class worlds, unable to step across class boundaries to understand Ellen and, perhaps, work with her for greater social justice. For Ellen's part, she holds fast to her position that not only do the White students in the class fail to understand her history as an excluded Black person, neither do they have any desire to understand her situation in economic terms.

Student and Teacher Reactions

When I spoke with students about the September 3rd discussion in separate interviews a few days later, I found that each recalled it very differently. Ellen said that when she left class, she promptly forgot it. Referring to Kathy Curtis, she explained, "I can't let people like that bother me. I wasn't upset at all." By contrast, Kathy said she felt bad about the exchange and wondered if she had offended Ellen. Keith rolled his eyes about Ellen's "hair comment," and Tonya said, "Ellen's right about some things, but she just wants to fight. She may be a girl from the projects." This latter comment was especially interesting to me since it illustrates what some researchers call the "nonsynchrony" of race, class, and gender. That is, Tonya, as an

African American, identified with Ellen regarding race and gender but distinguished herself in terms of social class (McCarthy, 1988, 1993; Hicks, 1981).

When I asked Fishman about the hooks class discussion, he said he felt the tension in the group and worried about where it might be headed. He was uncertain, he said, about how to respond to Ellen's apparent disdain for opinions that differed from her own. He remarked,

> Although I value her perspective as an African American woman who has experienced racism, I fear that her hostility may intimidate the other students. She may make those who want to disagree with her fearful to do so. . . . As much as I want her in the class, I hope she does not make it impossible for me to generate the open give and take I want.

In subsequent weeks, as Steve and I talked further about the September 3rd discussion, and both of us read more deeply in the Critical Race Theory and Whiteness studies literature, Steve began to blame himself, not Ellen, for what he saw as the discussion's failure. He lamented that he had been unable to help students articulate and explore—"inventory"—the different assumptions about race relations behind the conflicting stories they told (Gramsci, 1971, p. 324). He said he believed that if he had only had the appropriate language and conceptual understanding, he might have been able to help students position themselves within an historical framework, seeing themselves not just as telling personal stories but as representing particular moments in the national dialogue about racism and ways to decenter White privilege.

For example, he believed that Keith's "we're-all-the-same" position represented the philosophic basis of the Civil Rights movement of the 1950s and 60s, a movement that used this credo to justify the elimination of group classifications from public policy. With regard to Kathy's multiculturalism, Fishman said he might have pointed out that she seemed to represent another stage in the national conversation, one that began in the early 1970s. The Black History Month she mentioned is a token response to some Americans' growing realization that schools, in their historic role as vehicles of cultural assimilation, carried the not so hidden message that some cultures are better than others. From his later-in-the-semester vantage point, Fishman understood that critics of the program praised by Kathy would say that what is advertised in today's schools as multicultural- ism is nothing more than a rebaked version of 1920s cultural pluralism. That is, critics of the Black History Month approach would argue that such recognition of ethnic difference, although it may promote understanding among members of diverse groups, does not really alter our nation's cultural hierarchy. What is required if White, middle class ways of thinking are no longer to be privileged in allegedly "culturally unbiased" classrooms is a thorough overhaul of school materials and instructional methods at all levels. A few add-on units attached here and there to the main curriculum will not suffice. (For more on the cultural pluralism-multicultural debates, see Dewey, 1915/1999; Feinberg, 1998; Schlesinger, 1992.)

With regard to Ellen, Fishman said he now realized that she pre- sented a complicated amalgam of positions. When she disapproved of her White classmates' identifying her primarily as a Black woman and accused them of clutching their purses at the approach of a Black man, she seemed to be calling, like Keith, for color-blindness. However, when she spoke about the lack of Black judges, lawyers, and doctors, her comments could be seen as representing a later stage in our national discussion, one in which people came to under- stand that the color-blind policies of the 1950s and 60s could also function to hide and perpetuate White privilege, treating racism "as something that can be eradicated by simply ignoring it" (Thompson, 1998, p. 525). Given the failure of these color-blind policies to change the status quo—to bring about the proportionate represen- tation of minorities in the professions and other centers of power— Ellen seemed, like current Critical Race Theorists, to call for color- consciousness. That is, she appeared to want her classmates to go beyond arguing for equal opportunities for all individuals and push for equal outcomes for all groups. In calling for equal consequences of economic competition as well as equal opportunity to engage in such competition, Ellen was echoing not only Critical Race Theorists but also 20th century egalitarian liberals who argue that unequal consequences ultimately beget unequal opportunity (see Lichtenstein, 1984; Sandel, 1984).

Not only did Fishman lament his failure to position these students' comments within an historical context, he also realized he missed an opportunity to point out that Tonya McInnis's remark about racism's now being "better hidden" illustrated the central thesis of hooks's article, namely, how much easier it is to trace racism to individual bigotry rather than to identify its more insidious source in political and cultural institutions. That is, Tonya's comment suggested—mistakenly, hooks would say—that if we could just bring personal prejudice into the open so we could deal with it, the effects of 300 years of discrimination could be magically undone. In addition to interpreting Tonya's narrative as focusing on personal rather than institutional racism, Fishman also wished he had helped the class investigate the different philosophic assumptions underlying these two ways of explaining discrimination. These are the liberal assumption that individual agency determines human behavior, versus the Marxist assumption that economic and social structures play this role.

Of course neither Fishman nor I has any idea, since we cannot redo the class, whether, had he done what he wished, he could actually have altered what happened that day. What is clear, however, is that simply setting up a space in which students can tell stories does not guarantee collaborative inquiry or increased understanding by either the narrators or their listeners. In fact, stories that are simply presented and left unconnected, outside any larger framework to give them additional meaning, may lead people to turn deaf ears to one another.

A Productive Class Discussion: Competing Stories Put into Context

The next class discussion I describe took place three weeks later on September 24th and had very different effects on the participants. Whereas the early September session left Ellen dismissive of the course and Steve worried about it, the late September one, because Fishman could help students connect their narratives by placing them in a philosophic context, had positive residue for both.

On September 24th, the class was discussing a selection from Clarence Darrow's (1932/1973) autobiography in which Darrow attempts to refute William Paley's (1802/1973) teleological arguments for the existence of God. Ellen, to support her rejection of Darrow's atheist views, told the story of a serious car accident from which she walked away unscathed. She explained,

> This proves to me there is a God. No one but God could have kept me out of harm's way because I had no seat belt on. I didn't see it coming, and I didn't brace for it. . . . God has a time for everyone, and He wasn't yet ready for me to go. . . . There's a reason for everything.

When Ellen concluded, Steve's student assistant, Warren Murray, a 23-year-old, African American, business major who was videotaping the class, challenged her story, offering an alternative explanation. Although usually silent behind the camera, Warren piped up asking Ellen if she had considered the fact that maybe she was just lucky. "You say it's by faith that you didn't get hurt in the accident. But what about the atheist who walks away from the same accident? He would say it was luck, not God."

Ellen did not reply to Warren but chose, instead, to express her disdain for this type of inquiry. Apparently directing her question to the class in general, and using phrases that became among the most memorable of the semester, she asked,

> Why should I question my beliefs anyway when I am happy with them? If they're not broke, why fix them? Maybe if I was younger and didn't have other responsibilities. But I have a whole lot of other issues. I've got children. I work full time. If I was 21 years old, just hanging around with nothing to do, I too would suck this stuff up. But I've got other things to worry about.

The videotape shows students taken aback by Ellen's comments and then a moment of half-derisive laughter sweeping around the class circle. Fishman, however, instead of retreating from Ellen's challenge, as he had on September 3rd, reacted with a thoughtful nod. He was, in this situation, on familiar ground because Ellen had just sounded a theme well known to philosophers. Steve told the class, "Ellen's question is a good one," and he urged students to take it seriously. "Lots of people would agree with Ellen," he continued, "that philosophy is a waste of time," and he described the strong American tradition that argues that action is more important than reflection. "Critics like Ellen say," Fishman told the class, "'I have my ideas, and I am content with them. Why upset me with new ones?'" Referring to the two Platonic dialogues the class had read, Fishman concluded,

> Remember Socrates going around disturbing people? Ellen's right. Thinking is upsetting. It can even be dangerous. So how would you answer her? How would you justify philosophic thinking to people like Ellen and convince them of the merits of the questioning life?

In raising these issues, Fishman was encouraging his students to place Ellen's story in philosophic context, specifically, to inventory the traces of anti-intellectualism, the historical celebration of a life of action rather than contemplation, that had left its deposit in Ellen's account. In offering Ellen and the class new language with which to describe her unhappiness with reflective thinking, Fishman hoped to dignify Ellen's story and give her and her classmates a chance to reexperience and reconceptualize her sense that philosophic thinking is a waste of time.

In the class circle that day, if one thinks of it as the dial of a watch, Steve was sitting at the 6:00 position with Ellen to his right at 3:00 and Tonya McInnis to his left at 9:00. Tonya, like Ellen, was a frequent class contributor, so the fact she raised her hand to speak at this point did not seem unusual. However, her answer to Ellen's query, "Why question?" went down in the collective class history as something as striking—and as oft repeated—as Ellen's comments earlier that class period. Tonya, in fact, borrowed one of Ellen's phrases in a linguistic performance she herself later dubbed "Tonya's Preach." Tonya began,

> I don't know what anyone else thinks about what goes on in here, but I sucks it up! I sucks in everything you all say. Really. I'm a better person than I was when I came in here—the way I look at people,

listen to what they're saying. In here I've heard other people's beliefs, and I realize maybe mine isn't the only way of reaching the goal.

Pushing her chest out, shaking her shoulders, and laughing, Tonya pointed to Warren Murray behind the videocamera. "Hey, Warren, you keep that camera rolling," she said, and to the class she admonished, "Hey, y'all. Listen to me!" Once again picking up on Ellen's language, Tonya continued,

> I'm like Socrates. I do not claim what I do not know. I tell my daughter and my father about the conversations we have in here, and they want to know more. I don't know about anybody else, but this class has made me stronger. My mind, my intelligence. I leave out of here big and strong and proud, and I'm just waiting to get back here next time. I sucks it up!

The class was delighted by Tonya's "preach," someone yelling "Go, girl!" in the middle of it, and even Ellen smiled.

In Tonya McInnis's testimony, I hear her speaking not only about the importance of reflection but also putting her own response to the course in philosophic context. That is, by aligning herself with Socrates, Tonya takes her differences with Ellen out of the realm of personal disagreement and places them on the much richer canvas of diverse intellectual movements. In addition, she testifies to the intrinsic value she is finding in the class. Tonya is saying, in effect, to Ellen and many other classmates who are instrumentalists, that she is not treating the course simply as a means to a degree, nor is she doing her work with her eyes focused only on the grade. Instead, course ideas and conversation are a means of personal growth important enough to carry home and take to heart.

Not surprisingly, Tonya's testimony about the benefits of philosophic inquiry had no immediate impact on Ellen's resistant stance. As a matter of fact, at the close of that same period, Ellen once again contradicted Fishman in a seeming effort to distance herself from the course. When Steve tried to explain to students why he believes "writing intensive" courses are important, he mentioned that for him writing can be a "friend." As a person who lives alone, he said, he frequently uses writing to help him clarify his thoughts and feel less isolated. When he finished, Ellen raised her hand and again disagreed. She declared,

> You say writing is your friend. Well, writing is no friend to me. I might like it if I was just doing it for myself, but I have to do it for you. In here I'm pressured. The teacher is grading it, and that's a whole different thing.

Fishman nodded and said, "Yes, Ellen, I see your point. Ideally all writing would be voluntary, and there would be no grades." The class then concluded with Fishman handing out the assignment for next time.

Student and Teacher Reactions

When I spoke with Ellen three weeks later, in mid-October, I asked her what she recalled about this September 24th Darrow class session. She laughed as she described Tonya's preach and admitted that the class was beginning to make her think. She explained,

> Dr. Fisherman keeps my mind spinning all the time. He keeps the class flowing with various questions; you never know what to expect. . . . But I like it in there. There's a family feel, and I can say whatever I want. . . . The teacher respects us, so we respect him. . . . And there are so many ideas on the table. It makes you open up your own mind—even if you don't want to. . . . I'm more like Tonya now. I won't miss class unless I have to.

The change that Ellen reported in mid-October—her gradual opening to new ideas—was corroborated by a number of her class-mates. For example, Elizabeth Pritchett, a 19-year-old, White, sopho-more music major, told me that she, Ellen, and Robert Bullerdick—the 30-year-old, White, junior, health and fitness major with whom Neha Shah had corresponded about Plato—had recently been in a small group discussing their homework papers. Elizabeth volun-teered, "Ellen's great. She listened when I read my paper, and after-ward she asked me some good questions." Tonya McInnis concurred:

Ellen shows why you can't judge a book by its cover: people aren't always what you think they are. Although she sometimes still spurts out things and steps on people's toes, Ellen listens. And I know she's not just acting like she's listening; she's really hearing.

When I interviewed Fishman about the September 24th class, he said he was pleased he could use Ellen's account of her car accident and her negative view of philosophic questioning in productive ways. That is, he believed that by contextualizing Ellen's criticism of reflection—by showing that her query, "Why question?" has a long history in philosophy—he was able to dignify her concerns and use them to advance the class's awareness of some of the pros and cons of a contemplative life.

Steve also noted something that other researchers have observed: students are able to say things to one another that no teacher would dare say (Landsman, 2001). In this case, Tonya, as a returning African American woman, could take up Ellen's language in ways Fishman could never have done and, in a positive fashion, invite Ellen and the rest of the class to look at a reaction to philosophy that was opposed to Ellen's. In mid-October, Fishman told me,

> I have a sense we have all just gone through some test of fire, that we could have dismissed each other, and the class could have broken apart. But for some reason—and Tonya is important here—we have remained open to one another and are developing what I think Dewey would call likemindedness. We are able to communicate well enough now to feel some mutual care.

Thus Ellen's prophecy about always being an outsider in this academic setting was not fulfilled: her classmates did not, ultimately, see her only as a Black woman. To the contrary, they eventually saw her as a valuable contributor to class conversation, willing to listen to their stories and reveal aspects of her own life that many would hide. For example, she held her classmates spellbound as she recounted her trials and tribulations as a worker in the prison system, analyzed her own failed marriage, and described her deep affection for her mother who, as a young woman, had picked cotton in the fields of North Carolina.

The improved tone and productiveness of class conversation at mid-semester that was noted by Elizabeth, Tonya, Ellen, and Steve—their shared sense that students' conflicting stories were now generating mutual understanding—continued throughout the term. This development was bolstered by the second instructional support I now describe.

Instructional Support #2: Ungraded Writing

In addition to class discussion, Ellen mentioned ungraded writing as being helpful in promoting her turnaround, her moving from saying in early September that Fishman was "from another planet" to describing in mid-October her growing comfort in, even excitement about, his course. Specifically, the Class Reflection Log and in-class freewrites offered Ellen additional opportunities to present her views and narratives. More important, however, these opportunities were structured to encourage Ellen to gain critical distance from them and practice philosophic thinking.

Class Reflection Log (CRL)

In a kind of ongoing written conversation between teacher and students, Fishman required pupils to answer a series of nine questions, one every 10 days or so, in their Class Reflection Logs. These questions asked students to reflect on class events and issues as well as on their own thinking and learning in the course. As Steve read these informal journals, he responded in marginal comments and endnotes, but he did not grade them. (CRL questions are listed in appendix C. For further discussion of the efficacy of informal, self-reflective writing for returning women, see Tarule, 1988.)

To illustrate the way in which the CRLs gave Ellen a chance to gain critical distance on her views, I turn to her first entry, written in early September: a two-page, typed reflection on the unit on race. Steve asked students three questions:

> Please think back on our first unit, on your reading and our class discussion of the essays by Fanon, Carmichael, and hooks, and answer these questions.

a) What idea, anecdote, or insight comes to mind as you recall these authors' pieces?
b) What new insights, if any, did you get about racism from our class discussions?
c) Is there anything left over from our class discussions that you feel you did not get to say and would like to say now?

In Ellen's response, she tells Steve that she did indeed learn something new: "There are even more deferent [sic] types of racism than I realized." In this comment, Ellen seems to be referring to the notion of personal versus institutional racism. Although she did not speak to this issue in class, and she never pins the distinction down clearly in her Reflection Log, Ellen offers what appears to be an example of institutional racism. She writes that she recalls a classmate's statement that racism is an "individuals choice [sic]." She disagrees with this view, she says, and to support her contention that racism is more than just an individual matter, she describes a test she once took for prospective police officers that works against Blacks by assuming that everyone turns "purple and blue" when they are suffocating. Thus, provoked by Steve's CRL prompt, Ellen seems to be seeing the police test in a new way. She writes,

> There was a statement made by another student in class that "Racism was a human relations issue because it was a individuals choice." I remember taking many test that were very racism, for example On the N.J Police exam one of the question was if you arrived on the seen and found someone turning purple and blue what would you do? Many black people got this question wrong because of what? you tell me. It was tests like these that made Racism what it is which is not an individual, human relations issue.

In this entry Ellen is doing exactly what Steve hoped for. She employs the interplay between philosophic thinking and personal narrative to reconfigure the landscape in which she lives. That is, using Fishman's question to revisit her experience with the New Jersey police exam, Ellen is able to conceptualize it in new terms.

In a CRL question a month later, in mid-October, Steve again asked students to reexamine their experiences with America's racial and social hierarchies, this time teacher-student relations in his own classroom. Specifically, he wanted to know how their similarities with or differences from him affected their experiences in the course. Steve's prompt reads,

> Do you believe that my race, class, and gender give White, middle-class, male students in my classes an advantage over female students, students of color, or working class students? Please explain.

Ellen responds,

> I really do not believe that the teacher caters to any specific gender, race, or class. He appears to be very fair and open minded. To be honest, I have not had the time to think or concentrae on him treating people different.Now that I have had some time to think about this. I feel as though he really treats everyone equal.

This CRL question gave Ellen an opportunity to focus on an aspect of race and social relations—that between teacher and student —that she says she had not previously considered. Although this is somewhat surprising since she had immediately noted the contrast in financial and social capital between herself and her younger White classmates, I speculate that there are three possible reasons for her claim she has not focused on Fishman's and her differences. The first of them may result from Ellen's seeing Steve, as I reported earlier, as so different from her that he seemed to be "from another planet." That is, the fact that Steve is White may have been insignificant compared to the numerous oddities she named that made him seem to her so Other: his hair and hand motions, his strange language and choice of reading assignments. A second reason for Ellen's not having considered this question may lie in her own complex amalgam of views on race relations. That is, her own juggling of color-blind and color-conscious positions may lead her, on the one had, to berate her White classmates and, on the other, to believe that despite all the social and cultural differences that separate her and Fishman, it is possible for him to understand her and treat her fairly. A final interpretation of this CRL entry is that Ellen is not being candid about the racial situation in which she finds herself since she knows that Fishman will read what she writes.

Because of this latter possibility, I pressed Ellen about this CRL entry in an interview in mid-November. She did not waiver from her position that a professor can be color-blind in the best sense, viewing all his students as equally worthy human beings. She explained, "I just picked up on that Dr. Fisherman was a teacher, doing what he had to do, not that he was White. I always thought he had the best interests of his students in mind. It never occurred to me that he was singling me out or grading me unfairly."

In-class Freewrites

In addition to the CRLs, a second type of ungraded writing Fishman required was in-class freewrites. In about half of all classes, he asked students to do 10 minutes of writing at the start of class as a way of collecting their thoughts about an issue or assigned text. Ellen did not always do these freewrites because, as she explained to me, when she had not read the assignment, she was not going to pretend to know it.

However, on one occasion Ellen's in-class freewriting proved extremely valuable for her. In early November, Steve had students freewrite about a possible topic for their term essay. As he has already explained, these papers were intended to focus on a moral dilemma the student faced and/or cared about deeply as well as alternative solutions to it. As the freewrite began, Ellen whispered to Steve she had no idea what to write about. Steve responded, "Please give it a try."

As Fishman observed his students writing in the class circle, he noticed, as the 10 minutes drew to a close, that Ellen had become animated. In fact, the videotape shows her bouncing up and down in her seat as discussion began, barely containing her excitement. She raised her hand, and when Steve called on her, she told everyone, "I've got a great idea. I'm going to write about capital punishment—the freedom and responsibility thing we've been discussing." Indeed, class conversations the previous week had focused on human agency and the different theories behind punishment as retribution versus punishment as rehabilitation. During these sessions, Ellen had expressed her strong support for capital punishment and defended her position by telling stories of hardened criminals she had encountered as a prison guard. She also had a chance to hear students take opposing views. This oral practice prepared Ellen for her freewrite which, in turn, crystallized her thinking and jumpstarted her essay. Taken together, the class discussions and the freewrite were crucial to this novice writer's success with the term essay.

The in-class freewrites, then, in ways that paralleled the CRLs, gave Ellen a chance to practice reflective thinking and composing without worry about grades and, in many cases, without having to read and understand an assigned text. In the pre-essay freewrite I have just described, Ellen got support for her essay project, an assignment she repeatedly told me "intimidated" her, one she was far from eager to begin.

Instructional Support #3: Audiotaped Responses to
Students' Essay Drafts

The third instructional support that Ellen mentioned as being helpful was Fishman's audiotaped response to a draft of her capital punishment paper. This audiotape, like class discussion and ungraded writing, helped Ellen contextualize her stories. In Fishman's 12-minute taped response, he described his reactions to her draft, posed questions, and offered revision suggestions. Giving Ellen the same sort of help with philosophic exploration that he provided in class, he urged her to relate her story about capital punishment—that some criminals deserve to die—to alternative views and then see that all of these positions reflect certain underlying attitudes and assumptions. In recording oral responses to students' drafts rather than writing them, Fishman's intention was to model the sort of questioning and theorizing he wanted pupils to engage in. He also believed that through the expressiveness of his voice, he could better convey his enthusiasm for those aspects of student papers he found successful as well as make clear that his comments were suggestive rather than prescriptive. (For more on this response technique, see Fishman & McCarthy, 1998, chapter 10.)

When I met with Ellen a week before the final draft of the essay was due, I asked her about Fishman's tape. In response, she patted her pocketbook and said,

> It's right here. I've been carrying it around for a week but haven't had the courage to listen to it. I dread hearing what he has to say. . . . All this writing is driving me crazy. I procrastinate and procrastinate. I'm a person who prefers speaking. Give me a topic, and I'll have a speech ready for a hundred people in no time.

Despite Ellen's dread of what she imagined would be Fishman's suggestions for major revisions, when I compare her draft with her final paper, it is clear that Steve's tape was an effective way of communicating with her. She was able to make good use of a number of his suggestions, rendering the piece more coherent than it had been in draft form. My inferences from Ellen's finished essay about the tape's effectiveness were confirmed when, in a post-semester interview, she told me that when she finally listened to the tape, she found it more useful than she expected. Particularly helpful, she said, was Fishman's thinking aloud about the questions she might ask of people who hold views different from her own.

In sum, I believe that for novice writers who, like Ellen, prefer oral to written communication, the taped response works especially well. When Ellen finally did listen to the tape, she told me, it was in her car going home from school. "It was odd," she said, "to have Dr. Fisherman speaking to me while I was driving. But I liked it. I played it several times."

TEACHER AND STUDENT MEET AGAIN A YEAR AND A HALF LATER: THE IMPORTANCE OF STUDENT GOALS, MOTIVATION, TIME, AND TRUST

Although the three instructional supports I have just described— class discussion, ungraded writing, and audiotaped responses to drafts—helped Ellen with her compositions for Fishman's course, an irony is that Steve and Ellen had their best success with her writing a year and a half after the course was completed. The trust that Ellen developed in Steve's class that enabled her to experiment with new ways of knowing never led her to confide in him fully about her writing. She never admitted to Steve—as she did to me—that she struggled with her papers and had little confidence in her skills. In fact, when he approached Ellen early in the semester, urging her to get help at the Writing Center, he described her attitude as "I have no problem." According to Fishman, she said, "Oh, I didn't know you cared about the way I wrote. I can write well if I want to." Ellen did stop by the Writing Center on three occasions that semester, but the tutors reported that she was in such a hurry—and seemingly unwilling to think deeply about her pieces—that they made little progress.

By contrast with Ellen's "no problem" comments to Steve, she admitted to me from the beginning that her writing was "rusty" and she "could really use some help." However, at the same time, she confessed she had little interest in composing. She told me, "When I got into his class, and he said you gotta write, I was like, write? I'm not in here to write! Writing is just not me."

However, in spring 2000, nearly a year and a half after Fishman's course concluded, and as I continued to follow Ellen in subsequent semesters, she told me once more in a phone interview about her writing difficulties. She was struggling that semester, she said, in two courses that required a number of papers, a class in leadership and her senior research seminar in her major, criminal justice. After listening to her genuine distress, I took a chance and offered, "Dr. Fishman might be willing to talk with you about your writing for these courses." Although Steve and I had never mentioned such a plan, I knew he regretted having made so little headway with Ellen's writing mechanics and rhetorical understanding during his course. I also knew that in the intervening period he had worked extensively with another underprepared writer in a one-on-one situation (a tutorial we report in the following chapter).

Ellen, to my surprise, was open to my offer. Because she had decided to dip into her savings, she told me, she was not working this semester, and, thus, she "finally [had] time for this." So Ellen and Steve met for an hour on two occasions in February and March 2000, three months before her graduation. Together they focused on

Ellen's assignments, and, according to Steve, working with her this time was totally different. She was less defensive, he said, probably because he was not grading her, and he felt that for the first time they could both be honest about her compositions. He could show Ellen the difficulties he had reading them, and she no longer had to try to convince him, as she often had done in his class, that her writing was fine and deserved high marks and/or extra credit. Ellen told me she finally understood the value of Fishman's advice about being more careful of her audience, specifically, about paying close attention to the teacher's prompt and making herself clear in topic sentences as she moved from one idea to the next. She also claimed that she profitted from Steve's advice about indenting paragraphs and marking quotations. And, indeed, her revised papers do show improvement in these areas.

In my final interview with Ellen in May 2000, a week before she graduated, she described these individual sessions with Fishman:

> When Dr. Fisherman read my papers, he said, "What are you talking about?" He didn't say it in those words; he was tactful. But he's like, "Ellen, you leave out so much. You can't assume that people know what you're talking about. You have to tell them what you're going to say and then relate it to the question the teacher is asking.". . . I could see why he was having trouble. I thought, "Girl, no one would even believe you have a two-year degree."

Why could Ellen and Steve work together fruitfully on her writing in spring 2000 when, during his course in fall 1998, they could not? By the time Ellen met with Steve a year and a half after she completed his Intro course, a number of changes had occurred. First, she had come to see the value of effective written communication for personal growth and career preparation. That is, she wanted, as she put it, "to be able not just to talk to people but also to put [my] ideas in writing." This meant that she was no longer just trying to get through her written work as quickly and painlessly as possible. Instead, she had her own motives and goals for doing the work, not just the ones imposed by the teacher. (For the importance of motivation in underprepared students' learning to write, see Lazere, 1992; Leki, 1992.)

Second, by spring 2000 Ellen had decided to alter her priorities, quitting her job and "tightening [her] belt" so she could devote more time to her school work, and, as she said, "finally put my heart into it." Reducing out-of-school work hours was something that Neha Shah, as we have noted, was able to afford much earlier: back in the fall of 1998.

Finally, there was the trusting relationship Ellen had developed with Steve. A week before graduation, she told me,

> I really appreciated knowing there was one teacher I could talk to if I needed to who said "If you need help, I'll be there." And I was glad he didn't sugar-coat [his evaluation of my writing] and say, "Oh you're okay."

To summarize, teacher and student made progress in this post-class, non-graded, tutorial setting because Ellen came voluntarily with significant personal and professional goals. She was, thus, more motivated and willing to make changes in her writing strategies.

FOUR EVALUATIONS

Because we have focused in this chapter on the racial dynamics of Fishman's class, I will evaluate the teaching and learning that took place there in terms of Critical Race Theory and Whiteness studies. Then, following my pattern in Chapter 2, I will also assess Fishman's teaching and Ellen's learning in terms of Gramscian, Freirian, and Deweyan objectives.

An Evaluation by Critical Race Theorists and Whiteness
Studies Scholars

Critical Race Theorists analyze apparently neutral institutional practices and language in order to reveal their underlying ideological and cultural biases. An important foundation of this scholarship is "legal realism," an approach to jurisprudence that has, interestingly, been strongly influenced by the work of John Dewey (see Horwitz, 1992; Schlegel, 1995; Summers, 1982). Proponents of legal realism are skeptical that judicial decisions are simply the result of the logical application of self-contained legal principles. Rather, such decisions are shaped, they argue, by social and psychological forces outside the law.

One aspect of Critical Race Theorists' critique is their contention that legal language and reasoning marginalize people who prefer other ways of knowing. Thus, these theorists emphasize alternative discourses—for example, story, allegory, and personal narrative—as a means by which minorities gain voice (see Bell, 1992; Delgado, 1989/1995, 1995; Ladson-Billings, 1998; Williams, 1991). In this regard, I believe Critical Race Theorists would applaud the heteroglossic nature of Fishman's classroom discussions, his welcoming of stories and alternative ways of talking in class discussion. In addition, they might approve Steve's curriculum because of its inclusion of works by anti-racists like Fanon, Carmichael, and hooks.

On the other hand, these theorists, along with Whiteness studies scholars, would criticize Fishman's reliance on what he calls "careful, openminded, step-by-step argumentation" as the sole acceptable way to write in philosophy. They would fault him for ignoring the power of other written forms, including narratives, to explore philosophic issues and persuade readers.

Further, Critical Race Theorists would deplore Fishman's general color and power evasiveness. That is, they would criticize his failure to show students the bankruptcy of the color-blind, assimilationist model of race relations and the inadequacy of so-called multicultural curricula. They would also say he perpetuated White privilege by not explaining to students that the century-and-a-half-long effort by minorities to gain full legal rights in America has not only failed to ensure social justice for all Blacks, it has, paradoxically, accrued further advantage to Whites (see Ladson-Billings, 1998, p. 13). Specifically, Fishman never directly tells his class what Fanon, Carmichael, and hooks know very well: that simply letting Blacks and other American minorities have free access to compete in the American marketplace leaves the economic and political distributions of power just as they are. Given the institutional structures and pervasive cultural practices which favor Whites, there is no way that simply eliminating *de jure* racial segregation—or implementing token affirmative action programs—will significantly reduce the poverty and social inequities which plague America's minorities.

Finally, Critical Race Theorists and Whiteness studies scholars would likely be disturbed by Fishman's grading methods. He does nothing, they would say, to make up for the unequal playing field on which Ellen Williams has to compete. That is, he does nothing to reduce White privilege when he grades Ellen on what she does not know rather than what she does. Specifically, he evaluates her on an area of her weakness, her academic writing, rather than on her areas of strength, her oral and social skills and her preferred, confrontational style of debate.

Gramscian Evaluation

Gramsci would, like the Critical Race Theorists, find some things to praise in Fishman's teaching as well as much to criticize. On the positive side, Gramsci would be pleased that Steve's course improved Ellen's attitude, at least in limited ways, toward book learning, theory, and the power of contemplation to make everyday life more meaningful. Gramsci would, that is, appreciate Ellen's comments a week before she graduated when, in our final interview in May 2000, she said,

> You know what my thing always was. I was just here because I had to be, and I wanted to be left alone. I always felt like life experience just outpowered book learning, but now, where I am today, I don't think that as much. When I read something, I still want to know how I can apply it to my job or my life, but the two sorts of learning are now closer to each other.

On the negative side, Gramsci (1971) would point out that Ellen did not appear to be headed in the direction of becoming the "organic intellectual" he wants, the working class person who takes on the physical and intellectual discipline necessary to understand the history of intellectual movements and ideas (p. 6). That is, Ellen did not get a classical education in Fishman's course that enabled her to articulate values and ideologies that would counter the cultural hegemony of the dominant class and lead to social transformation. In fact, Ellen admitted, because of her "crazy, too-full" schedule, she often did not read Fishman's assignments carefully and sometimes did not read them at all.

Freirian Evaluation

Like the evaluations of the Critical Race Theorists/Whiteness studies scholars and Gramsci, Freire's assessment of Ellen's experience in Fishman's course would, I believe, be mixed. He would be impressed with the solidarity that actually developed among Ellen and her peers. Ellen spoke regularly on the phone with several classmates, including Tonya McInnis and Robert Bullerdick, discussing personal and philosophic issues, and these students often extended class discussion as they left the classroom, talking among themselves about the issues with which the class had just been engaged. In addition, Ellen arranged to meet with Tonya and Robert for dinner the night before the final exam so they could study together. Freire would also be pleased with the relationship that Ellen and Steve ultimately shaped. By mid-semester they were working well together in class discussion, and, a year and a half later, they collaborated in investigating Ellen's writing.

However, after praising the solidarity Ellen developed with classmates and the relationship she and Fishman forged, Freire, as in chapter 2, would criticize the texts or "codifications" in Steve's class. Fishman presented many readings, Freire would say, that were not particularly relevant to a working class, Black woman. Although Freire might agree with Critical Race Theorists that the readings by Fanon, Carmichael, and hooks were a step in the right direction, he too would criticize the way Fishman handled them, but for different reasons. Whereas Critical Race Theorists and Whiteness studies scholars would be upset by Fishman's failure to bring White privilege to the forefront of class discussion, Freire would focus on Steve's failure to speak about class conflict. Specifically, Freire would excoriate Fishman's failure to help Ellen see the many class contradictions in her own life, for example, the contradictions that pitted her need to work against the likelihood of getting the degree she needed to progress at work.

Deweyan Evaluation

As for Dewey, his evaluation of Ellen's learning and Steve's teaching would be significantly more positive than the assessments I have just outlined. Although Dewey would be unhappy with Ellen's failure to develop a strong interest in learning about the history of Western thought—Dewey believes that one aim of education should be transmission of the seminal texts and ideas of the culture—he would be pleased about a number of other features of Ellen's and Steve's interactions.

Along with Freire and the Critical Race Theorists, Dewey would applaud the opportunities Ellen had to teach her classmates as well as Fishman and, thereby, to establish solidarity with them. He would be even more gratified, however, that Ellen was able to integrate philosophic theory with her personal and professional lives. Dewey would be proud of this integration as well as of the critical attitude that Ellen adopts in her term essay and that she took with her from Steve's class. It is a deeper, more pervasive residue than anything Neha Shah took with her. Finally, Dewey would be pleased that Ellen and her classmates and teacher, at least at times, managed to communicate well enough across race, class, and gender lines to blend their various discourses so they could create a classroom space for cooperative inquiry.

Conclusion
STEVE FISHMAN AND LUCILLE McCARTHY

As a Deweyan, Fishman was, despite all the criticisms from various perspectives that McCarthy has just outlined, quite pleased with Ellen Williams's experiences in philosophy. As we have shown, Ellen, like Neha Shah, started out in Fishman's class reluctantly, seeing it as an annoying and insignificant means to her careerist ends. In fact, if anything, Ellen was more opposed than Neha to being in philosophy, and her expressions of opposition were directed not only at the subject matter and teacher but at many of her classmates as well. All this notwithstanding, Ellen, like Neha, found sufficient assistance from instructional supports in Fishman's class to achieve some of his specific objectives for students.

In Ellen's case, we have argued that her success was based upon Steve's acceptance of her preferred discourse—storytelling and accounts of personal experience—in class discussion, ungraded writing, and her final essay. However, we have also shown that Steve did not accept (or reward) Ellen's stories without asking her to work with them, to question them and/or place them in philosophic contexts so they could become exploratory tools for her and, at times, for her classmates as well. The result of Fishman's asking Ellen to use her stories in this way was twofold.

First, Ellen came to see the value of questioning as a means of knowledge construction, its usefulness in helping her reconceptualize her own experiences. Second, she developed a caring relationship both with her classmates and Fishman. That Ellen believed Fishman cared about her was evidenced by the fact that, in the three semesters following her course in philosophy, she turned to him twice for letters of recommendation and, in her final semester, for help with her writing. And Fishman felt that this care was not just one way— from him to her. On several occasions when Ellen came to his office or they met by chance on campus, she inquired about his well-being, smiling as she urged him to be less reclusive and work-oriented.

Fishman's and Ellen's ability to develop enough likemindedness—despite the obvious differences between them—to form a productive community of two is noteworthy. We say this because some educationists have suggested that the best way to overcome oppositions between White teachers and Black pupils is for teachers to immerse themselves in and identify with the culture of their students. For example, Ladson-Billings (1994) concludes that most of the White teachers she studied who were successful with African American pupils lived in Black neighborhoods, joined Black churches, and/or attended students' community events. Because these teachers altered their community identification, they were able to engage in what Ladson-Billings (1994) calls "culturally relevant teaching."

Fishman, however, made no such changes in his lifestyle and habits, and yet he and Ellen managed to develop a shared language, understanding, and friendship. In saying that Steve and Ellen succeeded in relating to one another without Fishman's doing what Ladson-Billings recommends, we do not mean to deny the signifi-cance of Ladson-Billings's call for White teacher transformation. But given the fact that the vast majority of American school teachers is White, and given the unlikelihood that many of these teachers would—or could—follow the implications of Ladson-Billings's research, we believe that careful study of successful community building of the sort that developed between Steve and Ellen is worthwhile.

∾

Coda

The Researchers Continue to Converse

STEVE FISHMAN AND LUCILLE McCARTHY

Although as co-researchers we agreed that Ellen Williams made significant progress toward achieving Fishman's goals, there remained, as in our study of Neha Shah, lingering and significant disagreements between us about Fishman's approach to underpre-pared students. With regard to Neha, as we outline at the close of chapter 2, McCarthy's conflicts with Fishman focused primarily on his failures to adjust his curriculum. That is, McCarthy thought Fishman showed little respect for the cultural diversity Neha brought to his classroom and the borderland perspective she applied to her homework and exam papers. With regard to Ellen Williams, McCarthy's disagreements with Fishman focused less on his curriculum and more on what she saw as inappropriate grading policies and ill-designed reading and writing assignments.

Regarding Steve's grading, McCarthy's frustrations were twofold. First, she thought Fishman made a mistake in *what* he evaluated: his focus on Ellen's academic achievements to the exclusion of her moral and social ones, such as expenditure of effort and improved interpersonal skills. Second, McCarthy thought when Fishman did focus on Ellen's academic achievements, he was mistaken in *how* he evaluated them. Specifically, she criticized his use of an across-the-board standard rather than an individual one, that is, a standard which would have measured the distance Ellen had travelled from her own baseline at the start of the semester. As McCarthy complained to Fishman during one of their more heated exchanges, "If you're such a Dewey man, you should be just as interested in rewarding Ellen for how far she has come as you are in maintaining some elitist, Ivy League standard."

For his part, Fishman admitted that he did indeed, in his grading, emphasize academic achievement over moral and social development. Although he granted that the latter are vitally important, he tried to justify their absence from his evaluation procedures by claiming that he lacked the ability to accurately measure them. However, in response to McCarthy's charge that he clung to a rigid, across-the-board standard and, thus, failed to properly reward Ellen for her individual academic growth, he strongly disagreed. To the contrary, he reminded McCarthy that in assigning Ellen Williams a "C" for his course, he actually worried he might have put too much weight on Ellen's personal growth, what he saw as her courageous 180 degree turn from disdain for critical reflection to its whole-hearted practice. He added that he tried to balance an individualized standard of academic progress for Ellen, as he did for all his students, with a more generalized one. In other words, he tried to look at each student's individual starting point and development while also comparing his or her work with that of other undergraduates. He was concerned that, to do otherwise, to omit all comparison to other students, might lead pupils, like Ellen and Neha Shah, down a primrose path to a false sense of their relative academic skills and accomplishments.

Regarding McCarthy's criticisms of Fishman's assignments, she complained that when he designed them he was insensitive to Ellen's academic level, interests, and need for feelings of success. Although McCarthy ultimately found that Fishman gave Ellen opportunities to present her own stories and opinions, McCarthy thought it foolish and self-defeating that Steve continued to insist that Ellen read original sources in philosophy. This material, McCarthy argued, was appropriate for most of Fishman's students but questionable for underprepared pupils like Ellen. Instead, McCarthy urged him to substitute selections from secondary sources since Ellen's difficulties with primary ones often led her to avoid doing the philosophy homework.

In addition, McCarthy believed that Ellen's academic confidence would have been bolstered, and her personal needs better met, if Steve had spent less time on enlightening Ellen and more time on nurturing and supporting her. In particular, McCarthy thought it unwise that Fishman required Ellen to discuss her personal narratives in relation to philosophic concepts and recast them in "academic" prose. In line with a number of sociolinguists (eg., Smitherman, 1989/2000), McCarthy thought Fishman's stance showed little sensitivity to the ideological cargo of Standard English and the historical role that Ellen's mother tongue, African American Vernacular English or Ebonics, has played in the struggle for social liberation. Thus, according to McCarthy, instead of requiring Ellen to place her personal narratives in academic context, Fishman should have allowed Ellen to present them in her own style.

Further, in McCarthy's view, Ellen should have been provided with alternative ways of demonstrating her philosophic understanding, perhaps through oral presentations or posters as substitutes for written work. As evidence of need to provide students like Ellen with alternative way for displaying their mastery of philosophic ways of thinking, McCarthy pointed to Ellen's ongoing resistance to his writing assignments. At one point, McCarthy, barely masking her deep frustration, asked Fishman,

> Why in the world won't you set up activities that build on Ellen's strengths so she can succeed and feel good about being back in

school? It isn't as if you teach math or biology where the subject matter needs to be taught in a definite sequence and students must have certain basic information before they can do advanced work. Quite the opposite, you have *carte blanche* in philosophy.

In attempting to defend his assignments, his requirement that Ellen read original sources and be graded on her writing about them in Standard English, Steve talked about the difficulty of tailoring his readings and homework for individual students. But more than that, he spoke of his unwillingness to water down his subject matter or alter his aims for students. Nevertheless, Fishman did admit it would be ideal if he could, as McCarthy suggested, impart philosophic ways of thinking to students like Ellen by focusing on their own narratives written in their own styles rather than on canonic materials. But, as Fishman recalled for McCarthy, his experiments in the past with using students' lives and stories as course texts, while downplaying primary materials, had felt like failures to him. Without primary source materials, he explained, he had found it hard to raise class discussions above the level of dorm bull sessions or help students challenge their own ideas by seeing them as part of broader historic and philosophic conversations (see Fishman & McCarthy, 1995). That is, Fishman said he discovered that so-called "philosophic ways of thinking" could not so easily be separated from the classic texts, conversations, and rhetorical styles in which they were embedded.

Not only did Fishman reject McCarthy's suggestion to focus primarily on students' own narratives, he also rejected her recommendation to substitute secondary sources for primary ones. He told her he feared such a substitution would imply that the point of the assigned readings was not to grapple with philosophic thinking but, rather, to memorize "predigested" material, learning, for example, five features of Platonism or six characteristics of American pragmatism. This desire to have his students stay away from what he called predigested summaries and, instead, confront the complexity of primary material was rooted, Steve said, in his own undergraduate experience. He described for McCarthy the seriousness that he observed in his own teachers who seemed uncompromising in their desire to pass on the best of philosophic inquiry. Although Fishman acknowledged that Ellen came to philosophy with different interests, skills, and resources than he did as an undergraduate, he said he did not want to shortchange her. "I believe," he told McCarthy, "that Ellen will have important positive experiences in my class if I can convince her of both my commitment to my field and my commitment to her."

McCarthy could only shake her head. But rather than give up, she tried again to convince Fishman of the rightness of her criticisms by backing them up with appeals to research. She told Steve he sounded like those hidebound teachers whom educationists and compositionists sometimes study, teachers who, under the banner of maintaining standards and allegiance to their disciplines, refuse to adjust to changing student populations. By contrast, adaptable teachers, those who see their disciplines as dynamic rather than fixed and who take their students' moral and social development as seriously as they take their academic progress, have significantly greater success with their students than instructors who avoid experimentation (see Ball, 1999, 2000; Feagin, Vera, & Imani, 1996; Fox, 1990; Katz, 1999; Mahiri, 1998; Stodolsky and Grossman, 2000; Sylvester, 1994).

Despite what McCarthy saw as the reasonableness of her arguments, Fishman held fast to his belief that he had an obligation to acquaint pupils with primary sources from his discipline's canon and to require them to practice philosophic writing. Neither would he surrender his doubts about the possibility of fairly measuring Ellen's, or any other student's, moral and social progress. As a consequence, the two of us continued to hold conflicting views of the academic demands that Steve made upon Ellen and the grades he assigned her. What Fishman saw as his obligation to give students a taste of the rigorous and noble adventure of philosophy, McCarthy saw as a mark of Fishman's narrowmindedness, his projections onto his students of his own idiosyncratic longings and personality. Conversely, what McCarthy saw as grading policies that would be fairer to Ellen's actual achievements and course requirements that would be more sensitive to her real needs—adjustments McCarthy believed would promote Ellen's feelings of success—Fishman viewed as lowering his aspirations for students.

In a final effort to justify his pedagogy, Fishman told McCarthy that despite all that went wrong, he believed something important went right between Ellen and him. He then recalled the last conversation he had with Ellen in fall 1998.

> She came by my office at the end of exam week to drop off her term essay. She told me she was running late, yet we talked a little about her own plans and about her children's schooling before she said goodbye. When she went to leave, she paused at my door, turned to me and said, "I'll never forget you, Dr. Fisherman. I really mean that."

Steve told McCarthy that he was not exactly sure what Ellen intended, but he thought she was acknowledging that, although he made her work hard, she was grateful about where it had taken her.

Common Goals, Deweyan Community, and the Resolution of Freire's Teacher–Student Contradiction

Education must begin with the solution of the teacher-student contradiction by reconciling the roles of the contradiction so that both are simultaneously teachers *and* students.

Paulo Freire (1970/1997, p. 53)

In our studies of Neha Shah and Ellen Williams we saw clearly the cultural and linguistic chasm that frequently separates teacher and underprepared student. Put differently, we came to see that Fishman's struggles with Neha and Ellen were as much about overcoming a cultural, class, and/or ethnic barrier as about reconciling different educational goals and aspirations. Thus, we were determined that when another underprepared writer enrolled in one of Fishman's classes we would pay close attention to the chasm between instructor and pupil: a disjunction that Freire calls the teacher-student contradiction. Indeed, such a student, Andre Steadman, did appear the following semester in Steve's advanced class, Philosophy of Education. In this chapter we tell Andre's story, and, employing Freirian lenses, we probe the impact of Fishman's Deweyan pedagogy on the contradictions that initially separated this student and Steve.

As we show in chapters 2 and 3, Neha Shah and Ellen Williams made progress in philosophy despite their lack of interest in the subject matter and despite having goals that conflicted with those of their teacher. They did this by drawing upon a variety of instructional supports that were available in Fishman's classroom. Andre Steadman, the 21-year-old, African American student and novice writer on whom we focus in this chapter, also made progress. However, Andre's gains were only partially attributable to instructional supports available to all of Fishman's students. Instead, because Andre and Steve were able to find, amongst their many differences, a number of common goals, they developed a cooperative, tutorial relationship that became the foundation of Andre's achievements. In this chapter, then, we explore an instructional dynamic—a weekly one-on-one tutorial, an extra help session between teacher and student—that is quite different from the whole-class interactions we featured in our accounts of Neha and Ellen. Whereas in the tutorial there is the obvious advantage of a teacher focusing exclusively on one individual's needs, there is also the disadvantage of no opportunity for the sort of productive interaction among students that played such a large role in Neha's and Ellen's cases.

Although the instructional dynamic between Andre and Steve was different from what it was with Neha or Ellen, Andre's experiences in philosophy, like these women's, were shaped by the particular array of resources—social, academic, and linguistic—he brought with him. With regard to academic capital, Andre fit somewhere between Neha and Ellen. Although he did not have Neha's past record of scholastic achievement, he had been making steady progress toward his bachelor's degree since he graduated from high school three years earlier. Although he was employed 40 hours a week in a 4:00-to-midnight job monitoring software at a local bank, he, unlike both Neha and Ellen, saw himself as a full-time student. Also, unlike Neha and Ellen, Andre told Fishman he was happy to be at UNC Charlotte.

Even more important than Andre's history of continuous schooling and positive attitude toward the University was the particular approach he adopted toward Fishman's course. Because of this posture, as we will show, it took Andre and Steve only two weeks to shape the cooperative relationship that it took Steve and Ellen almost a year and a half to develop and that totally eluded Steve and Neha.

Our story of Andre is divided, like those we tell of Neha and Ellen, into three parts. In Part One, Fishman presents the Deweyan-Freirian theory behind his tutorial arrangement with Andre. That is,

Steve outlines the way he uses Dewey's ideas about democratic community to ameliorate the chasm, or contradiction, between Andre and himself. In doing so, Fishman further develops the discussion he began in chapter 2 about the different strategies Dewey and Freire suggest for fashioning equitable school relations. Specifically, Steve fills out his explanation of why—despite his deep respect for Freire's radical vision of a transformed society—he adopts a Deweyan pedagogy and a gradualist approach toward social reform.

In Part Two, Fishman and McCarthy describe Andre's challenges and successes in Philosophy of Education as well as in his courses in three subsequent semesters. In this part, we individually author alternate sections, detailing Andre's experiences from both the teacher's and student's point of view.

Finally, we conclude this chapter, as we have the preceeding two, with a coda in which we once more bring into the open our disagreements. This time, our differences focus on McCarthy's charge that Fishman, in his responses to Andre, underappreciated the depth of America's history of radical politics and the dangers of our present capitalist and consumerist culture. She claims that, as a result, Fishman missed important chances to work for increased social and economic justice.

Part One

Linking Dewey's Community and Freire's Liberatory Classroom

STEVE FISHMAN

As we said in chapter 1, the task of explicating, comparing, and applying Dewey and Freire is a challenging one given the vast corpus of these theorists' work and the complex strands of thought woven into their politics and pedagogies. As we also said, we believe our characterizations of them—Dewey as gradualist social reformer and Freire as radical transformer—are justifiable, although the richness of their philosophies means they can be read and characterized in different ways.

Therefore, as I began my work with Andre Steadman in spring 1999, I relied on our characterizations, and I hoped that by enacting Dewey's conception of democratic community[1] I could succeed in softening the teacher-student contradiction that Freire deplores. Attempting to carry out Deweyan theory to achieve Freirian ends may seem surprising because Dewey's political orientation and approach to the classroom is, as I have noted, quite different from Freire's. Despite the fact that they share the same goal—extension of democracy from the political to the economic and civic spheres—their analysis of human history, and, thus, their means of achieving this goal are diverse.

Dewey understands history as a series of clashes between inherited social institutions and contemporary developments. He sees the challenge for both the individual and society at large as setting aside or altering habits developed in an earlier time that, in present conditions, are no longer appropriate. For example, he (1935/1991) explains the inequitable distribution of wealth in capitalism as the result of outdated institutions—in particular, the legal property system that allows industrial entrepreneurs "to reap out of all proportion to what they sow"—frustrating the potential of modern science and technology to better the lives of all (p. 53). Dewey's solution to this inequity rests on expanding the democratic aspects of capitalism—that is, reforming outdated legal codes and moral attitudes through the application of scientific method or "organized intelligence" (p. 56; 1934, pp. 73–79; 1936/1987, p. 132, 141–45).

By contrast, Freire (1970/1997) views history as a continuous conflict between social classes. He understands economic inequities to be the result of deliberate subjugation of one class by another and sees little positive in capitalism upon which to build social reform. Given that, for Freire, class conflict is the key to historic change, and proletarian struggle, rather than application of scientific method, is history's primary liberalizing force, his hope for increased social justice lies in freeing, or "humanizing," the oppressed.

Although Freire (1994) does not altogether discount the possibility of a "broadening of democratic spaces" within capitalism, spaces where the bourgeoisie and the proletariat can negotiate (p. 92), he is steadfast in his claim that workers and the dominant class are caught in serious contradiction. He tells us that while there are exceptional situations in which the oppressed and oppressor classes may act in concert, we must never forget that "when the emergency which united them is past, they will return to the contradiction which defines their existence and never really disappears" (1970/1997, p. 125). Since Freire (1994) believes that capitalists are, by nature, "dehumanizers" who cannot participate in liberating the oppressed, he argues that they will always impede the human "ontological vocation" of increased equity and justice (pp. 98–99). In short, as I read Freire, the only time real harmony between different social classes will occur is when the bourgeoisie disappears and a classless society emerges. (For further discussion of Freire's views of class polarizations, see Taylor, 1993.)

Because Dewey's approach involves less class polarizing than Freire's, I believed it offered me, in the current North American climate, a practicable way of softening Freire's teacher-student contradiction. That is, the gradualist approach underlying Dewey's pedagogy—his view that there are democratic and progressive forces within capitalism on which to base class reconciliation—made his classroom orientation more useful to me than Freire's. This is because Dewey's theory can account for my students' and my own complex and often overlapping mixtures of opposition and accommodation to the values of the dominant elite. In *Liberalism and Social Action*, Dewey (1935/1991) explicitly warns against the use of static and polarized class affiliations. He writes,

> In spite of the existence of class conflicts, amounting at times to veiled civil war, any one habituated to the use of the method of science will view with considerable suspicion the erection of actual human beings into fixed entities called classes, having no overlapping interests and so internally unified and externally separated that they are made the protagonists of history . . ." (p. 56; see also Eastman, 1959, p. 292).

In sum, I believed that, applied to my classroom, Dewey's analysis of class relations within capitalism—his conception that classes are dynamic and overlapping rather that static and mutually exclusive—provided me with a practicable basis for reducing Freire's teacher-student contradiction. Put another way, Dewey's analysis is less vulnerable to the postmodern charge that has been leveled at Freire's conception, namely, that it neglects the ambiguous and shifting social spaces that North American teachers and students actually occupy (Glass, 2001; McCarthy, 1988; Taylor, 1993; Weiler, 1994, 1996. For more general criticism of conceptions of worker and owner classes as distinct and monolithic, see Gottlieb, 1992, pp. 141–145.)

Freire's Approach to the Teacher-Student Contradiction

According to my reading, Freire (1970/1997) wants liberatory teachers to focus on the way capitalists have foisted distorted pictures of reality onto the working class in order to maintain their power. Freire (Shor & Freire, 1987) also wants teachers to learn from their working class students how these students see the world and to become sensitive to "the beauty of their language and wisdom" (p. 30; Freire, 1994, pp. 68–85). This is in line with his belief, shared by Dewey, that teachers should become learners and learners should become teachers (1970/1997, pp. 53, 61; 1970/2000, p. 27; Shor & Freire, 1987, p. 33; see also Dewey, 1916/1967, p. 160). Unfortunately, Freire finds that in most schools teachers assume they have all the knowledge and students none. In other words, he finds teachers attempting to fill their students with information as if they were bank accounts designed for receiving knowledge deposits. He (1970/1997) calls this sort of banking approach a "contradiction" (p. 53).

However, Freire obviously does not mean that teachers are involved in a logical contradiction when they encourage student docility. Rather, building on Gramsci (1971), he sees education as a site of conflict, one in which teachers, consciously or unwittingly, serve the dominant class by transmitting capitalist values as transcendent truths. In other words, Freire extends Marx's (1932/1978) analysis of class antagonism to cultural institutions like public schools. Traditional teachers in capitalism, Freire (1970/1997) suggests, serve the same oppressive function regarding proletarian children that police and soldiers serve regarding colonized natives. He writes, "A careful analysis of the teacher-student relationship at any level, inside or outside the school, reveals . . . a narrating Subject [the teacher] and patient, listening objects [the students]" (p. 52). Freire adds that this sort of banking pedagogy is not just an innocent mistake but an effort by the oppressor class to render students passive so they can more easily be dominated (p. 55). In a political and human sense, then, as opposed to a narrowly logical sense, teachers and students are, for Freire, in contradiction. The continued existence of the teacher means the dehumanization of the student. Freire states his radical means for reforming this situation most starkly when he suggests that if teachers are to overcome the teacher-student contradiction they must "die" to their middle-classness (p. 114). (I note that, in later work, Freire [Shor & Freire, 1987] suggests that the teacher-student contradiction can work in converse fashion: students who want to maintain the status quo resisting the transformative ideology of their "revolutionary" teachers [p. 69]).

I find three specific pedagogical features of traditional, banking education at the center of Freire's charge that teacher and student are caught in a contradictory relationship. The first is that teachers fail to promote active problem-posing and critical consciousness among their students (1970/1997). Second, teachers lack respect for pupil competencies that lie outside orthodox school measures (1993, 1994). And, finally, teachers distrust students' judgment and discount students' ability to orchestrate their own liberation (1970/1997, 1994; Shor & Freire, 1987).

Freire's (1983) solution to the traditional teacher-student antinomy starts with problem-posing education, helping students use "their reading and writing of the world" to "read and write the word" (p. 7). In other words, Freire (1970/1997) says that teachers should help students see their social environments as laced with exploitive relationships, and they should make these inequities the subject matter of their literacy instruction. It is Freire's hope, as I interpret him, that as teachers adopt a problem-posing pedagogy they will begin the process of "dying" to their bourgeois values and being "reborn" in solidarity with their working class pupils (pp. 113–14; see also 1996, p. 163).

Dewey's Approach to Teacher-Student Tensions in Contrast to Freire's

I believe that Dewey would not deny the importance of Freire's starting point: his problem-posing approach. To the contrary, as I have said, Dewey (1916/1967), very much like Freire, wants students to become teachers and teachers to become students in the classroom (p. 160). Although Dewey, like Freire, decries docility in students, he sees banking education not as a nefarious political plot but simply as the result of teachers having an inadequate grasp of learning theory. As a consequence, instead of Freire's radical call for the dissolution of teacher's bourgeois loyalties, Dewey (1935/1991) urges teachers to help pupils employ "the method of intelligence" in collaborative projects and inquiry. In fact, Dewey says that the scientific method—"the method of cooperative experimental intelligence"—should be enacted in every branch and detail of school learning (p.35). The upshot is that whereas Freire's vision of the role instructors might play in resolving our present social dilemmas focuses on their unveiling the realities behind the oppression of the proletariat, Dewey's vision focuses primarily on teachers encouraging student use of "organized intelligence" in the context of cooperative, democratic classrooms.

This analysis, by Dewey, of what teachers might do to prepare students to liberalize American society undergirded my decision to begin my tutorial with Andre Steadman by attempting to fashion a democratic community with him, one in which we might practice Dewey's notion of intelligent, collaborative thinking. Before turning to the details of Andre's and my experiences in Philosophy of Education, I offer a brief exposition of Dewey's conception of democractic community.

Dewey's Conception of Democratic Community

Dewey (1927/1988a) tells us that the cure for the problems of American democracy is more democracy. And by "democracy" he does not just mean popularly elected officials, rule by law, and due process. Rather, for Dewey (1916/1967), democracy is "a mode of associated living," a way of working together that depends upon mutual consent and respect for the aims, emotions, and habitual responses of those with whom we associate (p. 87, 5). In fact, community and democracy are so closely tied in Dewey's view that he calls democracy "the idea of community life itself" (1927/1988a, p. 148).

In describing a desirable community, Dewey specifies three interwoven and recursive features: (1) common purpose and goals, (2) likemindedness, and (3) mutual care. By *common purpose*, Dewey (1916/1967) means more than just people's achieving shared goals by using one another, as is the case, for example, with many employers and employees. Instead, he envisions individuals working toward common ends who also respect one another's "emotional and intellectual dispositions" and seek one another's consent (p. 5). By *likemindedness*, Dewey refers to people's having enough common experiences to understand the meaning of each other's words and diverse perspectives. And by *mutual care*, Dewey envisions individuals encouraging the development of each other's unique abilities for the benefit of the whole. Mutually caring communities are those in which each person has "an equitable opportunity" to give to and receive from others, and, thus, what counts as progress for one has genuine value for all (p. 84; 1927a/1988, p. 149).

Essential to the development of common purpose, likemindedness, and mutual care, according to Dewey, is successful communication. Dewey's (1925/1989) example of such communication is one person, A, beckoning to another person, B, to bring a flower. To understand each other, says Dewey, person B must learn to see the world as person A sees it and vice-versa. He writes,

> The characteristic thing about B's understanding of A's movement and sounds is that he responds to the thing from the standpoint of A.

He perceives the thing as it may function in A's experience, instead of just ego-centrically. Similarly, A in making the request conceives the thing not only in its direct relationship to himself, but as a thing capable of being grasped and handled by B (p. 148).

Put differently, people who communicate successfully are, to use a popular expression, on the same wave length. They respond in sufficiently similar ways to social events, requirements, and expectations that they are able to form communities that carry out common projects. Applied to the classroom, such communities engage in cooperatively organized inquiry and are akin to Pratt's (1991) "safe houses." However, in contrast to Pratt's safe houses which are homogeneous, with members sharing ethnicity, gender, race, or class, Dewey (1916/1967) wants to create communities of comfort that are transethnic. He wants the sort of "intermingling in the school . . . of different races, differing religions and unlike customs" that will create "a new and broader environment" (p. 21). That is, Dewey seeks to develop shared language and common cause while, at the same time, promoting exchanges among the variety of cultural and racial traditions represented by America's "hyphenated" citizenry (1916/1976a, 1916/1976b). In sum, Dewey believes that we can use our differences to expand the number of safe houses to which we belong.

In speaking of Deweyan community as a promising way of ameliorating Freire's teacher-student contradiction, I do not underestimate the obstacles to even modest liberalization of American schools and society. However, given the absence of any deeply rooted, radical tradition in the U.S.—as well as the hybrid aspirations and overlapping social locations of most teachers and students—the progressive movement within which Dewey writes seems to me a more realistic and hopeful basis for school reform than Freire's emphasis upon class conflict. That is, without denigrating the radical vision of proletarian triumph behind Freire's work, I believe Dewey's (1935/1991) gradualism, his trust in the further development of organized intelligence and democratic institutions within capitalism, offers a more practicable basis for classroom liberalization (p. 59).

As applied to my work with Andre Steadman in spring 1999, my hope was that by fashioning democratic community with Andre, I would have a reasonable chance of softening the classroom contradictions Freire describes, a reasonable chance to better promote Andre's active learning, recognize and build on his competencies, and take seriously his own aspirations. I also believed that, if I succeeded, I would be taking a small step toward the reform which will, in Dewey's (1916/1967) words, "produce in schools a projection in type of the society we should like to realize, and by forming minds in accord with it gradually modify the larger and more recalcitrant features of adult society" (p. 317).

In the section immediately following, I set the stage for McCarthy's and my study of this third novice writer by reiterating my specific classroom objectives and, then, articulating the ideology, or political orientation, that underlies them.

OBJECTIVES FOR ADVANCED PHILOSOPHY STUDENTS AND THE IDEOLOGY UNDERLYING THEM

My goals for advanced students are much the same as for my Intro students. First, I want my advanced students to read texts carefully, identifying authors' stances and their defenses of them (argument extraction). Second, I want students to practice critical reflection, to assess an author's position by looking at it from a distanced or analytic perspective (argument evaluation). Third, I would like students to contextualize their views (intellectual reconstruction), and, fourth, I urge them to use philosophy to reconceptualize their experiences (application of philosophy). Finally, I expect pupils to display mastery of academic composition in Standard American English (coherent writing).

These five objectives reflect my view of the defining features of philosophic literacy, the rules and conventions which I see as governing philosophic meaning-making. However, my approach is hardly ideologically neutral. Rather, the way I introduce students to philosophy of education is located within broader political goals that are more my own than universal features of my discipline.

The ideology undergirding my classroom approach echoes Dewey's gradualism as I have described it above. That is, I share

Dewey's faith that American democracy can be extended by further developing the forces of liberalism and collaborative inquiry that already exist in our society. I adopt this ideology for two reasons. First, both my students and I, despite the overwhelming grip of the dominant class, occupy ambiguous and overlapping social spaces, ones that provide chances, albeit limited and narrow, to resist as well as accommodate mainstream life. That is, based on considerable anecdotal data, my students are, by and large, critical of American racism, sexism, and classism and, at the same time, hell-bent on using the exchange value of their anticipated diplomas to maximize their economic wealth. Thus, "to launch a politics of refusal" with my students, as some critical pedagogists advise, by focusing primarily on the ways schools "reproduce the discourses, values, and privileges of existing elites" would be to do a couple of things I am disinclined to do (McLaren, 1994, p. 197). It would force me to either ignore my students' expressed desire for further entry into the mainstream or to dismiss their aspirations as "false consciousness," a case of the oppressed appropriating the ideology of the oppressor. (For the dangers of false consciousness, see Freire, 1970/1997; Williams, 1977).

Second, my gradualist ideology not only allows me to take my students' mainstream aspirations seriously it also allows me to present them with some realistic visions of social change. Given the conservative nature of our society's history and current political trajectory, I am not sure how students and I can construct radical alternatives to capitalist America that would not invite ridicule or seem impossibly difficult to achieve. I fear that for me to make untenable claims about the sort of political transformations my students, colleagues, and I can actually accomplish might lead to the very despair that Freire (1970/1997) himself wants to overcome (pp. 43–48; see also Giroux, 1992, p. 105). This is not to deny the importance of radical visions for those who, like myself, advocate more piecemeal reform. Such visions are essential for keeping us from complacency, for keeping our more centrist inclinations from blinding us to our society's terrible inequities. However, at this moment, from our present situation within advanced capitalism, I believe our best chance for an improved future rests upon gradualism: a steady expansion of the progressive, cooperative forces in our society that lead to reforms in education leading to a more liberalized culture leading to more reforms in education and on and on in a continuing liberalizing cycle (see Dewey, 1916/1967, pp. 91, 317).

In sum, when I combine my students' aims—their intended writing of the world, to borrow from Freire (1983)—with my own reading of America's political climate, I find myself unwilling to make radical transformation the primary focus of my pedagogy. I say this with sadness because of my own longings and my deep respect for visions of a society in which all people can "control the social and economic forces that determine their existence" (Giroux, 1991, p. 5). However, since the success of a radical political movement in America—one that effects a transfer of power from owners to laborers —does not seem a live possibility in the foreseeable future, I take a more gradualist, Deweyan approach. I attempt to develop in students those skills that will give them at least modestly increased chances of collaboratively shaping and controlling their destinies.

Part Two
Dewey's Communal Ideals as Applied to Teacher–Student Relations
STEVE FISHMAN AND LUCILLE McCARTHY

Because we believe that the relationship between college teachers and their underprepared students is important to these students' success in particular courses as well as over the long haul of their college careers, we now explore, in a series of single-authored sections, the relationship that Steve Fishman and his pupil, Andre Steadman, developed in Steve's advanced philosophy course. Our aim is to discover the extent to which Fishman's effort to establish Deweyan community with Andre succeeded in softening Freire's teacher-student contradiction.

At the outset of our study, in spring 1999, Fishman worked alone, collecting data in his own classroom: student texts; class observation notes; and transcripts of his and Andre's ten, hour-long work sessions. However, since Steve was Andre's teacher, a situation in which Andre may well have felt constrained, we believed we needed additional information to crosscheck and augment the data Steve gathered. So when the semester ended, McCarthy asked Andre if he wanted to continue reflecting, in interviews with her, about his learning and writing at the University. He readily agreed, and McCarthy spoke with Andre bi-monthly from May 1999 until his graduation in December 2000.

Fishman begins our account by showing the importance of a positive initial encounter between teacher and novice writer. This is essential, we have found, if they are to find common goals and alter orthodox teacher-student relations. Thus, Fishman's first approach to Andre was conducted with caution, and in it we see a necessary ingredient for ameliorating Freire's teacher-student contradiction: the teacher must respect student aspirations and competencies. When Fishman first spoke to Andre about his writing, he sought his cooperation and carefully avoided suggesting that Andre's difficulties with the dominant code were a mark against his capabilities or that his existing skills were unworthy. Rather, Fishman wanted to convey this message: "Andre, I suspect you are in some ways underprepared for my course, but instead of my urging you to drop, we can, despite the limitations imposed by our school situation, find spaces to converse, develop common goals, and help one another."

DEVELOPING SHARED GOALS: THE TEACHER'S PERSPECTIVE
Steve Fishman

In my spring 1999, "writing intensive" section of Philosophy of Education, when I read my 25 students' initial homework assignments and in-class freewrites, Andre Steadman's work stood out. (For the writing assignments in this course, see appendix D.) That is, in Andre's compositions were so many rhetorical and mechanical mismanagements that I was uncertain I was correctly following his thinking.

The fifth session of my Philosophy of Education course was on a Thursday, and at the close of the period, I motioned to Andre as the other students were leaving. He waited by my desk for a moment while I gathered my papers, and then we left the room together. In the hallway just outside—and sensitive to Freire's warnings about middle class teachers and their hegemonic roles—I said softly, "I think you've got a problem with your writing." Andre and I are about the same height—6' 2"—and our shoulders almost touched as we walked slowly beside one another down the corridor. I had no idea how he would respond, and, despite my authority, I felt vulnerable, like I had just asked a new neighbor to my house party. I was presenting an invitation to someone I did not know, someone who was, in obvious ways, very different from me. At the time, Andre was 21 and I was 60. He is from the South; I am from the North. He is Black; I am White. He is a computer science major; I have trouble accessing my department's web site. And on and on.

However, I was implicitly asking Andre to build upon our differences, to agree that if we could be open with one another—I admitting that, as a philosopher, I was no expert in teaching novice readers and writers and he being candid about his inexperience with academic composing—we had a decent chance to resist the typical teacher-student relationship. Instead of just keeping the normal, college instructor distance from Andre, I hoped I could convince him to join me in shaping a shared, albeit two-sided goal: improved philosophic thinking and writing for him and improved teaching for me. These were goals I believed neither of us could achieve without the other's help.

Out of the corner of my eye, I searched Andre's face and body language for reactions, but his demeanor told me little. After a few more steps, and still looking straight ahead, he finally nodded. Relieved, but still feeling unsure, I found myself saying, "I'd like to talk with you about it. Would you be willing to meet this Friday at 2:30?" Andre matched my slow pace for a few more steps, and then, without change of expression—and just before speeding up to go his own way—he nodded a second time.

As I have indicated, when Andre and I left the classroom together, as strange as it may seem, I felt vulnerable and fearful of rejection. Since I suspect that most novice writers at the college level lack confidence about their writing but, understandably, do not want to admit it to a teacher who must grade their work, I was heartened by Andre's first nod. It indicated to me that the news I had brought did not surprise him and that he was at least somewhat open to me. When Andre nodded a second time, indicating his willingness to meet with me, I took it to mean he wanted to work on his writing and was willing to spend time on it despite what I suspected was a busy schedule. With these initial gestures, Andre and I made our first start toward a community of common purpose. That is, we had, I believed, with a minimum of words, tentatively shaped a shared project and negotiated a joint activity for achieving it.

But what was Andre thinking? How did he describe the first beginnings of the community he and I were forging? Lucille McCarthy reports on Andre's perspective.

DEVELOPING SHARED GOALS: REPORTING THE STUDENT'S PERSPECTIVE
Lucille McCarthy

Fishman saw his relationship with Andre progressing cautiously toward shared goals, and, according to what Andre told me in post-semester interviews, he agreed. In his comments, however, he focused less on Steve's respect for his aspirations and competencies than on another element that must be present, according to Freire, if the teacher-student contradiction is to be altered: a problem-posing approach.

In Andre's initial conversation with me, in May 1999, he explained that Fishman did not lecture but instead questioned students as they all sat in a circle. Despite being a quiet person, Andre said, he liked being asked for his opinion, liked expressing himself, and he found it interesting to hear his classmates' views as well. This was, he told me, at least part of why he accepted Fishman's invitation to meet with him. Andre explained,

I saw from the beginning that in class Steve wanted our opinions, and he helped students say their ideas. He asked us what *we* learned from the readings; it wasn't just "Read because you have to." He was trying to figure out what *we* got out of it. . . . And he called on me every day all semester! In my other schools teachers called on me, but this never happened here at UNCC.

In addition to the open dialogue Andre said he enjoyed in class discussions, several other factors shaped his decision to meet with Steve. There were Andre's own doubts about his writing as well as the positive comparison between Fishman and some teachers he had at the two small, historically Black colleges he attended before transferring to Fishman's large university. Andre told me,

I make a lot of errors with grammar. I use my own method of grammar rather than what I was taught in junior high and high school. I've gotten bad grades in other classes for my writing, so I've gotta get better, and I saw Steve wanted to help me out. Why not take his offer? Basically, it was free of charge. . . . I didn't expect that a teacher at UNCC would care about me like that. It's a big school, and most professors just lecture and don't care if you get it. He's more like teachers at my other schools. He wants me to learn.

Not only did I question Andre about why he agreed to meet individually with Steve, I also asked him why he signed up for Philosophy of Education in the first place. I assumed he did so to satisfy the university's writing intensive requirement—ninety per cent of the students who enroll do so for this reason—but I was wrong. Andre had other, less instrumentalist, more personal, goals in mind. His comments suggest that he wanted to expand his skills and interests, but he wanted to do this in a community of likemindedness, to use one of Dewey's categories. He told me that his friend, Craig Stock, a former student of Fishman who is, like Andre, African American, recommended the course because of its open collegiality. Andre explained,

I signed up for philosophy because all I took in high school was business and math and science. I didn't read much and would write only a paragraph for homework maybe. And I used to talk only about money. But recently I have become interested in learning other ways of thinking about things. I know Craig Stock, and he had Steve's course last semester. On Saturdays, when Craig and I work together, he talked about Aristotle and other authors, and he said they also discussed race issues in this course, and he felt good about that.

With help from his friend, then, and with an eye for what was happening in class, Andre seemed to know more about Fishman during their initial exchanges than Steve knew about him. However, for both of them the germ of successful community—common purpose—had been planted. Fishman's respect for Andre's aspirations and competencies, his care not to suggest Andre's problems with academic literacy indicated deficiency, and Steve's problem-posing pedagogy had all set the stage for reshaping the teacher-student relationship. Steve now describes how his and Andre's relationship developed from this seed of common purpose.

DEVELOPING LIKEMINDEDNESS AND MUTUAL CARE
Steve Fishman

In our early meetings, I found that Andre's and my common goal was helping us gradually generate a community of likemindedness and mutual care, one built, in Dewey's (1916/1967) terms, on the "intellectual and emotional dispositions" we were able to share in our conversations (p. 5). This went a long way toward allowing us to communicate sympathetically and learn more about our locations on the oppressor-oppressed continuum. Despite my respect for Freire's analysis of teacher-student oppositions, I found that the places Andre and I occupied were less contradictory than Freire's analysis might lead us to believe.

For example, as Andre and I conversed, we learned about the places where our lives overlapped. Given that I am the grandson of non-English-speaking, lower class Jewish immigrants, a child born at the outset of World War II—a particularly anti-semitic period—who grew up in a dominantly Jewish section of the Bronx, and that

Andre is the son of a working class, African American family and grew up in a dominantly black section of Columbia, South Carolina, there were ways in which I identified with Andre as an outsider to mainstream American life. In saying this, I do not want to neglect the important distinction, following Ogbu (1988), between voluntary and involuntary immigrants to America. Nor do I intend to ignore Freire's insights about oppressor-oppressed conflicts. On the other hand, I do not want to go in the opposite direction and deny the importance of Andre's and my commonalities.

This ambiguity about our social locations was evident in Andre's post-semester interviews as well when he too seemed to refer to that place where our outsidernesses overlapped. When McCarthy asked Andre about the consequences for his and my relationship of his being considered Black and my being considered White, Andre seemed surprised McCarthy called me White. Andre told her that he knew that I grew up in the Bronx, and, therefore, he assumed I was Italian. "In my mind," Andre said, "Italians and Asians aren't White."

As I have indicated, the specific intention of my early meetings with Andre was not just to discover where our lives overlapped but also to learn more about his background so I could better step into his shoes and understand his aspirations and goals. We therefore spent considerable time talking about his previous school experiences, especially his college writing courses. In Freire's terms, these conversations enabled me to learn how Andre was reading the world and, thus, avoid imposing my own reading of it on him. In Dewey's terms, they were helping me see things from Andre's point of view so I could promote likemindedness.

Andre explained that he took two semesters of composition at Morris College in Sumter, South Carolina. Mrs. Hunter, his first semester comp teacher, combined explicit grammar lessons with a variety of assigned essays, including "declarative and descriptive" ones.

During our first meeting Andre talked so softly and in such clipped sentences that, although we sat almost knee-to-knee, I had to lean forward to hear him.

"Mrs. Hunter cared," Andre told me.

"What do you mean?" I asked.

"She wouldn't go on unless everybody got it. She was like you. She wanted us to learn. In other classes I just cared about grades but, with her, I cared about learning."

Andre told me that although he had trouble with "sentence structure" in that class, he ultimately received a B.

In those early meetings, I also asked Andre several times how he felt about mastering the writing conventions of Standard American English. I told him I worried that stress on these conventions ("cultural arbitraries," as Bourdieu and Passeron [1977] put it) might ruin his chance to compose the way he wanted, to express his ideas in his own fashion, in a literacy different from the one prescribed by the dominant class. (For more on such worries, see Gilyard, 1991; Giroux, 1991; Goldblatt, 1995; Horner & Lu, 1999; Smitherman, 1977, 1999.)

I explained to Andre, "A lot of educational researchers say that for some students learning the standard code is a betrayal, a rejection of their own culture's way of speaking and telling stories. Are you sure I'm not pressuring you into this?"

Andre's answer surprised me. He said that although he is a computer science major, he really hopes to become an entrepreneur. He needs to write better because he wants to own small businesses, like car washes and grocery stores, something he frequently reads about in a magazine he gets in his hometown, Columbia, South Carolina.

Just as I tried in our early meetings to understand Andre's views of school writing and his motives for wanting to move his compositions closer to Standard American English, so I tried to grasp his views of my course texts. He wanted to know these, he told me, because he did not want to be narrow in his thinking, and he saw reading authors like Plato (1997), Locke (1693/1997), Dewey (1902/1997a, 1916/1997b, 1938/1997c), Freire (1970/1997a), Kozol (1992), Delpit (1995), Baldwin (1963/1988), and Oakes (1985) as an opportunity to learn about other people's ideas.

From these early conversations with Andre, then, I sensed that he had had good experiences with some of his teachers and had developed communities of mutual care with them. It was especially significant, I thought, that he saw similarities between Mrs. Hunter, his first semester English teacher at Morris College, and me. In my class, like hers, Andre said, he focused more on learning than on grades. This made it easier for him and me to approach his writing from a similar perspective. Our common focus on learning—as opposed to a teacher-student debate about test scores and evaluations—meant that Andre could talk honestly with me about how much time he was putting into his homework, and I could talk honestly with him—without worry about making him defensive—about my reactions to his papers. This growing likemindedness made it easier for us to have the type of communication which Dewey (1916/1967) sees as central to fruitful community, a communication open enough to stimulate a "widening of the area of shared concerns," a breaking down of barriers so Andre and I could better understand the consequences of our exchanges upon each other (p. 87). Further, as Andre's and my growing likemindedness allowed us to develop the widened communication that Dewey wants, we were also forging something like the solidarity that Freire wants. However, I felt that it was not only I who was developing care for and solidarity with Andre. I felt Andre was also developing care for and solidarity with me.

Alternatively put, I thought our softening of the teacher-student contradiction was less a case of my dying to my class identification and being reborn to Andre's than of both Andre's and my doing some travelling from our home territories. Just as I was crossing my own boundaries to enter into Andre's student world, so Andre was making similar efforts to travel into my teacherly world. I thought his care for and increasing solidarity with me could be seen in the wordless manner in which he made clear he appreciated my working with him. This was evidenced by his perfect class attendance, by his willingness, despite being shy, to accept my daily calls upon him in class, and by the sincere effort I believe he made with every reading and writing assignment. I speak of mutual care and travel, because, put bluntly, I thought that Andre was trying to help me out, or care for me, by holding up his end of the implicit understanding between teacher and student about classroom attendance, preparation, and participation. In addition, Andre was always on time for our weekly meetings, and he was, I believe, candid in his answers to my (and later McCarthy's) questions about his learning and writing. Finally, there was the easy laughter between Andre and me, something I took as a sign of our willingness to be vulnerable with one another, to create spaces which defied the institutionally prescribed ones.

It is possible that Freire might see Andre's stepping into my teacherly world as cooption, as my doing him a disservice by altering his ways of thinking and speaking and, thus, modifying his identity. Yet, in light of the ambiguous spaces Andre occupies, his position as both inside and outside mainstream culture, it is not surprising to me that our conversations would result in a mutual movement of this sort. In other words, I am not ashamed of Andre's moving into my world because I believe it reflected some of his own genuine aspirations rather than ones that I imposed on him.

Freirian Problem-Posing in a Deweyan Community: Learner as Teacher, Teacher as Learner

In our ten, hour-long, Friday afternoon meetings, as Andre and I worked toward a Deweyan community of common purpose, like-mindedness, and mutual care, we were also employing a Freire-like, problem-posing, learner-as-teacher, teacher-as-learner method for exploring his writing concerns. Particularly important in helping Andre and me become co-investigators was a research tool I call "dialogic think-aloud protocols." I wanted to use these protocols to understand the logic behind Andre's writing, so I started each of our Friday afternoon sessions by having him read his homework papers outloud. I was recording these sessions, and I believed that the transcripts of Andre's reading his own work and "thinking aloud" about it would give me useful information about his linguistic code. In thus trying to understand the logic behind Andre's writing, I was building on Shaughnessy's (1977) and Bartholomae's (1980) contention that to help students bridge successfully to the target language, teachers need insight into the rules students are employing rather than assuming them to be *tabulae rasae* upon which to impose the dominant forms.

Although I originally saw these protocols only as investigatory tools for my use, they quickly became powerful investigatory tools for Andre as well. This is because, instead of just recording data for a researcher to analyze later on, Andre began to actively participate with me in interpreting the data he generated during his think-alouds. Together, he and I posed questions about what he had said, and we collaboratively theorized about his thinking and writing processes. Because neither of us had anything like a clear under-standing of what was going on, we genuinely needed one another and the very different perspectives we brought to our inquiry. It was this problem-posing collaboration that enabled Andre and me to discover three competencies that even Andre himself did not know he had. These were his abilities (1) to use the dominant code, (2) to summarize texts in his own words, and (3) to elaborate on his understanding of philosophic issues and theories.

Bringing Forward Student Competencies Regarding
the Dominant Code

What Andre and I discovered was that often he could orally edit his own compositions as he read them aloud, reading correctly—despite errors on the page—what he intended to say. This showed us that Andre knew more about the writing mechanics of Standard American English than his papers indicated. (This pattern is noted by a number of writing researchers, including Bartholomae, 1980; Butler, 1980; Lu, 1994/1999b; Leki, 1992; Perl, 1980; Shaughnessy, 1977, pp. 172–75; Shor, 1987, p. 112.)

An example of Andre's and my collaborative, problem-posing inquiry occurred in mid-February when he read aloud his two-paragraph homework paper about an article titled, "Women's Ways of Going to School" (Holland & Eisenhart, 1988). Early in his home-work, Andre writes: "Personally I am in college *somethat* I can learn more about the computer science industry to enhance my capable in this field" (emphasis mine). On Andre's first read through—one he did without stopping to edit—he rendered the words, "I am in college somethat I can . . ." exactly as he had written them. However, on his second rendering, he orally corrected himself and read, "I am in college *so that* I can . . ." I then recommended to Andre that he read aloud more slowly, urging him to read exactly what he had typed. Yet, twice more he rendered "somethat" as "so that," even after I pointed my finger at the word "somethat" to make sure Andre was focusing on it. Finally, I suggested to Andre that if I were doing the reading, I would not render "somethat" as "so that." To this comment, Andre responded, "Oops, my mistake."

At this point, I explained to Andre that I was perplexed by his ability to make oral corrections—in the case of "somethat" in three of four readings—without knowing he had made them, and I asked him how he would account for it. He was, at first, as puzzled as I was. After thinking about it a while, he explained that he really had "so that" in mind while composing but, as he read, he was totally focused on his meaning and, therefore, did not see the discrepancy between what he intended and what he wrote. Unfortunately, this meant he did not realize that what he had just spoken would be, if written, a valuable improvement, and, in this case—although not always—it was left unchanged.

Although, in the course of the semester, Andre and I were never able to fully tap into his ability to make oral corrections to help him edit his papers, I believe this portion of our work was worthwhile. The dialogic think-alouds helped us develop some shared language for discussing and theorizing about his writing concerns. They also showed Andre that if he paid close attention to his compositions, he could find discrepancies between what he intended to write and what he actually wrote. Put another way, although we did not have immediate results in terms of papers with dramatically improved surface features, our collaborative inquiry helped Andre see his own strengths, and this was something he was able, gradually, to build on in my course and in others in subsequent semesters.

Bringing Forward Student Competencies Regarding Argument Extraction and Use of One's Own Words

Just as the dialogic think-alouds helped Andre and me discover that he knew more about standard writing mechanics than his compositions showed, so our discussions also helped us realize that when he summarized texts he could rely less on the language of the assigned readings and more on his own. To show his development in this area, I present excerpts from three of our early-semester meetings in February and March. In the homework papers we investigated together in these sessions, Andre increasingly risked using his own words and, thus, writing outside the dominant code rather than presenting more correct prose that he lifted straight from the assigned reading. A superficial look at these three home-work papers might suggest that Andre's writing is deteriorating across time rather than getting better. However, a closer look reveals a student attempting to understand and summarize difficult theoretical material in his own voice.

February 5: Borrowing Author Language for Argument Extraction. Early in February, I assigned a selection from Freire's *Pedagogy of The Oppressed* (1970/1997a). The homework prompt—designed to encourage argument extraction and argument evaluation (my classroom objectives 1 and 2)—asks students to explain what they have learned by reading this selection and to conclude with a question they would be willing to present to the class as a discussion leader.

Andre's response is three paragraphs long: a short introduction and brief conclusion framing a seven-sentence main paragraph in which he relates what he understands about Freire. I reproduce it just as he typed it.

> Paul Freire's, "Pedagagy of the Oppressed", is an article that argues for the liberation of the teacher/student manifestation. In doing this Freire argues against the banking concept of education and for the liberation of students and in many cases teachers.
>
> Freire's denounces the banking concept of education in that he sees the students as the oppressed and the teacher as the oppressor. He argues in this concept that knowledge is a gift bestowed by those who consider themselves knowledgeable upon those whom they consider to know nothing. In this model, the teacher presents him-self to his students as their necessary opposite; by considering their ignorance absolute, he justifies his own existence. In so doing this, the students are alienated, and forced to accept their ignorance. However, although Friere denounces such a system, he also gives a solution or what he feels would " liberate" the students capabilities. He argues that education must begin with the solution of the teacher/student contradiction, by reconciling the poles of the con-tradiction so that both are simultaneously teachers and students. He believes the solution is not to integrate them into the structure of oppression, but to transform that structure as they can become

beings for themselves. Such a transformation would undermine the oppressor's purposes, thus undermining the banking system.

After reading the article, I agree in many ways that the banking system is such a system of oppression and further more I agree with Friere's solution to change the banking system. However, the question that I pose is, how do we actually go about changing a system that has dominated the classrooms for so many years?

The question Andre poses at the end of his homework about how to change long-established, oppressive systems is clearly a good one, and I praise him for it in my marginal comments. I realized that if we used it in class, it could bring our discussion from a theoretical to a more practical level. The question also suggested to me that Andre had not only read the piece but had responded to it in a serious way. However, what disappointed me was that, in his main paragraph, five of his seven sentences contain extensive unacknowledged quotes from Freire. The language is so obviously not Andre's that the problem was evident to me at my first reading.

Andre and I met to talk about this homework paper on Friday, February 5th, and we began, as usual, with Andre's reading his work aloud to me in a dialogic think-aloud protocol. The tone of Andre's and my conversation was, in this, our third session, no different from that in our earlier ones, and in no way was I upset with him because I trusted that he was making a good faith effort and doing the best he could. That is, I began our conversation with no desire to criticize him for using unacknowledged quotes. In fact, in a later meeting, Andre himself introduced the word "plagiarism" to describe what he sometimes did, but this is a pejorative word I would never have thought to use in this situation. In other words, it never occurred to me that Andre was trying to trick me or pretend that someone else's writing was his own. Rather, my disposition as Andre and I investigated his writing in our February 5th meeting was one of curiosity, a desire to find out what Andre was thinking as he completed his Freire homework.

After Andre had read his composition aloud, I asked him about two of the five unacknowledged quotes he incorporates into his own sentences, quotes taken almost verbatim from Freire's text. These are

[Freire] argues that education must begin with a solution of the teacher-student contradiction, by reconciling the poles of the contradiction so that both are simultaneously students and teachers. He believes the solution is not to integrate them into the structure of oppression, but to transform that structure as they can become beings for themselves.

Attempting to learn what Andre understood of Freire, I asked him what he meant by saying that the poles of the teacher-student contradiction must be reconciled. Andre was unable to say much, so I briefly discussed Freire with him, recalling our class discussions of the previous week in an effort to be helpful. We talked about the ways students and teachers are unequal in the classroom, and, ultimately, we agreed that teachers and students reconcile their differences when they face problems together in a cooperative and trusting environment.

I then asked Andre several more questions about his homework. In particular, I wanted to know if it seemed different to him from his previous papers in my class. He responded, "Do you mean the grammar?" I said, "No, I'm thinking of the tone, the sound of it," and he answered, "I guess it doesn't sound much like me." I agreed and asked why he stuck so closely to Freire's language. He said, "I didn't understand him. Rather than make a mistake, I said it the way he does."

I appreciated Andre's honesty, and I hastened to assure him that other students—and even I myself—have difficulty reading Freire. I then offered him specific advice about how he might work to understand texts and bring forward his own voice as he summarizes them. "In philosophy," I said,

> a failure to understand is a good starting point. If there are sentences you can't figure out, start your paper with them and then offer a number of interpretations, but put them in your own words. I'll bet you'll get a lot closer to the author's meaning than you think you can.

I also suggested that he use the triple-entry notetaking technique I had introduced in class (see appendix E) and reminded him that this technique would help him be a more active reader and give him chances to come up with alternative interpretations of the text.

Andre responded in his usual quiet way. He said, yes, he would try the triple-entry technique on his next homework. He also told me he would try to write more in his own voice.

February 19: Trying to Summarize the Text in One's Own Words. Andre's next paper that I discuss, an assignment focusing on a selection from Dewey's *Child and Curriculum* (1902/1997a), provides insight into Andre's nascent efforts to summarize texts in his own language. My homework prompt asked students to write a letter to a designated classmate with answers to two questions. It read:

> Dewey divides educators into two groups: those who emphasize subject matter and those who emphasize student growth.
> 1. Which of these, subject matter or student growth, has been dominant in your own schooling?
> 2. How does Dewey suggest we reconcile these different approaches?

At the start of the next class session, students exchanged their letters with their partners and responded in writing to one another. In this assignment, I was trying to encourage my pupils, first, to apply philosophy to their own lives and, second, to summarize Dewey's argument from his text (my objectives 4 and 1, respectively). I now reproduce the letter Andre typed for his classmate, Melissa, a letter in which he offers a paragraph-long answer to each of my questions. (The emphases are mine.) Andre writes,

> Dear Melissa,
> Subject matter has been a dominated force in my educational process. I've been taught from day one to separate subjects into different groups. I've been taught math separate from science and so forth. Although, I feel when you grow older you automatically learn more and at a faster beat. I also feel you understand different things if their are broken into different categorizes. You consume and focus more on one subject at a time, whether than two or more subjects. I feel that a lot of subjects need to be separate from one another because they can be confusing.

Dewey's suggest we reconcile education *life-terms* instead of present-terms. He argues learning should be a connection between the student and what is being taught. It should be a *purely formal and symbolic* of the child. Secondly, he feels it should be a motivating change. He has a strong belief in interaction with the student and what they are tiring to learn. Thirdly, he feels presentation should be *external*. His opinion is the lessons are water down by the time they get to the student. The faculty should eliminate some of the authority in the designing process of its curriculum. Finally, he feels the mind and spiritual aspects should have connections in the learning process. These suggestions would bring interest into the minds of the children's who are capable of learning at any level.

Thanks for reading.
Andre Steadman

When I read the second of Andre's two paragraphs, his summary of Dewey's solution to the student-curriculum dichotomy, I was puzzled. At times, I believed Andre really understood Dewey. For example, he says, correctly, in his second sentence, that Dewey believes there "should be a connection between the student and what is being taught." In the fourth, he says there should be a "motivating change," and, in the fifth, that there should be "interaction with the students and what they are tiring [sic] to learn." All this sounded like Andre had grasped some of Dewey's central themes. Granted, he had not directly answered the question about how Dewey resolves the student-curriculum dichotomy, but he appeared to understand at least something of Dewey's argument.

By contrast, the other sentences in Andre's second paragraph made me uneasy. In the first, he says Dewey wants to "reconcile education life-terms instead of present-terms." Although there is a resonance of Dewey in this sentence—Dewey frequently speaks about the need for continuity in experience, for finding connections between present, past, and future—I was not really sure what Andre meant. Does he, I asked myself, understand this point in Dewey but is simply unable to express it clearly? Has he worked hard on this paper, coming to grips with difficult ideas upon which, at this point, he has only a shaky handle? If so, I certainly wanted to credit and praise him for such effort. But I was not sure.

Similar uncertainties accompanied my efforts to understand what Andre meant by his third sentence, "It should be a purely formal and symbolic of the child." I interpreted Andre's "It" to refer to education itself. But why in the world he believed Dewey wants education to be "purely formal and symbolic of the child," I did not know. That is, I could not figure out what in Dewey's text would lead Andre to make this claim.

Because of my confusion about Andre's letter, I was looking forward to our discussion of it on February 19th. I wanted to learn how Andre viewed his work, how he explained his written product and the process he followed to achieve it. At the beginning of our session, before he read his paper aloud, I asked Andre about this process. He explained that he spent about an hour reading the text and approximately 30 minutes writing his response. In addition to doing triple-entry notetaking, he said he underlined phrases he thought he might be able to use in his answer.

Andre then read his piece and, after we had discussed several features of it, I spoke about my own puzzlement. "Andre," I said, "I had some trouble figuring out what you were trying to say in a couple of places. For example, I couldn't understand what you meant by 'life-terms' and 'present-terms,' 'formal and symbolic,' and 'motivating change.'" Andre responded by assuring me that he had "gotten his ideas from the book." When I heard this, I replied, "Well, why don't we both take a close look at Dewey's text?"

The two of us read silently for a while, each looking at our own copy of Dewey, when Andre suddenly hit pay dirt and pointed at Dewey's phrases, "life-terms" and "purely formal and symbolic" (1902/1997a, p. 285). He also pointed out that, on the same page, Dewey talks about the educational evils of "lack of motivation" and teacher presentations conducted in "external, ready-made fashion." This cleared up the opacity of Andre's writing for both him and me because we realized that Andre, in an effort to use his own language, was still borrowing from the text, but this time only a few phrases that he wove together with his own words, not whole sentences as he had done earlier. His attempt to use his own voice, while still using some of the author's phrases, meant that his Dewey homework, on the surface, seemed less accomplished than his Freire paper. However, Andre and I knew better, and we were both pleased with his effort.

In addition, we were satisfied with our collaborative investigation of it. Throughout our February 19th conversation, Andre and I seemed to share the view that figuring out his writing was our joint challenge, and when he orchestrated our moment of clarification, we celebrated together. In short, the dialogic think-alouds and our collaborative problem posing about Andre's texts allowed us to abandon our designated roles as teacher and student and take on the less contradictory identities of problem-posing co-investigators.

At the close of our February 19th meeting, I asked Andre what else besides the triple entry technique he might do to get more of his own voice into his work. He immediately spoke about starting his papers earlier so he could spend more time on them. He said that by waiting to write his papers until the night before they were due he had too little time to digest the material so he could say it in his own way. Naturally, I applauded this idea and reminded him about acknowledging what he does not understand and then using that as a focus for his writing. I also asked him to read his next homework response to a friend to see if it sounded like him.

March 5: Continuing to Employ One's Own Voice in Argument Extraction. The next meeting I describe took place two weeks later, on March 5th, and centered on an assignment from Dewey's *Experience and Education* (1938/1997c). When Andre and I met to discuss it, he told me in considerable detail about his girlfriend's reading of his draft, how she pointed out sentences which did not sound like him and how he revised in an effort to explain his ideas better in his own words. I was excited about this because Andre seemed to be taking more control over his writing.

My homework prompt asked students to choose a paragraph from the Dewey selection and discuss its significance for them: again a request for argument extraction and application of philosophic theory (my objectives 1 and 4). Andre chose a paragraph from *Experience and Education* in which Dewey describes "miseducative experiences." Although Andre never explains why he found this concept personally significant, I could see that he had tried hard to distinguish Dewey's voice from his own. I now reproduce Andre's homework response.

> While reading Dewey, the second paragraph on page 330 caught my interest. It basically talk about the indirect experience of education and he argues how some experiences are not educational. However, Dewey starts this paragraph by saying, "the belief that all genuine education comes about through experience does not mean that all experiences are genuinely or equally educative." I feel Dewey is saying all experiences have purpose, but some are mis-educated. Uneducational experiences may affect one's future and their thought process. One's experience may not connect or service a purpose and may even discourage one's progress. Uneducated habits will inability one to control its future experiences. To overcome mis-educated experiences, one must initialize self-control and have an purpose in society.

As Andre and I talked about this piece, I praised his effort. I said he had put into his own words a couple of core Deweyan concepts. In fact, I told him that his third to last sentence—"One's experience may not connect or service a purpose and may even discourage one's progress."—was so good that "it made me dance."

However, I do not want to give the impression that Andre's ability to summarize a difficult text in his own language was a straight-line process. When he and I discussed his second to last sentence, the one following the sentence I had just praised, we realized he had returned to his earlier practice of piecing together the author's words with his own. Specifically, Andre takes Dewey's sentence, "The consequences of formation of such habits is *inability to control future experiences*" (p. 331, emphasis mine) and turns it into "Uneducated habits will inability one to control its future experience." Although this might seem like a setback, I took it as a developmental error, one to be expected as Andre, a computer science major and underprepared writer, struggled to expand his academic literacy. (For more on students' "interlanguage" as they move toward the target language, see Kutz, 1986.)

Of course Andre's progress in understanding and summarizing texts did not result only from our time together on 10 Friday afternoons. It was also the consequence of numerous other factors, including his willingness to try out new ways of reading and composing. For example, regarding his *Experience and Education* assignment, he told me that he "slowed down" and "started earlier," did triple-entry notetaking, and had a reader look at and question him about his draft.

Bringing Forward Student Competencies Regarding Elaborating on Philosophic Subject Matter

Andre's and my dialogic think-alouds helped us not only discover that he knew more about standard writing mechanics than he thought and set the stage for practicing argument extraction in his own voice, our discussions also revealed that Andre often knew more about philosophic subject matter than his texts indicated. I believe this also impressed him. It showed him another strength he possessed which he was underutilizing, and, as Andre explained to McCarthy in one of their post-semester interviews, he left my course determined to put down on paper more of what he now realized he could say.

A tutorial session in which Andre and I came to appreciate his greater understanding of course readings occurred on the second Friday in April as he and I discussed one of his final homework papers for Philosophy of Education. In this session we discovered hidden competencies in two additional areas I list as my objectives for student thinking and writing: argument evaluation (objective 2) and intellectual reconstruction or the ability to contextualize a position (objective 3).

In this mid-April session, Andre and I focused on his response to an assignment about Hansen's (1995) *The Call To Teach*. My prompt asked students to characterize the pedagogies of three inner city high school teachers, each of whom is described by Hansen in a chapter-length naturalistic account. I wrote, "Please present your own analysis of these instructors' teaching using any categories you find appropriate." Andre's homework consists of three typed paragraphs, one devoted to each teacher:

After reading Hansen's account of the three teachers and their class-rooms, I find all three to have a unique style of teaching. To begin with my category for Mrs. Payne is "FOLLOW MY RULES IN MY CLASSROOM." She seems like the kind of teacher that state rules that each student must be govern by. Before the class day starts, she has an objective that must be completed during that class and no greater or less is accepted. I feel Mrs. Pain classroom setting is very demanding because is very procedural. Everything happens in a sequence format. You come into her classroom and you have to do A before you can B, etc. I feel that is would be very difficult to learn in her class because everything is predictable. There is no think process done other than following rules. I feel if she loosens up her rules, her class will be more beneficial than procedural.

My category for Mr. Peters is "WILLINGNESS." I picked this category for Mr. Peter because of the uneducated background and the course is teaching. As we all know that Mr. Peter is not a certified teacher, but has the force to teach a religious course. Mr. Peter's class-room is more of a group and gives your own belief type of situation. He frequently asks student their opinions and he also gives his opin-ions on the topic at hand. I feel that his type is teaching has a future, it just needs some years and guidance. I feel that once he has more confident in what are doing and become even more open minded. He will be very successful in the future.

My category for Mr. James is "DETERMINATION." I feel under his conditions he is handling is job in a professional way. He seems well organize with the way he handles himself and his students. I analysis Mr. James has a determine and understanding individual. He is determine because he wants give up on the his student. I understand he has a person who believes that everyone can learn under any conditions. In the reading, we see that something in his class he has problems with behavior and attention. I feel with his years and experience with dealing with trouble students he held his ground. He handles each a has a separate individual. He respects them and their situations better than the other teachers they have encountered, Mr. James gets the up most respect from me in the way he handles himself and the students he is involve with.

As usual, we began our meeting with Andre reading his work outloud. In his first paragraph, Andre categorizes one teacher as employing a pedagogy Andre calls "Follow My Rules In My Classroom." At the close of this paragraph, Andre claims that it would be very difficult to learn in such a classroom because "every-

thing is predictable. There is no think process done other than following rules. I feel if she loosens up her rules, her class will be more
beneficial than procedural." When I asked Andre about why he was
critical of this teacher's approach, he told me that if students do not
figure things out on their own, they will not learn very much.

Andre's answer pleased me, for it made clear that he had a strong
grasp on what he had read and written (objective 1) and that he
could reflect critically upon it (objective 2). By "reflect critically," I
mean that Andre was able to generalize about the details he had
read, to step back and see them as representative of a certain pedagogical approach. Put differently, his act of characterizing Hansen's
first teacher as a "follow the rules" instructor showed he had generated what amounts to a "grounded theory" (Glaser & Strauss, 1967),
organizing Hansen's data under a broad concept or idea.

As our meeting progressed, I continued to press Andre about his
paper in hopes he would explain why being less strict about class
procedures would benefit this teacher's students. I asked, "If, as you
suggest, the teacher that Hansen describes loosens her rules, how
will that be beneficial?" Andre repeated,

> Unless students do some thinking on their own, they will learn very
> little. This is because, if you don't do things on your own, whatever
> you learn is worthless since it won't stick with you. You won't
> remember it.

At this point, I was delighted. Andre's spoken elaborations not
only revealed careful reading and critical thinking, they also reflected progress toward my third classroom goal for students: the ability
to do synthetic, or contextualizing, work. Andre's comments, I
believed, were informed by his mid-February work with Dewey's
Experience and Education (1938/1997c). In written and oral discussions, with me and in class, Andre had focused on Dewey's belief
that lack of student involvement causes much school learning to be
forgotten or stored in relatively inaccessible "watertight compart-
ments." Two months later, Andre's analysis of the Hansen book
echoed these earlier discussions about Dewey. This was especially

remarkable—and I pointed this out to Andre—since our meeting to discuss his Hansen paper did not occur until two weeks after he had turned it in. That is, Andre's ability to remember his Hansen homework two weeks after he wrote it—and the Dewey principle a couple of months later—was a sign that he had significant understanding of both.

Appreciative of the critical and synthetic work behind Andre's characterization of one of Hansen's teachers, I asked Andre, "But why didn't you put those comments in your paper? Look how much richer your answer could have been if you had just added a few sentences." Andre nodded and smiled at me, "I know. I know," he said. "I need to add more sentences. I need to elaborate more in my own words."

Andre's responses during our mid-April meeting thus showed both him and me that his underelaborated compositions sometimes cloaked hidden competencies, unarticulated understandings of course issues and methods. This realization that he knew more than he wrote in his homework was an important discovery for Andre, I believed, a possible confidence booster as he moved on to future academic work.

My intuition about Andre's increasing self-confidence was on target, as McCarthy reports in the next section. In addition, she found another, equally important residue from Andre's and my work together that I did not foresee. Andre was, in our late-semester discussion of the Hansen book starting to articulate his own Freire-like critique of banking pedagogy and student docility. Drawing upon Dewey and Freire—as well as his own student experiences—Andre was giving voice to his opposition to traditional teacher-student relations. It is a resistance that he further articulated—and enacted—in subsequent semesters. In sum, then, McCarthy will offer evidence that my approaching Andre as a learner myself, someone who genuinely needed Andre's interpretations, allowed him not only to play teacher to me but also, in a way Freire would applaud, to use philosophy to probe his own opposition to traditional schooling.

Residue
STEVE FISHMAN AND LUCILLE McCARTHY

We take the title of this section from Dewey (1938/1963a) who says that the test of any experience, including an educational one, is the residue or deposit it leaves with the individual. He writes, "Every experience lives on in further experiences. Hence the central problem of... education... is to select the kind of present experiences that live fruitfully and creatively in subsequent experiences" (pp. 27–28). Similarly, Freire (1970/1997) is concerned with the outcomes of teacher-student interactions. He tells us, "Since it is [in] a concrete situation that the oppressor-oppressed contradiction is established, the resolution of this contradiction must be *objectively* verifiable" (p. 32, italics in original).

In this section, McCarthy analyzes the consequences or residue for Andre of Fishman's and his work together. That is, she explores the impact on Andre's academic literacy of their Freirian efforts to bring forward his competencies, honor his aspirations, and promote his active learning. Drawing upon her recorded interviews with Andre, McCarthy reports the ways in which Andre's and Steve's Deweyan community not only softened Freire's teacher-student contradiction but also helped Andre achieve his own goals for Philosophy of Education and become more articulate about his schooling in subsequent semesters. Following McCarthy's report of the residue Andre took from his sessions with Fishman, Steve discusses his own learning, the ways in which his pedagogy profited from his conversations with Andre. He then reflects on their collaboration's implications for Freirian classroom reform.

RESOLVING THE FREIRIAN CONTRADICTION:
SIGNIFICANCE FOR THE STUDENT
Lucille McCarthy

In interviews during the year and a half following Fishman's class, Andre recalled for me his experiences in Philosophy of Education and described events in subsequent courses. In evaluating his comments, I focus on two consequences of his and Fishman's efforts to resolve the teacher-student contradiction. First, I discuss how their discovery of Andre's hidden understandings of the dominant code helped Andre write in his subsequent courses. Second, I show how their appreciation of Andre's ability to understand and summarize pedagogical theory helped him become a more critical knower. This latter development was evident in his reflections on his schoolwork in the semesters following Fishman's course.

Building on Student Competencies: Improved Writing and
Extension of Academic Literacy

As we have seen, early on in Fishman's class Andre expressed his desire to write more effectively in the dominant code. Steve's and Andre's collaboration helped Andre progress toward this end by boosting his confidence about what he already knew concerning Standard written English, knowledge he both underappreciated and underused. Their collaboration also gave Andre a sense that he could digest difficult texts and discuss them in his own voice. The semester following Fishman's course, Andre took a required, writing intensive class in his major, "Computer Science for Today's Society," and he told me about his continuing motivation to speak for himself and to write so his readers could understand him. In October 1999, he explained,

> I'm trying to be aware of other people reading my writing and make it more clear what I'm trying to say, the point I'm trying to get across. Before [Steve and I worked together], I would just write down whatever came out of my head the morning before the paper was due. I didn't want to think about the mechanics of it. . . . [But] my meetings with him helped me see my writing better. . . and because he wanted to help me, I spent more time. . . . Now when I am writing, I think about the person who might read my paper.

I then asked Andre what techniques he was using to get his own points across, and he referred to several habits and attitudes he had developed in philosophy. "Basically, I'm still doing the same things I did in that class: reading my draft out loud, expressing the topic a little more [elaborating], trying to stick to my topic, and getting help proofreading."

A year later, in November 2000, when Andre and I met for our last interview before he graduated, I had followed his writing for three semesters, so I knew a good deal about it. However, I asked him for one final assessment. "Andre," I said, "in two months you'll be out of college and into a job. How do you feel about your writing now? Will you be okay writing in whatever job you take?" Andre smiled and replied:

> Yeah, I'm getting there. I mean, pretty much, as long as I take my time, and I understand what my purpose of writing is and who I'm writing to. And I still ask someone to look it over for me. . . . But when I write now, it's more about me getting a point across, where before, I was just getting a grade.

In short, Andre's comments in the semesters following Fishman's course indicate that, as a result of Steve's and his work together, Andre was taking steps toward realizing his goal to express his thoughts better through his writing.

Building on Student Competencies: Thinking Critically about Teaching and Learning

As Steve pointed out, Andre's and his conversations about Hansen's (1995) *Call to Teach* was an important moment in helping Andre realize his own ability to reflect critically. As time passed, Andre became increasingly aware of oppressive teacher-student relationships and able to articulate his preference for active learning within a caring community. Freire would be pleased, I believe, that instead of blind opposition to the status quo, Andre was using ideas from philosophy to speak about his resistance with increasing insight. In our final interview, he explained,

> Before Steve's class, I didn't know that you could look at how people teach kids and how kids grasp things and how environment affects that. I doubt I could be a teacher myself, but every once in a while I think of it. If I did, I would be more like Steve, teaching and learning

at the same time. In class, he heard all our opinions, and they didn't always match his. So he learned. . . . It's a better environment if there is more interaction, if the teacher asks the student to think.

Andre applied this pedagogical standard to classes he took in the three semesters following Fishman's course. About his writing intensive computer science course in fall 1999, Andre commented, "It's okay. I'm learning something. But it's mostly listening. When the teacher [and student presenters] ask questions, they already have their opinion of the answer, so there's really no reason to speak." In addition, Andre must have decided there was little reason to attend. Although he did not mention it to me, when I spoke to the teacher of this course, I learned that, in contrast to Andre's perfect attendance in philosophy, he had missed a substantial number of these classes.

An even more striking lack of dialogue existed, according to Andre, between him and the director of his senior project in computer science in fall 2000. He felt totally alone in that class, he indicated, without community of any sort, without the kind of give-and-take between teacher and student that helps each learn about and from the other. Instead, according to Andre, that teacher was all "ego," seemingly interested only in displaying his own knowledge. "He cares about opinions all right," Andre said, "but only his own. . . . And he seems to think we should all live and breathe computer science like he does. But we don't, and it's hard for him to understand that." To provide further evidence of the gap between teacher and student, Andre explained that this instructor had not had the "respect" to return students' papers, "so I can't even get information about what I may be doing wrong."

By contrast to these courses, Andre spoke positively about the technical writing class he had taken in spring 2000. In that class, apparently, the teacher, like Steve, worked to overcome the teacher-student contradiction. Using a familiar phrase, Andre told me: she "wanted us to learn." Rather than maintaining her distance, according to Andre, as if she had all the knowledge and students none, she strove for classroom community and student participation. In particular, Andre explained, this teacher had students work in groups, and she tried to make the assigned audiences for their papers come alive. At one point, she even brought in her 12-year-old son for whom students were to write operating instructions for a computer game. Andre and his group spoke with the child, and he, along with Andre's teacher, actually read and gave them feedback on their instruction manual. It was the sort of active learning within a community of inquirers that Andre had come to value.

In sum, as Andre developed his ability to reflect critically on his own education, his classes became, to use Freire's term, "codifications." As with the portrait of the teacher he criticized in Hansen's *Call to Teach*, Andre was able to step back and see his own classes as objects of analysis. Using theory he had learned in philosophy, he placed his experiences in a larger context, and, rather than just being oppositional, feeling angry and alienated, Andre could "read" these pictures of his own world in critically insightful ways.

RESOLVING THE FREIRIAN CONTRADICTION: SIGNIFICANCE FOR THE TEACHER
Steve Fishman

Lucille McCarthy has spoken about the consequences for Andre of his and my work together. I now speak from my perspective about the importance of our collaboration. At the outset, as I have indicated, he and I agreed upon a double goal: improving his ability to read and write in philosophy and improving my ability to work with novice writers. In addition, in the back of my mind, if not Andre's, was the desire to develop a Deweyan democratic community and soften the traditional teacher-student antinomy.

Regarding my goal of improved pedagogy for underprepared writers, the residue I take from Andre's and my collaboration is twofold: first, a set of ambitious, yet reasonable, expectations for novice writers who take my philosophy courses and, second, a sense of the common purposes and mutual care—the teacher-as-learner, student-as-teacher exchanges—needed to support and encourage such students. Of course, helping these students make progress toward my classroom objectives is important. However, efforts to do this will fall short, I believe, if there is little attention to the community developed by student and teacher (see Grego and Thompson, 1996). That is, thanks to Andre, it has become clearer to me that helping novice writers develop increased self-confidence as students and better attitudes toward writing and learning is more important than bringing about, for example, immediate improvement in the surface features of their papers.

Regarding my more ambitious goal—using Deweyan community to resolve Freire's teacher-student contradiction—I believe Andre and I also made progress. We did this by establishing a climate in which Andre could practice active and critical knowing. As McCarthy points out, in learning to place his own beliefs and experiences in a broader, philosophic context, Andre not only understood something about my discipline, he also experienced a Freirian critical "reading" of his own world.

This is not to claim that Andre and I acted, as Freire would ultimately wish, like political and cultural change-agents. That is, we did not succeed in significantly transforming my university or any other institution reproducing the values and practices of the dominant class. To the contrary, as I have already indicated, Andre, like myself, was an accommodator as well as resister of mainstream values. As evidence of this ambivalence in my case, I ask my Philosophy of Education students to read the work of contemporary critical educators like Freire, Kozol, and Delpit while, at the same time, continuing to assign Plato, Aristotle, and Locke. As for Andre, despite my occasional suggestions that he give up his goal of accumulating wealth and, instead, work with children as a coach, teacher, or a school principal—careers I was sure he would be good at—he remained adamant about what he wanted. Looking back, I acknowledge that I could have pressed more vigorously upon Andre the idea that we both had internalized too many of the values of the very class that has been for centuries our oppressors. However, I did not. To do so, I felt, would have been to diminish my respect for Andre's aspirations and, thus, hurt my chances of achieving one of Freire's other goals: helping students orchestrate their own destinies.

Just as Andre and I did not act as revolutionaries, neither did I answer Freire's call to die to my own middle-class life in order to be reborn in solidarity with the proletarian aspects of Andre's. However, as I hope is evident by now, it is not clear just what form such a rebirth would have taken since Andre and I occupy complex, shifting, and sometimes overlapping locations on the oppressor-oppressed spectrum. Andre's post-semester interviews with McCarthy underline the complexity of his allegiances and identity. Across time, as he was progressing toward his entrepreneurial goals, he was also deepening his understanding of America's injustices toward African Americans. He told McCarthy in their final interview that he was not only reading about computer science. He was now also studying Malcolm X and Frederick Douglass "to learn more about our dream."

I recognize that Andre's and my accomplishments might be dismissed as extremely modest. However, in terms of a gradualist ideology in the Deweyan mode, I believe our achievements are note-worthy. I say this because they are set in the context of realistic educational goals and are the result of a pedagogy for reform that is within the grasp of most teachers and set within an ideological framework deeply rooted in America's cultural history. This is not to diminish the importance of talking with our students about the radical transformations and proletarian victory envisioned by Marx, Gramsci, and Freire. Nor is it to denigrate the value of debating with students about alternatives to capitalism's exploitiveness, hierarchical relationships, and income inequities which many of them see as "natural." However, despite the importance of such radical perspec-tives, the proletarian victory these theorists envision seems out of reach. By contrast, Andre's and my collaboration is a problem-posing pedagogy that builds upon and seeks to expand the liberal, reforming forces of cooperative inquiry that already exist within capitalism. Given our current political climate, this approach in the classroom is, I believe, my best opportunity for promoting more equitable relations and institutions outside the classroom.

FOUR EVALUATIONS
Lucille McCarthy

As I have done in earlier chapters, I will now evaluate, with regard to
Andre, the teaching and learning in Steve's classroom. I will do this
from the perpectives of the theorists who have shaped and provided
analytic distance on the student-teacher stories we tell in this book:
the Critical Race Theorists and Whiteness studies scholars from
chapter 3 as well as Dewey, Gramsci, and Freire, upon whom we
draw throughout this book.

An Evaluation by Critical Race Theorists and Whiteness
Studies Scholars

From the Critical Race Theory point of view, I suspect these
theorists would find it inexcusably negligent on Steve's part that, in
a course on philosophy of education, he assigned no texts focusing
on the Civil Rights movement and its effect on U.S. public education. From their standpoint, it is bad enough that Steve did not
explore the implications of the 1954 *Brown* case but, even more
surprising, given the location of Steve's university, that he omitted
discussion of the 1971 *Swann v Charlotte-Mecklenburg Board of
Education* decision.

However, these same theorists and scholars would, in my view,
also make some entries on the ledger's positive side. First, Critical
Race Theorists would be pleased that, as Andre noted, Steve
welcomed students' opinions and stories in class discussion. In fact,
this was, as I reported, a feature of Steve's Philosophy of Education
course that appealed to Andre from the outset. Second, I believe
both Critical Race Theorists and Whiteness studies scholars would
applaud Steve's ability to use the texts of writers like Delpit, Hanson,
and Kozol to bring issues of race and schooling to the center of his
students' focus. In particular, Andre told me in our first post-semester interview that the Kozol text was especially rewarding because he

was able to use it to reconsider his own educational journey. In both his homework paper about Kozol and in class discussion, he was able to revisit his experiences in primarily White, well-funded schools (from first through third grades) as contrasted to his experiences in primarily Black, underfunded schools (from fourth grade through high school).

Given that Andre was the only African American in Steve's advanced class, I speculate that Critical Race Theorists and Whiteness studies scholars would find Andre's testimony noteworthy. Not only did Andre say that Steve's class was a safe place to productively consider race relations, he also reported that many of his White classmates were surprised to learn about the different levels of resources available to predominantly White and Black public schools. Following Andre's lead, they were beginning to acknowledge, at least in modest ways, that Whiteness is indeed a valuable property.

Gramscian Evaluation

Whereas I claimed that Gramsci would record mixed evaluations of Steve's work with Neha and Ellen, I believe he would be much more positive about Steve's time with Andre. True, Andre does not leave Steve's class as an organic intellectual or revolutionary intent on transforming civil society, but he seems far more committed to serious reading and critical reflection than do either Neha or Ellen. Steve can hardly take credit for the fact that Andre came to his class wanting to learn about philosophy and concerned to write more in line with the academic code. Nor can Steve claim that he directly influenced Andre, as he left his class, to read Frederick Douglass and Malcolm X in subsequent semesters. Nevertheless, I believe Gramsci would say that Steve's demanding syllabus, weekly writing assignments, high standards, and individual sessions with Andre encouraged his scholarly aspirations. In fact, in one of our last interviews, Andre mentioned that, despite his entrepreneurial ambitions, one of his primary goals was to become more of an "intellectual."

Freirian Evaluation

In Steve's part of the immediately preceeding Residue section, he anticipates what I believe would be Freire's strongest criticism of his approach to Andre. Freire would lament Steve's failure to challenge Andre's stated desire to be a successful entrepreneur, an owner of multiple businesses. Although Fishman adopts a pedagogy that is much more in line with a problem-posing than a banking model, he does not help Andre, anymore than he helped Ellen, see the contradictions in his life caused by class conflict. In addition, Freire would be chagrined by the absence from Steve's reading list (except for pieces of Freire's own work) of radical educators, those who argue, for example, that America's schools are tools of social control, unjust sorting devices that help the bourgeoisie exploit worker and minority classes (see Bowles & Gintis, 1976; Karier, 1975; Katz, 1971).

Despite these shortcomings, however, I believe Freire would also see three important silver linings in Andre's experiences in philosophy, positives that balance, if not outweigh, the negatives. First, although Steve, admittedly, does not die to his middle-classness, he does try to get into Andre's shoes and develop solidarity with him. During their weekly conversations, they discover, in addition to their common concerns about Andre's class work, areas of shared interest outside academics—for example, sports—which add to their mutual understanding. Evidence of this is that long after Steve's Philosophy of Education course concluded, Andre continued to stop at Steve's office for informal chats, chances to share his own progress and check on Steve's.

Second, as I report in my part of the Residue section, Andre, as a result of taking philosophy, was able to reflect on his education in following semesters in Freirian ways. That is, after Steve's course, Andre was able to draw upon ideas from various texts he read in philosophy, especially those by Dewey and Freire, to transform his felt opposition to banking education into articulate, informed resistance. Finally, I believe Freire would be pleased with Steve's strenuous attempt to do what Freire himself sees as crucial for the liberatory teacher's mission: honor student competencies and aspirations as well as apply a problem-posing approach to the study of academic subject matter.

Deweyan Evaluation

Earlier in this chapter, Steve quotes Dewey (1916/1967) to the effect that teachers should modify their "methods of teaching" to "retain all the youth under educational influences" until they have developed the ability to make intelligent decisions (p. 98). In Steve's effort to build democratic community with Andre—to find common purpose, likemindedness, and mutual care—and in his effort to establish a collaborative form of inquiry, I believe Dewey would see an honest attempt by a teacher to adjust his "methods of teaching" to meet a particular student's needs.

Dewey would also laud Steve's and Andre's tutorial for two additional reasons. Not only is it an illustration of a teacher modifying his pedagogy in an attempt to retain a student under "educational influences," it is also an example of a teacher and student communicating and finding likemindedness across class, ethnic, and generational lines. Further, I believe Dewey would see their collaboration as evidence that schools can be agencies of progress, helping to realize the democratic potential of U. S. society. That is, I believe Dewey would argue that Steve's and Andre's tutorial is evidence that within the school structure—a structure that radical theorists often describe negatively as an institution designed to control the poor and eliminate cultural diversity —there is space for teacher and student to nurture collaborative, critical thinking while working toward a more equitable distribution of our society's cultural, intellectual, and material goods.

Coda
The Researchers Continue to Converse
STEVE FISHMAN AND LUCILLE McCARTHY

Although we agreed that Andre Steadman enjoyed his tutorial with Steve and profitted from the course, McCarthy once again had reservations about Fishman's pedagogy. Whereas her questions about Fishman's teaching of Neha Shah and Ellen Williams centered on the inappropriateness of his curriculum, grading policies, and assignments, her criticisms of his work with Andre focused on Fishman's gradualist ideology and the way this affected his teaching.

To begin with, according to McCarthy, Fishman underestimated America's strong radical tradition, and this limited what he said to and did with his students. McCarthy disagreed with Steve's view that wholesale, dramatic political change is out of the question in America's future. Objecting to this claim, she pointed to the history of worker revolt in the United States, citing the Haymarket Square riot of 1886, the Homestead steelworkers battle with Pinkertons in 1892, and the two-month long strike of textile workers at Lawrence, Massachusetts in 1912. She also referred to well-known American journalists like Lincoln Steffens and John Reed who vigorously supported Bolshevism after the 1917 Revolution and Communists like Earl Browder and Theodore Brameld who, in the 1930s, promoted school focus on class struggle and class consciousness (see Draper, 1957; Karier, 1986).

In addition, she reminded Fishman that as early as 1828, Robert Dale Owen—whose Scottish father started the first kindergartens and co-ed schools in America—called for material as well as formal educational equality for all of America's youth. His demand was for campuses that would provide the same food, clothing, and shelter so that "the orphan boy should share the public care equally with the heir to a princely estate" (qtd. in Cremin, 1951, p. 41). According to

McCarthy, Owen's proposals, had they been adopted, would have profoundly altered the way children were raised and, ultimately, would have led to the abolition of American class differences.

Although McCarthy was upset that Fishman said nothing in Philosophy of Education about the possibility of dramatic social upheaval in America and failed to draw upon the tradition of Owen, Steffens, Browder, and Brameld, she was hardly surprised. Steve's gradualist liberalism, she thought, was consistent with what she understood as Dewey's notion of social reform, one that boiled down to individuals pursuing their own interests to the neglect of group solidarity. She reminded Fishman that for all of Dewey's talk about the possibility of reconciling individual goals and the larger social good, Dewey himself never took the personal risks necessary to truly shake the capitalist system. She told Fishman, "It's telling that despite Dewey's strong sympathy for Debs and the Pullman workers who were on strike the year he arrived at the University of Chicago, he never spoke out publicly in their defense. In fact," she said, "Dewey even urged his colleagues to remain quiet so as not to offend the capitalist nabobs who were funding the university."

McCarthy then directed a similar attack at Fishman himself. She told Steve that rather than risk his comfortable, tenured position by leading his students in protests on his own campus, he was, like Dewey, sitting on his hands and doing nothing publicly to confront social injustice. For example, McCarthy, invoking Robert Dale Owen's worry about material differences among students, pointed to the obvious discrepencies between the computer resources of rich and poor students on Steve's own campus. It was a classic case, she said, of the university's masking its sorting function as it reproduces America's class divisions. McCarthy suggested that the least Steve could have done was lead his students in seizing one of the few computer labs on campus to bring this inequity to the public's attention and force administrators to do something about it. (For examples of such activist pedagogy, see Hadden, 2000; Orner, 1992; Shor, 1992).

Taking McCarthy's charges seriously, Steve attempted to answer them in order. First, he acknowledged our nation's history of labor violence and the influence of the American Communist party.

However, while admitting that certain aspects of capitalism have had horrific consequences for countless people worldwide, he repeated that he saw no reasonable alternative to working for gradual reform from within the present American system.

Second, Steve addressed McCarthy's contention that Dewey was more concerned with saving his job than building solidarity with fellow workers. He confessed that, despite Dewey's overall record as a courageous public intellectual, he saw no way to justify Dewey's failure to support the Pullman strikers in the summer of 1894. However, Steve went on, even though Dewey denied that proletarian violence and triumph was the cornerstone of social reconstruction, he reminded McCarthy that Dewey sought the same ends as America's radicals. That is, Dewey (1935/1991) sought the extension of democracy from the political to the social and economic realms of life by urging the establishment of a "socialized economy" that would serve liberty and individual development (pp. 63–65). And, Steve added, "So do I."

Third, regarding his own unwillingness to lead his students in political confrontation, Steve said he had no simple response. He told McCarthy that he fully supported Robert Dale Owen's plea for more equitable student opportunities. He even quoted Dewey (1916/1967) as wanting something similar when Dewey advocated "such supplementation of family resources as will enable [all] youth to take advantage of [school facilities]" (p. 98). Nevertheless, and despite Fishman's own recoil at the ways in which his university reproduces current class inequities, he said he thought it inappropriate to make a computer lab sit-in a requirement in Philosophy of Education. To contextualize his position, Fishman offered a different gloss than McCarthy on the 1930s arguments about teachers and the appropriate politics of the classroom. According to Fishman, there were many, not just communists like Browder and Brameld, but also liberals like George Counts and John Childs, who believed teachers had a duty to develop student attitudes that favored a new world order based on international socialism. By contrast, there were also conservatives who thought school teachers were public servants with an obligation to encourage values that reflected the existing society and the attitudes of the majority (see Violas, 1973). Fishman told McCarthy,

> Although you have made clear that you would have sided with Browder and Brameld, I would have sided with those like Dewey, who wanted to avoid both extremes. Like him, I would have spoken out against efforts from both the left and the right that looked like student indoctrination. [See Dewey, 1934/1986b.]

Steve added that in the spirit of Dewey he took his first obligation as a teacher to be not the imposition of his own views but the encouragement of open classroom discussion with the aim of developing what Dewey (1934/1986b) calls "continuous inquiry" and "intelligent scepticism" (pp. 160–161; see also Bode, 1938).

Applying this principle of student deliberation to his Philosophy of Education classroom, Fishman said that asking for a computer lab sit-in would defeat the purpose of student give and take and be especially unfair to pupils who held conservative ideologies, those who, for example, see democracy as primarily about "negative liberties" and hands-off, laissez-faire government (see Berlin, 1970). But even if all his students did have radical orientations, he said, he would still be uneasy about exposing them to suspension or expulsion, not to mention jeopardizing his own career. Steve concluded by relating his ideology to his own life and career trajectory:

> Political confrontation has just not been part of my own personal narrative. I'm afraid I have never seen myself as a revolutionary leader. I know this sounds like a cop-out, but I went into teaching because I felt that, given my personality, my best chance of working for a better society was to help students become more reflective, articulate, and intellectually aware about the world in which they find themselves. That is, despite schools being controlled by the dominant elite, I believed there was still enough loose play within them, at least in most North American situations, for students and teachers to develop critical consciousness.

In addition to McCarthy's charge that Fishman's gradualist ideology ignored the radical tradition that actually exists in America and caused him to say and do too little in this regard with his students, she believed it hurt his teaching in a second way. McCarthy told Fishman that she thought he engaged in "teacher malpractice" when he refused to deconstruct Andre's professed, capitalist aspirations. She said she was disturbed by his complacency in response to Andre's entrepreneurial ambitions. "It may seem like a success story to you and Andre," she said, "but in my view Andre is simply serving the interests of the ruling class, just another case of keeping the disempowered hopeful while reducing their appetite for revolt." McCarthy explained to Steve that, in her view, he had an obligation as an educator to show Andre the ways he was being manipulated by capitalist interests, the ways in which his idea that money equals success is a mask for what is really going on: he is being trained by bourgeois culture to want goods that he does not need. McCarthy concluded: "Andre's success is not going to change the sad fact that 10% of our richest citizens own 86% of our nation's wealth" (see Spring, 1996, p. 4; West, 1993, pp. 10–11).

Attempting to answer this final criticism by McCarthy, Fishman began by acknowledging her condemnation of our capitalist and consumer culture. He said he too thinks it criminal that so few have so much while so many have so little. However, in an effort to defend his approach to Andre, he recalled for McCarthy that in various indirect ways—both in class and in one-on-one sessions—he had suggested to Andre as well as his classmates that, as college students, they were privileged and, thus, had an obligation to help those less well-off. He also argued once again that to push much harder against Andre's goals was to disrespect Andre's right to make his own decisions. Fishman said, "Even if I were absolutely certain that I knew what was best for Andre—which I am not—I would avoid intervening if I thought doing so might interfere with his independent judgment or injure his sense of self-worth."

Steve then conceded, as he had when reflecting on his experiences with Neha and Ellen, that he had, no doubt, made many mistakes. For example, he agreed that in Philosophy of Education he should probably have assigned selections from radical educational historians as well as texts dealing with the school court cases initiated by the

Civil Rights movement. Yet, despite these and other shortcomings, he said, he remained positive about his collaboration with Andre. He told McCarthy he believed that by working in the spirit of Dewey, Freire, and Gramsci—encouraging Andre to become more critical, to inventory his ideas, and to work cooperatively with others—he had, in his own modest way, contributed to the extension of democracy and to social reform.

CHAPTER FIVE

Conclusion: Sorting Conflict, Weaving Hope

> [P]hilosophy is . . . a kind of intellectual disrobing. We cannot permanently divest ourselves of the intellectual habits we take on and wear when we assimilate the culture of our own time and place. But intelligent furthering of culture demands that we take some of them off, that we inspect them critically to see what they are made of and what wearing them does to us.
>
> *John Dewey (1925/1989, p. 35)*

When Fishman asked McCarthy to observe his classroom so he could improve his instruction of underprepared writers, he expected her to help him understand students' composing processes and ways he might bring student papers in line with Standard American English. As we have shown, things did not turn out to be that simple. Instead, our study of three novice writers led us into debates about the proper function of public education in a democratic society, controversies that have at least a 150-year history in America. As we discussed these controversies, we were forced to consider our own answers to our title questions: Whose goals? Whose aspirations? To our discomfort, we discovered we had diverse responses. The area that caused the most conflict for us was social reform, the school goal about which our answers were more different than similar.

Regarding our similarity, we both found ourselves to the left of center in terms of a reformed social order. Neither of us is conservative or reactionary. Rather, we both want to extend democracy beyond due process, freedom of speech, and popularly elected government to other civic, economic, and cultural areas of our society. In other words, although we both worry about the dangers of large state bureaucracies, we favor more worker and democratic control of industry, more equitable incomes, and a less hierarchical social structure.

Where we clashed was over the proper role of individual teachers in helping promote our vision of social reform. For example, in Fishman's class, where McCarthy saw ways to increase cultural and ethnic parity, Fishman saw potential Balkanization. And where Fishman saw possibilities for reform resulting from conversation across class and ethnic lines, McCarthy saw continued hegemony of the dominant elite. This clash between McCarthy's Freirian radicalism and Fishman's Deweyan gradualism gave each of our chapters a distinct hue and focus.

In chapter 2, our conflict was about how multiculturally sensitive Fishman and his curriculum should be in Intro to Philosophy. In chapter 3, we argued over the significance of color-consciousness for Fishman's class, especially his grading criteria. Lastly, in chapter 4, we debated Fishman's level of class consciousness and whether it was appropriate for his course in Philosophy of Education. Before Fishman offers specific advice to discipline-based teachers about instructing novice writers across the curriculum, we summarize the conflicts between us and look back on Fishman's interactions with three inexperienced writers.

MULTICULTURALISM IN INTRO TO PHILOSOPHY: HOW MUCH? HOW LITTLE?

As we studied Neha Shah, our focus student in chapter 2, it quickly became clear that we had diverse views about the appropriateness of Steve's curriculum for a recent immigrant like Neha. McCarthy, sounding very much like a 1990s advocate of multicultural education, argued that Steve failed to appreciate and make use of the borderland perspective Neha brought to his class and her papers. McCarthy saw Steve's syllabus as provincially Eurocentric in its orientation, sending the hidden message that white Euroamerican culture is somehow superior to all others, including Neha's.

Underlying the difference between us was our conflict about the appropriate way to promote social reform in Intro to Philosophy. For McCarthy, it meant using Steve's classroom to celebrate and support Neha's native culture—its practices, language, and literature. However, Fishman resisted McCarthy's suggestions for redesigning his reading list, saying he was not sure he should or could do this. Not only did he not have time to modify his curriculum to meet particular students' special needs, there was also the matter of his limited expertise. He felt he knew too little, for example, about Neha's culture and the Indian philosophic tradition to construct a set of assignments built around her home community's literacy. That is, if equitable instruction for Neha meant a redesigned curriculum, Steve claimed it was out of his reach. Instead, he thought the best he could do was use his expertise to familiarize her with some of the philosophic texts, social and moral issues, and ways of constructing knowledge that were an important part of the warp and woof of her newly adopted country.

Thus, although McCarthy characterized Fishman's actions toward Neha as those of an assimilationist—going so far as to accuse him of having "Rodriguezed" Neha—Steve did not agree (Rodriguez, 1982). He protested that his ideal was not, as McCarthy implied, a homogeneous America, one built around an alleged Anglo Saxon tradition of initiative, industriousness, and thrift. Instead, he simply did not see it as his responsibility in Intro to Philosophy to be an advocate for or informant about Neha's home traditions. This did not mean he believed the preservation of minority ethnicities was solely a family or private organization affair as did the "cultural pluralists" in the 1920s (see Kallen, 1924). Nor did it mean he wanted to be insensitive to Neha's special challenges as a recent immigrant. However, given that he took his main teaching goal as the exploration of Western philosophic literature and the introduction of its distinctive ways of thinking and writing, he thought it unwise to make major adjustments in his classroom objectives for and requirements of Neha. As a result, and contrary to McCarthy's suggestions, Fishman asked Neha to do the same reading and writing he assigned all his Intro students, and he defended his position by arguing that to do otherwise was both impracticable and a disservice to Neha and his discipline.

Making Progress Even When Goals Don't Match

Although we disagreed about how best to promote social reform in Intro to Philosophy, we agreed that Neha made progress toward Fishman's classroom objectives. To Steve's surprise, McCarthy discovered that the key to Neha's achievement was not the many situations that he provided for students to use writing to explore his curriculum. Rather, these writing-to-learn exercises were effective only when accompanied by chances for Neha to discuss them with classmates in small groups and pairs. In these contexts, she could practice philosophic discourse in ways that were less threatening to her than whole class discussions and more helpful to her than Fishman's marginal notes on her papers.

A Social Motive: The Importance of Talking With Classmates about Writing-To-Learn Homework

Not only did Neha's small group and one-on-one exchanges with classmates help her understand course material, they also gave her what we have called a "social motive" for doing Steve's assignments. When she was writing for her classmates as well as the teacher, Neha was no longer just an instrumentalist completing her classwork to get a passing grade. She was also doing it because she was motivated to serve and please her peers. From Fishman's standpoint, one significant result of Neha's being socially motivated was that his and Neha's goals overlapped, even if only modestly and by default. That is, although exploration of cultural knowlege was never an end in itself for Neha, it did become an important means for achieving her genuine desire to please her small group and letter-exchange partners. This was, in Steve's view, a gratifying result of his effort to nurture a Deweyan form of cooperative student inquiry. Although Fishman could make little headway softening the contradictions that separated him and Neha, the fact that his pedagogy gave Neha chances to bridge some of the gaps between herself and her class-mates was crucial for sustaining her motivation to do the assigned work and helping her achieve, in limited measure, his goal of exploration of cultural knowledge.

COLOR-CONSCIOUSNESS IN INTRO TO PHILOSOPHY: HOW MUCH? HOW LITTLE?

Our second focus student, Ellen Williams, was Neha Shah's classmate. Like Neha, Ellen was an underprepared writer who saw philosophy as nothing more than an annoying and irrelevant requirement for graduation. In contrast to Neha, however, Ellen, as a native born African American, was a member of a minority group that has long been victimized by American race prejudice. Thus, McCarthy's criticisms of Fishman's instruction of Ellen focused less on his Eurocentric curriculum and more on what McCarthy saw as the unfair way Fishman evaluated the progress of this working class, returning student.

McCarthy claimed that for Fishman to be effective with non-mainstream pupils like Ellen, he needed to expand his evaluation criteria to include not just their academic development but their moral and social growth as well. Furthermore, McCarthy insisted, when Fishman did evaluate Ellen's academic progress, as opposed to her moral and social growth, he was doing so too narrowly, paying too little attention to her particular circumstances, the great barriers she had to leap just to gain entry to his university and attend his class. In addition, McCarthy felt Fishman overvalued the importance of Ellen's written work in philosophy, failing to offer her other ways— such as oral presentations—to display her progress in his course.

The larger issue behind our debate regarding Fishman's instruction of Ellen was the same one that underlay our conflicts about Neha: our ongoing disagreement about the school goal of social reform, specifically, what constituted justice in Steve's class. McCarthy, reflecting a major turn in the national conversation about race discrimination in the 1970s, claimed that promoting justice in Intro to Philosophy meant Steve's giving up his color-blindness and becoming color-conscious. That is, he needed to do more to make up for the terrible imbalance between the greater social, cultural, and economic opportunities afforded most American Whites as compared to those available to most American Blacks. That is, McCarthy thought that what at the surface looked like a level field of competition in Steve's class was really heavily weighted against someone like Ellen. The greater public funds expended on her White classmates' primary and secondary schools—as well as these students' family financial resources and, thus, the time they could devote to their education—were all the result of White privilege. As McCarthy viewed it, because such privilege gave Ellen's White classmates enormous advantages over Ellen, Steve should evaluate her differently.

In response, Fishman said he was embarrassed to discover he had been color and power evasive, insensitive to the ways in which Whiteness was a hidden but valuable property in his classroom. However, he disagreed with McCarthy about the best way to deracialize his teaching space. Although he was sympathetic with McCarthy's stance regarding evaluation of Ellen, Fishman worried about the consequences of the identity politics McCarthy was advocating, specifically, its potentially negative effect upon the collaborative form of student inquiry he wanted to nurture in philosophy. He was not sure how he could handicap the grades of his pupils without destroying students' trust that he was treating each of them fairly.

Although Fishman saw no easy strategy for using his course to compensate for past and continuing race inequities, he thought his best hope for justice for Ellen rested on an approach that combined color-blindness and color-consciousness. In other words, Steve believed that a fair and race-cognizant pupil evaluation required measuring student performance against both the student's personal situation (color-conscious) and against an across-the-board (color-blind) standard. This meant that he sought, first, to weigh each student's academic progress against an individual measure, namely, how far each had come toward his classroom objectives from his or her initial starting point. Second, he tried to blend this individual evaluation with another that measured each student's performance against a broader criterion, namely, the average work of other undergraduates he had taught during his 30-year career in philosophy. Applied to Ellen, he thought that to evaluate her performance solely against an individual standard risked misleading her about how her work compared to that of her peers. As much as he was gratified by Ellen's individual progress in his Intro class, he insisted to McCarthy that Ellen's grade needed to reflect not just the substantial obstacles Ellen had to overcome once she got inside his classroom but also how well she had actually mastered the skills needed to read and write perceptively about philosophy.

When Storytelling Is Not Enough: The Importance of Contextualizing Student Narratives

Our study of Ellen Williams supports the claim of Critical Race Theorists that storytelling is an important means of helping long-silenced minorities gain a voice. Ellen told McCarthy in their interviews that the instructional supports in Fishman's class that most enabled her to open to philosophic questioning were ones that gave her chances to tell her stories. However, we also found that for Ellen's narratives to generate mutual understanding and critical reflection, they had to be contextualized. In other words, as hooks (1989) and Giroux (1992) note, storytelling by itself is not enough to establish fruitful dialogue. To be effective, student stories must be connected to broader political, social, and economic issues. As Gramsci (1971) describes this process, the philosopher's task is to help people analyze their narratives, creating an "inventory" of the intellectual ideas and movements which have left their deposit in these stories but have done so without their authors' awareness (p. 324).

Unfortunately, as McCarthy's accounts of Steve's Intro class show, Fishman was not always able to contextualize Ellen's narratives. For example, on the day his class focused on an article by hooks (1981/1995), Steve had too little historical and theoretical understanding of our country's debates about race to help students inventory their accounts and place them in a larger framework. As a result, student positions hardened, and their differences remained personal instead of reflecting broader philosophic and political points of view.

By contrast, when Steve was able to help students explore the ideas behind their diverse perspectives, students could re-examine their different positions and revisit their experiences wearing new conceptual lenses. As an illustration, McCarthy described the day Steve's Intro class discussed a text by Clarence Darrow (1932/1973) who argues against the existence of God. Because Fishman was familiar with the controversy surrounding this issue, he was able to help his class find the philosophic significance in Ellen's charge that studying views like Darrow's was a waste of time. As a result, as the class discussed Ellen's thesis—"If it ain't broke, don't fix it"—it was no longer just Ellen's view they were considering but the substantial history of challenges to philosophic questioning that began with the trial of Socrates.

A Social Motive: The Importance of Nurturing A Community of Student Inquiry

As McCarthy has reported, the effect on Ellen of successful contextualization of student narratives was noteworthy. She became a valued member of a group that she herself began to enjoy, one she saw as a source of personal growth, a class she said did not want to miss. She discovered that she needed her classmates and they needed her, and, as they worked together, their initial stereotypes started to fall away. As Ellen's classmate, Tonya McIinnis, also a returning African American woman, told McCarthy: "I have to admit I was wrong about Ellen. She is not a closedminded person who only wants to fight. Ellen is really listening now."

Successful class discussion not only gave Ellen a new social and non-instrumentalist motive for attending philosophy, it also helped her experience some of the rewards of philosophic questioning. Alternatively put, as she was bridging the gap between herself and her classmates, she was also reducing the distance between herself and Fishman, forging a relationship between herself and her teacher and his discipline that never developed between Neha and Steve. As McCarthy has reported, Ellen was establishing new "for-whats" or goals in philosophy, ones that overlapped with Steve's. Whereas Ellen initially told McCarthy that the chasm between Fishman and herself was so great she thought Fishman was "from another planet," by the time Ellen began work on her final essay for his course she told McCarthy she was now asking questions like Fishman and trying to emulate his "tactfulness."

Although Fishman never directly helped Ellen with the surface features of her writing while she was a student in his course, the success of his pedagogy in enabling her to become part of a community of inquiry meant that this underprepared writer took significant residue from his class. She left with an appreciation of the value of philosophic questioning and was starting to open, more generally, to the possible rewards of book learning. Put differently, Ellen achieved something of Fishman's overall goals for students, exploration of cultural knoweldge and, most notably, personal growth.

CLASS CONSCIOUSNESS IN PHILOSOPHY OF EDUCATION: HOW MUCH? HOW LITTLE?

Our original research question focused on how Fishman could become a more effective teacher of underprepared writers who enroll in his philosophy classes. We learned that making progress with the surface features of the work of novice writers is extremely difficult in the short span of a single semester. As a result, instead of seeing improved mechanics as a discipline-based teacher's first objective, we discovered that a more realistic aspiration is helping inexperienced writers become interested in course content and setting conditions so that they and their classmates learn from and teach one another. If such a classroom community can be nurtured, it is possible, as our studies of Neha Shah and Ellen Williams show, for novice writers to develop increased motivation and enthusiasm for their work.

Although we learned that moving novice writers' compositions closer to Standard American English is difficult, especially in courses like philosophy which focus on demanding texts, we also discovered that progress, albeit modest, can be made if teacher and student manage to establish writing improvement as a common goal. This is our major finding from our study of Andre Steadman, our third focus student. As a consequence of Steve's and Andre's tutorial work together, Andre developed new understanding of his writing process. In post-semester conversations with McCarthy, Andre said he applied what he learned about writing in philosophy to assignments in subsequent semesters. In particular, he began his papers earlier so he would have time to rewrite, shared his drafts with peers for reader feedback, and edited more carefully to make sure that what he put down on paper was what he really wanted to say.

Andre's new writing process was stimulated, at least in part, by the dialogic think-aloud protocols he shared with Fishman in their one-on-one weekly sessions. These helped him develop a co-investigator stance with Steve as he explored his compositions, a perspective from which he could "see [his] writing [problems] better." Of course, tutorials like the ones Andre and Steve shared are time consuming and hardly practical for large numbers of students given most instructors' course and pupil loads. Further, it is not easy to initiate tutorials, as we have seen in the cases of Neha and Ellen, because many students have neither the time for nor the interest in improving their writing. Yet, when teacher and student do share this goal, our study of Andre suggests that dialogic think-alouds are an effective way of making progress, not only with novice writers' composing processes but also with their mastery of course subject matter.

Reform Through Activism and Identity Politics Versus Reform Through Conversation and Common Purpose

Although Fishman and McCarthy agreed about the benefits for Andre Steadman of the dialogic think-alouds and his tutorials with Steve, we discovered further disagreements between us as we studied this third novice writer. McCarthy's unhappiness with Fishman's teaching of Andre was with Steve's lack of political activism, his failure to encourage students to confront injustices in the communities in which they lived. She argued that Fishman's reluctance to do this had the effect of perpetuating our society's hierarchical and inequitable status quo. The 10% of Americans who own 86% of our nation's wealth, she maintained, are not going to surrender their power and influence voluntarily. In her view, without well organized civil disobedience, or even more aggressive forms of worker protest, any hope for increased democracy in America is a pipe dream. By contrast, Steve, following Dewey, pinned his hopes for social reform on intelligent inquiry and expanded give and take across class and ethnic lines.

However, our disagreement was not just about how politically active Fishman should be or how aggressive teachers in general should be in getting their students' political views into alignment with their own. Our disagreement was also about how someone like Fishman—a White, middle-class, Euroamerican male—should go about becoming an effective instructor of students like Neha Shah, Ellen Williams, and Andre Steadman who are, to borrow from Lisa Delpit (1995), "other people's children." In keeping with McCarthy's identity politics, she argued that if Steve were to become a culturally sensitive teacher, he needed to do what Ladson-Billings (1994) and Freire (1970/1997) suggest: immerse himself in and incorporate into his curriculum the practices, values, and ways of knowing of his students. That is, just as McCarthy thought Fishman needed to work harder to understand Neha's home community, so McCarthy believed Fishman needed to surrender his White, middle-class identity if he were to successfully instruct Ellen and Andre. This was the only way, as McCarthy saw it, that Fishman could avoid making Neha feel that Euroamerican traditions were superior to her native Indian ones and making Ellen and Andre feel that White, middle-class language and values—and existing social injustices—were legitimately the American norm.

In the end, we had to accept that at times the two of us simply interpreted our data differently. For his part, Fishman ultimately judged his work with Neha, Ellen, and Andre as largely successful. Especially with regard to Ellen and Andre, Fishman thought our study showed Dewey to be correct: people can honor their differences while developing a substantial degree of likemindedness. Drawing once again on his Deweyan orientation, specifically Dewey's distrust of binary distinctions, Fishman thought McCarthy's NonEuropean/ European, Black/White, lower-class/middle-class distinctions were too hard and fast. Steve saw lots of variation within these categories, saw places where the identities of people from apparently distinct groups overlapped, places where their practices coincided and their interests merged. To imply, as McCarthy did, that only if Fishman became Indian could he truly be fair to Neha, and only if he "died" and were reborn Black and working class could he effectively teach Ellen and Andre was, in Steve's view, to exaggerate the ways he differed from his students and underestimate their chances of forging common goals and aspirations.

ADVICE FOR DISCIPLINE-BASED TEACHERS OF UNDERPREPARED WRITERS
Steve Fishman

Emphasize Content Over Form

If I am correct that Neha Shah, Ellen Williams, and Andre Steadman are representative of students I am calling underprepared, then the idea that should be first and foremost in the minds of discipline-based teachers is that such students are intelligent and, when properly motivated, hardworking. However, these instructors should also know that, for a variety of reasons, these students' acquisition of academic literacy presents significant hurdles for them, and there is no quick fix. In other words, when teachers explain in marginal comments or face to face that these pupils' writing is outside the standard code, these students are often unable or unwilling to immediately follow their instructors' suggestions for writing in the target language.

Therefore, I urge teachers—and this is hardly new advice—to direct most of their attention to the content rather than the form of their underprepared students' papers. I believe this is a way of showing them that a teacher is taking their work seriously and also a way of increasing their motivation. When I have adopted this approach, and when pupils have gotten excited about course subject matter, I have discovered that novice writers can do quite wonderful things. I am thinking of Ellen Williams's paper on capital punishment and

Andre Steadman's written analysis of Hansen's (1995) book, *The Call to Teach*.

Establish Cooperative Relationships With and Among Students

In addition to urging teachers in the disciplines to attend primarily to the substance rather than the form of their underprepared students' work, I also suggest they try to establish cooperative relationships between themselves and these pupils and among these pupils and their classmates. My recommendation about the first step in this process is based on my experience that underprepared writers are often defensive about their work. As a result, I advise instructors to be cautious and gentle with any offers of help for fear these students will see such offers as criticisms, as signs that the teacher believes they are somehow inferior, unable to do the coursework. After the initial teacher-student encounter, however, a multitude of factors shape the teacher-student and student-student relationships that ensue.

In Ellen's case, the most important factor was that she felt encouraged to speak her mind and bring her personal experiences into class discussions. In Andre's case, I attribute our good teacher-student relationship, at least in part, to the dialogic think-alouds and co-investigator stance we developed in our tutorial sessions. Regarding Neha, although my own relationship with her remained more distant, her success in my class was, as we have shown, the consequence of her rewarding interactions with classmates. In short, underprepared writers' feelings about their teacher and their class-mates—the degree to which these students sense they are valued participants in a shared inquiry—is central to the effort they put forward and, ultimately, to their academic success.

Provide Opportunities for Students to Bridge from Familiar Literacies to the Target Literacy

The instructional supports we have shown to be helpful for our three focus students all involve opportunities to use their familiar literacies to bridge to my academic one. Some involved writing, some involved speaking, but nearly all allowed students to mix familiar discourses with the philosophic one I was urging them to master. In Neha's case, she said she profited from the letter exchanges with classmates, the small group sharing of homework, and student-generated exams. For Ellen, the opportunities to practice philosophic thinking she found most helpful were whole class discussion and various types of ungraded writing, including her entries in her Class Reflection Log and her in-class freewrites. Andre also mentioned the significance of his participation in whole class discussion, but most of all, he said, he valued his chances to talk about his papers in one-on-one sessions with me.

Expand What Counts as Academic Progress

Finally, perhaps the most important piece of advice I can offer discipline-based teachers is that they expand their view of what counts as academic progress in their classes. I say this because it can be depressing for teachers as well as students if instructors define novice writers' progress solely in terms of improved writing mechanics. Rather, in determining the value of their course for their underprepared students— the residue their novice writers take from it—a much more encouraging picture emerges if teachers consider other signs of increased academic literacy as well. I have in mind Neha Shah's modest gains in critiquing patriarchy, Ellen Williams's increasing ability to consider alternative positions, and Andre Steadman's emerging skill in seeing his own educational experiences in a larger and more philosophic context.

Notes

CHAPTER THREE
(p. 68)
1. Neha's and Ellen's off-campus work hours were not that unusual among UNCC students who, according to the University's Provost, work an average of 30 hours per week. However, we do not know how many students are, like Neha, working for non-necessities and, therefore, able to reduce their hours and how many are, like Ellen, unable to cut back. We suspect that more UNCC students fall into the former category than the latter.

CHAPTER FOUR
(p. 119)
1. I acknowledge that the term community is often used honorifically or, to quote Williams (1976), as a god-word. I am also cognizant of the potential problems with conceptions that present communities as organic but hierarchical wholes, different parts performing different functions in the service of a higher good. Such conceptions can lead to idealizations of societies—like the Athenian polis of ancient Greece, the medieval European village, and the New England colonial town—that, despite their orderliness and achievements, were, in fact, caste-like and repressive of minority languages and cultures (see Dewey, 1916/1967, pp. 152–54; Noddings, 1996; Phillips, 1993; Pratt, 1987). Dewey (1916/1967) himself acknowledges the multiple ways in which the word community is used (pp. 20–21, 80–83), recognizing that there are communities that produce evil as well as good: communities of thieves and, by contrast, communities

of respectful and welcoming families (1927/1988a, p. 150). Thus, Dewey attempts to fashion a conception of community that is realistic enough to present a live hypothesis but also ideal enough to be a standard against which to evaluate competing social forms.

Appendix A
Research Methods

DATA COLLECTION AND ANALYSIS PROCEDURES FOR CHAPTERS 2 AND 3

Data Collected in Introduction to Philosophy, Fall 1998

Class Observations

- Teacher-researcher insider, Fishman, observed all classes and recorded notes after each session.
- Outside composition researcher, McCarthy, observed four classes and took notes during and after each session.
- Videotapes of all classes were made for later study.

Teacher Log

- Fishman wrote his impressions of class events and their meaning after each session.

Interviews

- Four 45-minute interviews were conducted by McCarthy at regular intervals throughout the semester with 10 students: our two focus students, Neha Shah and Ellen Williams, and eight of their classmates. Two interviews with each student were done in person and audiotaped for later transcription, and two were conducted on the phone with McCarthy taking notes.
- Two 20-minute conversations between Fishman and Neha Shah were audiotaped when she came to Fishman's office to discuss her writing.

Texts

- All of our 10 informants' in-class and out-of-class assignments were collected for analysis.

Follow-Up Data on the Two Focus Students

Neha Shah (Spring 1999)

Post-Semester Interview
- One 45-minute telephone interview was conducted by McCarthy in May 1999, six months after Fishman's course concluded.

Ellen Williams (Spring 1999 - Spring 2000)

Post-Semester Interviews
- McCarthy's interviews with Ellen. Five 45-minute interviews were conducted during the three semesters following philosophy. Four of these were done on the phone; the final one was conducted in person and audiotaped.
- Fishman's tutorials with Ellen. Two hour-long, tutorial sessions with Fishman were audiotaped in February and March 2000.
- Interviews by McCarthy and Fishman with Ellen's professors in semesters following philosophy. McCarthy interviewed two of Ellen's professors—one in criminal justice and the other the instructor of her leadership class. These interviews were conducted in person after the course was finished and lasted 45 minutes with McCarthy taking notes. Fishman audiotaped two 30-minute interviews with another of Ellen's criminal justice professors after Ellen's course with this instructor concluded.

Texts from Subsequent Courses
- McCarthy collected Ellen's writing from her courses in the three semesters following philosophy for analysis and subsequent discussion with Ellen.

Data Analysis for Chapters 2 and 3

Early in the fall of 1998, McCarthy began reading and rereading our data from Intro to Philosophy looking for themes and patterns (see Lincoln & Guba, 1985; Miles & Huberman, 1984; Spradley,

1980). Several of the categories that emerged focused on students' difficulties with Fishman's writing assignments. Neha Shah, as Fishman's only non-native speaker, was particularly interesting in this regard as was Ellen Williams, whose outspoken resistance to Fishman and his assignments was unusual. Thus, McCarthy made these two students a focus of her attention.

As data collection and analysis continued during the semester, Fishman and McCarthy added to their original interest in these students' writing a concern with their reading. Further, as we explored the literature on ESL and "basic" writers, we encountered recurring discussions of social justice, student empowerment and student right to their own language, and student and teacher transformation. These resonated with philosophies of education we had read over the years, resulting in our using the theories of Freire, Gramsci, and Dewey to help us name, explore, and explain what we were seeing. Later, as we analyzed Ellen's data and struggled to understand the racial dynamics in Fishman's classroom, we found the perspectives of the Critical Race Theorists and Whiteness studies scholars helpful and added them to our set of theoretical tools. Throughout our three-year process of data collection and analysis, we worked cooperatively to honor our quite different interpretations as we shaped our hypotheses, narratives, and conclusions.

DATA COLLECTION AND ANALYSIS PROCEDURES FOR CHAPTER 4

Data Collected in Philosophy of Education, Spring 1999

Tutorial Sessions

- 10 hour-long tutorial sessions between Fishman and focus student Andre Steadman were audiotaped for later transcription and analysis.

Teacher Log

- Fishman wrote his impressions of each tutorial session soon after it concluded.

Follow-up Data Regarding Focus Student Andre Steadman, May 1999–December 2000

Post-Semester Interviews

- McCarthy's interviews with Andre. Eight 45-minute interviews were conducted at regular intervals during the three semesters following his philosophy course. Four were done on the phone; four were done in person and audiotaped for later transcription.
- Fishman's interviews with Andre. Two 30-minute, audiotaped interviews were conducted by Fishman in June and August 2000.
- Interview by McCarthy with Andre's professor the semester following philosophy. One 45-minute interview was conducted with the teacher of Andre's writing intensive computer science class. It was done in person after the course concluded with McCarthy taking notes.

Texts from Subsequent Courses

- McCarthy collected Andre's writing for his courses in the three semesters following philosophy and later analyzed them and questioned Andre about them.

Data Analysis for Chapter 4

Our analysis of our data on Andre Steadman followed the same general theme and pattern analysis we describe above. However, unlike our studies of Neha Shah and Ellen Williams, Fishman worked alone during spring 1999 when Andre and he were doing their tutorial sessions. McCarthy joined Steve in May 1999 to collect follow-up data and read his emerging data reduction drafts. We thought it important to bring McCarthy aboard to interview Andre so we could elicit information that would augment and crosscheck that which Steve had obtained. We also wanted to follow Andre across time. Between May 1999 and Andre's graduation in December 2000, Fishman and McCarthy worked together, collaboratively constructing our narratives and conclusions while attempting to preserve our diverse points of view. (See Fishman & McCarthy, 2000, for further discussion of our research processes.)

Appendix B

Writing Assignments in Introduction to Philosophy

GRADED ASSIGNMENTS

- Homework assignments that ask students to respond to reading. Fishman gave twenty-one assignments of various genres requiring pupils to summarize and evaluate the readings and apply them to their own lives. These homework pieces often provided the basis for in-class interactions among students in groups and pairs. The homework assignments are listed below.
- Multi-draft essay. In the final month of the semester students were asked to write a multi-draft essay applying philosophic methods to a personal or public moral dilemma.
- Mid-term and final exams. These were student-generated essays exams (as described in chapter 2.)

UNGRADED ASSIGNMENTS

- Class Reflection Logs (CRLs). Nine times during the semester, Fishman asked students to reflect on their learning in the class. He collected the CRLs periodically, responding to them but not assigning a grade. The CRL questions are listed in Appendix C.
- Classnotes. Once during the semester each student served as class notetaker. He/she wrote up and made copies of his/her notes, distributing them to classmates at the beginning of the next session. The classnotes, which were read aloud and were often funny and entertaining, provided continuity and allowed all students but

one to participate in class discussion without having to take notes. Each day's notetaker, at the end of his/her notes, nominated the next scribe.

- Ten-minute, in-class freewrites. Fishman used freewrites regularly across the semester to allow students time to gather their thoughts before class discussion. He did not collect them.

HOMEWORK ASSIGNMENTS

Assignment #1 - Choosing and Defending One Side of a Debate (Frantz Fanon)

Please note that all homework is to be typed. Handwritten work is not acceptable.

After reading Max Hallman [1995], pp. 1–6 (in Hallman) and Frantz Fanon [1965/1995] (in Hallman, pp. 189–93), please choose one side or the other of the following debate and type a three or four paragraph defense of your position.

1. Fanon's view of capitalism as a form of colonization in which educators and clergy keep the exploited in submission is a distortion. It only serves to promote unrest among different races and social classes.

2. Fanon's view of capitalism as a form of colonization spotlights an important but usually hidden truth about White, Euro-America's treatment of Native Americans and African Americans.

Assignment #2 - A Summary and Question about Stokely Carmichael

Please type a brief summary of Carmichael's [1966/1995] argument against racial integration of White and Black in America (in Hallman, pp. 194–99). Conclude your summary with a question about Carmichael's position which you would be willing to present to the class discussion leader.

Assignment #3 - Short Essay on bell hooks

Please type a brief summary of what you consider to be bell hooks's [1981/1995] main points (in Hallman, pp. 199–209). Then indicate whether or not you believe there is such a thing in America as "White privilege." Have you yourself ever been a victim or beneficiary of such privilege?

Assignment #4 - Letter Exchange on Plato

All homework is to be typed. Hand-written letters are not acceptable. Two copies of your letter are required. One copy is to be given to me and the other copy is to be exchanged with your letter-partner at the start of class.

Reflect on your reading of Plato's *Apology* and *Crito*, and then write a 200-300 word letter to your partner in which you describe some aspect of the dialogues that you are having trouble understanding—a specific area you are having difficulty interpreting or fully comprehending.

You should make distinctions where you can—that is, describe what you understand and what you do not understand. You should refer to one or more particular passages in the dialogues where you are experiencing difficulty. Don't just say, "I don't understand the passage beginning at line 10 of page 64." In other words, you should provide a context for what you do not understand so your reader can see your difficulties and thereby give you some assistance.

I hope this assignment will help you clarify your thinking about the Apology and Crito dialogues as well as describe a particular problem or problems to a classmate that you really want to know more about.

Assignment #5 - Letter Response

Please bring two copies of your typed response letter, one for your letter partner and one for me.

Write a response of at least 200-300 words to the letter you received from your classmate. You may draw upon our class discussions as well as your own reading of Plato's dialogues. Please suggest possible answers to your classmate's questions and raise any other issues which you believe are relevant.

Assignment #6 - Short Essay and a Question about J.H. Holmes

Please write a short essay explaining what you got out of Holmes's [1929/1973] article (in Edwards and Pap, pp. 250–260). Please conclude with a question you have about his piece, one you are willing to share with your classmates and explore as class discussion leader.

Assignment #7 - Study Questions about Lin Yutang

Please type your answers to these study questions about Yutang's [1937/1995] article (in Hallman, pp. 286–292).
1. What does Yutang mean by calling himself a "pagan"?
2. Why does Yutang maintain his belief in God but surrender his belief in Christianity?
3. Yutang talks about "bending to the will of Heaven" (p. 292). What does he mean? Is this something you yourself want to do? Please explain.

Assignment #8 - A Question about William Paley

After reading the Paley [1802/1973] selection (in Edwards & Pap, pp. 419–434), please focus on a portion of the text or one of his arguments you find puzzling or difficult to understand. Please formulate a question which gets at the center of your puzzlement. Then type this question at the top of a blank page. We will form small groups, select the best question in each group, and pass it to to the next group for a collective answers.

Assignment #9 - A Debate about Clarence Darrow

Please type a brief essay after reading Darrow [1932/1973] (in Edwards & Pap, pp. 446–453) in which you defend one of these contrasting positions.
   1. Darrow's position may be depressing, but it is an accurate one with which we need to learn to live.
   2. Darrow's position is a one-sided, superficial view of human experience and our relationship to the world.

Assignment #10 - Study Questions about Carol Christ

Please read Carol Christ's [1978/1995] article (in Hallman, pp. 268–278). After discussing the study questions with a classmate (to be assigned), type your answers the following questions.
   1. What surprises you most about Carol Christ's article?
   2. Which of your own beliefs about the dominant Western religions and prevailing views about women in our culture does the article challenge?

Assignment #11 - Letter Exchange about Bertrand Russell

Bertrand Russell's work, including *Marriage & Morals* [1929/1970], has been controversial, although about 25 years after this book's publication Russell received the Nobel Prize. Please reflect on the assigned sections of the text (chaps. 3, 5, 6, 10, 16) and then write a 200-300 word letter to a classmate in which you describe some aspect of the text that you are having trouble understanding— a specific area you are having difficulty interpreting or fully comprehending.

Please bring two copies of your typed letter. Refer to specific passages in the text. However, don't just take a sentence out of context and say you do not understand it. Indicate what you do understand and what you do not understand. That is, try to help your letter correspondent by indicating what you do understand of the general argument in which the specific and troubling quotation appears.

Assignment #12 - Letter Response

Please bring two copies of your response letter, one for the class-mate to whom you are responding, the other for me.

Write a response of at least 200-300 words to the letter you received from a classmate. In your response, you may draw upon our class discussions as well as your own reading of the assigned sections of Russell's *Marriage & Morals* (chaps. 3, 5, 6, 10, and 16). Please suggest possible answers to your classmate's questions, and raise any other issues which you believe are relevant to her or his questions.

Assignment #13 - Short Essay and Question about Simone de Beauvoir

Please compose a brief essay explaining what you have learned by reading de Beauvoir [1949/1995] (in Hallman, pp. 25–31). Conclude with a question you have about de Beauvoir's article, a question you believe is important, one you are willing to explore as discussion leader with your classmates.

Assignment #14 - A Question about Mary Daly

After reading the article by Mary Daly [1973/1995] (Hallman, pp. 159–171), please generate a question which goes to the heart of the issues in Daly's article. Since we will be using these questions in small groups during class, please also provide enough background material so that your reader can understand why you think your question is important or why you believe answering it will be instructive.

Assignment #15 - Letter Exchange about Dewey (*Reconstruction*, chap. 2)

John Dewey (1859–1952) is America's best known philosopher and is considered the driving force behind the pedagogical reform movement known as "progressive education." The most accessible overview of his philosophy is *Reconstruction in Philosophy*

[1920/1962]. This book was written in 1919 and is the result of a series of lectures Dewey gave on a visit to Japan. *Reconstruction* was, therefore, not written for students but for an audience already familiar with the ongoing conversation in philosophy. Our assignments from this book are, thus, an important step forward in our efforts to become familiar with philosophy and to develop the skills to eventually contribute to its community of readers and writers. So make an extra effort with this book and be patient if the reading is difficult going in certain places.

Please reflect on chapter 2 of *Reconstruction*, and then write a one to two page letter to a classmate in which you describe some aspect of Dewey's chapter 2 that you are having trouble understanding—a specific area you are having difficulty interpreting or fully comprehending. Refer to specific passages in Dewey's text. Indicate what you do understand and what you do not understand. That is, try to help your letter-correspondent by indicating what you comprehend of the general argument in which the specific and troubling quotation appears. Please bring two copies of your typed letter to class.

Assignment #16 - Letter Response

Write a one to two page letter in response to the inquiry you received from a classmate this past Thursday. In your response, draw upon our class discussions as well as your own reading of chapter 2 of Dewey's *Reconstruction in Philosophy*. Please suggest possible answers to your classmate's questions and raise any other issues you believe are relevant to her or his questions. Bring two copies of your typed response letter, one for the classmate to whom you are responding and one for me.

Assignment #17 - Short Essay and Question about Paul Ree

Please write a short essay relating what you have learned from Ree's article [1885/1973] (in Edwards & Pap, pp. 10–27). Please conclude your essay with a question you have about Ree's piece, one you are willing to investigate as discussion leader with the rest of the class.

Assignment # 18 - Study Questions about John Stuart Mill

John Stuart Mill, godfather to Bertrand Russell and England's most famous intellectual of the 19th century, distinguishes between fatalism and determinism in his article, "On Liberty & Necessity" [1843/1973] (in Edwards & Pap, pp. 52–58).

1. After discussion with a classmate [to be assigned], please outline Mill's distinction between fatalism and determinism and show the importance of this distinction for Mill's defense of human freedom.
2. Compare and contrast Mill's position with Ree's. Do you find any significant differences between Mill's and Ree's views on freedom of the will?
3. If you had to pick between Mill's position and Ree's, which would you choose? Please explain.

Assignment #19 - Study Questions about William James

Taking a very different stance than Paul Ree or John Stuart Mill, William James [1884/1973], a famous American philosopher who taught at Harvard in the first part of this century, "hopes to persuade us" that we should assume that freedom of the will is true. James attempts to do this by examining the moral implications of the position he wants to resist, namely, determinism. His article, "The Dilemma of Determinism" is in Edwards and Pap, pp. 34–46.

1. Please explain how James understands determinism and indeterminism.
2. Does James persuade you that we have free-will? If so, why? If not, why not?

Assignment # 20 - Letter Exchange about Dewey
(*Reconstruction*, chap. 1)

We end our readings for the semester with chapter 1 of Dewey's *Reconstruction in Philosophy* [1920/1962]. It brings us full circle to questions we faced at the start of the semester, for in chapter 1

Dewey provides an interpretation of the trial of Socrates and concludes with a discussion of his own definition of philosophy, its methods and subject-matter.

Please read Dewey's chapter 1 and write a one or two page letter to a classmate describing some aspect of this chapter that you are having trouble understanding—a specific area you are having difficulty interpreting or fully comprehending.

Assignment # 21 - Letter Response

Please write a response of at least 200-300 words to the letter you received from your classmate about Dewey's chapter 1. In your response, draw upon our class discussions as well as your own reading of Dewey's chapter to suggest possible answers to your classmate's questions and raise any other issues which you believe are relevant.

Please bring two copies of your typed response letter to class. One will be given to the classmate to whom you are responding; the other is for me.

Appendix C

Class Reflection Log (CRL) Questions

Entry #1

   a) Briefly describe the quality of your education so far (K-college).
   b) Which teachers or events have been especially helpful for your development and learning?
   c) Which teachers or events have been especially harmful for your development and learning?

Entry #2

   In our opening class sessions, we discussed Fanon's, Carmichael's, and hooks's ideas about racism in America.
   a) What idea, anecdote, or insight comes to mind as you recall these authors' pieces?
   b) What new insights, if any, did you get about racism from our class discussions?
   c) Is there anything left over from our class discussions that you felt you did not get to say that you would like to say now?

Entry #3

   a) Approximately how much time do you spend on the written assignments for this course?

b) Has this writing helped your comprehension of the readings? Has it helped you participate in class discussion of these readings?

c) Have my responses to your written assignments been helpful? Are there steps you can take to improve the quality of your written work?

Entry #4

a) What goals do you have for yourself in Intro to Philosophy?

b) What goals do you think I have for my students in Intro to Philosophy?

Entry #5

Do you believe that my race, class, and gender give White, middle-class, male students in my courses an advantage over female students, students of color, or working class students? Please explain.

Entry #6

1. What, if anything, have you learned so far in Phi 2101?
2. Please comment on your mid-term exam.
   a) Did you learn anything by preparing for the exam?
   b) How did you respond to my evaluation of your exam?

Entry #7

This semester we have tried to learn about the ways in which philosophers think, read, speak, and write.

a) Please describe these ways as best you can.

b) Which aspects of philosophic thinking, reading, speaking, and writing have been the most challenging for you?

Entry #8

1. Please describe how you have gone about doing your homework assignments this semester.
   a) How do you do them?
   b) How do you go about the reading? Do you underline?
      Take notes? Write in the margins of the text?
   c) Where do you normally complete the homework assig-
      ments and how much time do they usually take?
2. Please describe why you are in school.

Entry #9

1. What, if anything, have you learned in philosophy this semester? What will you take away from this course as you move on
to the next semester?
2. What grade to you expect to receive in this course?

Appendix D

Writing Assignments
in Philosophy of Education

Assignment #1 - What is the Purpose of Education? (Plato [1997], pp. 54–77 in Cahn)

Please evaluate Plato's approach to education in a typed letter to a classmate. At the close of your letter, ask your classmate a question concerning any portion of Plato's text about which you are not clear. In order to help your letter partner, please explain the source of your confusion and the exact part of Plato's text that is in question. We will exchange letters at the beginning of the period, and you will have a chance to answer your letter partner's question and get an answer to your question.

Assignment #2 - What are the purpose, content, and psychology of education? (Locke [1693/1997], pp. 144–16 in Cahn)

Please choose *either* side of the debate below, and defend your position with a brief typed justification.
1. John Locke's approach to students and education is extremely harsh and traditional.
2. John Locke's approach to students and education is enlightened and progressive.

Assignment #3 - What are the politics of education? (Freire [1970/1997a], pp. 460–470 in Cahn)

Please type a short essay summarizing Freire's main points as you understand them. That is, explain what you learned about Freire's educational principles by reading this section. Conclude your essay with a question you would be willing, as discussion leader, to help the class explore.

Assignment #4 - What is the proper relation of student and curriculum? (Dewey [1902/1997a], pp. 274–288 in Cahn)

Dewey divides educators into two groups: those who emphasize subject matter and those who emphasize student growth. Please type a letter to a classmate responding to the following two questions. We will exchange letters at the start of the period, so you can respond to your partner's letter.
   1. Which of these emphases has been dominant in your education?
   2. How does Dewey suggest we reconcile these different approaches?

Assignment #5 - What sort of education is appropriate for democracy? (Dewey [1916/1997b], pp. 288–309 in Cahn)

After reading this selection from Dewey's *Democracy and Education*, please type a question which you would be willing to share with a small group of classmates. Each group will then select its best question to be circulated to another group for a collective answer.

Assignment #6 - What characterizes a good educational experience? (Dewey [1938/1997c], pp. 325–343 in Cahn)

Please pick one paragraph from this Dewey selection, a paragraph which stands out for you, one you agree with, disagree with, or just plain cannot figure out. Please then type a brief summary of your response to this paragraph.

Assignment #7 - Is America democratic? (Baldwin [1963/1988], pp. 3–12; Mura [1988], pp. 135–153; and Reed [1988] pp. 156–160)

James Baldwin suggests that America is a racist country, one founded on lies that mask the systematic oppression of minorities for the sake of the majority's economic and political advantage. David Mura says that until Whites accept their collective guilt over the oppression of Native Americans, African-Americans, and Asian-Americans, they will never understand themselves or others (see especially, pp. 144–153).
  1. How does Mura support his position?
  2. Do you agree with Mura that there is such a thing as "White privilege" in America? Have you either been a victim or beneficiary of such privilege? Explain.

Assignment #8 - Which theory is most fruitful to apply when analyzing the classroom? (Sleeter and Grant [1988], pp. 144–160 in Weis)

When you think about your own successes and failures, how much do you attribute them to your own skill and determination (or lack thereof) and how much to your race, class, gender, and ethnic background? Please type a short essay in response to this question.

Assignment #9 - What characterizes a good student? (Holland and Eisenhart, pp. 266–301 in Weis)

After reading about the three catregories of college student which Holland and Eisenhart [1988] use as analytic tools in their study, indicate in which category you would place yourself and why. Also, has college forced you to change your self-image, your "worker identity" (to borrow Holland's and Eisenhart's phrase)? Explain.

Assignment #10 - What constitutes a good teacher? (Hansen, *The Call To Teach*, pp. 67–90)

After reading Hansen's [1995] account of three teachers and their classrooms—Ms. Payton, Mr. Peters, and Mr. James—please write your own analysis of these intructors' teaching using any categories you find appropriate.

Assignment #11 - What does it mean to treat students equally? (Delpit, *Other People's Children*, pp. 105–134 and pp. 167–183)

After typing a paragraph about Delpit's [1995] suggestions for improving minority education in America, please conclude with a question about Delpit's views which you would be willing, as discussion leader, to help our class explore.

Assignment #12 - How do we achieve equal educational opportunities? (Oakes [1985], *Keeping Track*, Chaps. 1, 2, and 10)

Please type out the best defense you can for the side of the following debate which you most favor:
1. Tracking in all of its forms can and should be abolished.
2. We need some form of tracking in our schools if not the present one.

Appendix E

Triple-Entry Notetaking Assignment

[Given to Philosophy of Education students in early spring 1999]

Please do fifteen minutes of "triple-entry" notetaking on any 5 pages of Plato's *Republic*. After completing your notetaking, take ten minutes to freewrite a brief essay about this section of the text.

The "triple-entry" notetaking technique is a way of responding to a text that helps you voice you own views. It does not ask you to memorize the text or to guess what someone else finds important about it. To do "triple-entry," divide a blank page into three columns.

1. In the right-hand column copy from the text a passage that strikes you (plus the page number where it appears). By "strikes you," I mean a passage with which you disagree, which you don't understand, which you wholeheartedly endorse, or which triggers an association with something else.
2. In the middle column, write your response to the passage you chose, telling why it strikes you.
3. In the third or left column, write a response to your response. That is, reread what you wrote in the middle column and muse about it, reflecting further on what you said, why you said it, any further associations, etc.

How can you generate an essay from "triple-entry" notes? One suggestion involves going back through your triple-entry notes and circling anything which surprises or especially interests you. Then look over what you have circled, pick out one phrase to put at the top of a fresh sheet of paper, and begin your short essay.

References

Anderson, G.L. & Herr, K. (1999). The new paradigm wars: Is there room for rigorous practitioner knowledge in schools and universities? *Educational Researcher, 28.5,* 12–21.

Anzaldúa, G. (1987). *Borderlands/La frontera: The new mestiza.* San Francisco: Aunt Lute.

Baldwin, J. (1988). A talk to teachers. In R. Simonson & S. Walker (Eds.), *The graywolf annual five: Multi-cultural literacy* (pp. 3–12). St. Paul, MN: Graywolf Press. (Original work published 1963)

Ball, A.F. (1992). Cultural preference and the expository writing of African-American adolescents. *Written Communication, 9,* 501–532.

Ball, A.F. (1999). Evaluating the writing of culturally and linguistically diverse students: The case of the African American vernacular English speaker. In C.R. Cooper and L. Odell (Eds.), *Evaluating writing: The role of teachers' knowledge about text, learning, and culture* (pp. 225–248). Urbana: National Council of Teachers of English.

Ball, A.F. (2000). Empowering pedagogies that enhance the learning of multi-cultural students. *Teachers College Record, 102.6,* 1006–1034.

Bambara, T.C. (1984). Salvation is the issue. In M. Evans (Ed.), *Black women-writers (1950–1980): A critical evaluation* (pp. 41–47). Garden City, NY: Anchor Press.

Banks, J.A. (1968). A profile of the Black American: Implications for teaching. *College Composition and Communication, 19,* 288–296.

Barnett, T. (2000). Reading "Whiteness" in English studies. *College English, 63,* 9–37.

Bartholomae, D. (1980). The study of error. *College Composition and Communication, 31,* 253–269.

Bartholomae, D., & Petrosky, D. (1986). *Facts, artifacts, and counterfacts: Theory and method for a reading and writing course.* Portsmouth: Boynton/Cook Heinemann.

Belcher, D., & Braine, G. (Eds.) (1995). *Academic writing in a second language: Essays on research and pedagogy.* Norwood, NJ: Ablex.

Belenky, M.F., Clinchy, B.M., Goldberger, N.R., & Tarule, J.M. (1986). *Women's ways of knowing: The development of self, voice, and mind.* New York: Basic Books.

Bell, D. (1987). *And we are not saved: The elusive quest for racial justice.* New York: Basic Books.

Bell, D. (1992). *Faces at the bottom of the well.* New York: Basic Books.

Benesch, S. (1991). *ESL in America: Myths and possibilities.* Portsmouth, NH: Boynton/Cook.

Berlin, I. (1970). *Four essays on liberty.* New York: Oxford University Press.

Betz, J. (1992). John Dewey and Paulo Freire. *Transactions of the Charles S. Peirce Society, 28.1,* 107–126.

Bode, B.H. (1938). Dr. Childs and education for democracy. *Social Frontier, 5,* 38–40.

Bourdieu, P. (1982). The school as a conservative force: Scholastic and cultural inequalities. In E. Bredo & W. Feinberg (Eds.), *Knowledge and values in social and educational research* (pp. 391–407). Philadelphia: Temple University Press.

Bourdieu, P., & Passeron, J.C. (1977). *Reproduction in education, society, and culture.* Thousand Oaks, CA: Sage.

Bowles, S., & Gintis, H. (1976). *Schooling in capitalist America.* New York: Basic Books.

Brint, S., & Karabel, J. (1989). *The diverted dream: Community colleges and the promise of educational opportunity.* New York: Oxford University Press.

Brown v Board of Education. (1954). 347 U.S. 483.

Butler, J. (1980). Remedial writers: The teacher's job as corrector of papers. *College Composition and Communication, 31,* 270–277.

Campbell, K.E. (1997). "Real niggaz's don't die": African American students speaking themselves into their writing. In C. Severino, J.C. Guerra, & J.E. Butler (Eds.), *Writing in multicultural settings* (pp. 67–78). New York: Modern Language Association.

Carmichael, S. (1995). Excerpt from What we want. In M. Hallman (Ed.), *Expanding philosophical horizons: A nontraditional philosophy reader* (pp. 193–199). Belmont CA: Wadsworth. (Original work published 1966)

Christ, C. (1995). Why women need the goddess: Phenomenological, psychological and political reflections. In M. Hallman (Ed.), *Expanding philosophical horizons: A nontraditional philosophy reader* (pp. 268–278). Belmont CA: Wadsworth. (Original work published 1978)

Christian, B. (1987). The race for theory. *Cultural Critique, 6,* 51–63.

Cochran-Smith, M., & Lytle, S. (1993). *Inside/outside: Teacher research and knowledge.* New York: Teachers College Press.

Cremin, L. (1951). *American common school.* New York: Teachers College Press.

Cross, P. (1971). *Beyond the open door: New students to higher education.* San Francisco: Jossey-Bass.

Cummins, J. (1986). Empowering minority students: A framework for intervention. *Harvard Educational Review, 56,* 18–36.

Daly, M. (1995). Excerpt from *Beyond God the father.* In M. Hallman (Ed.) *Expanding philosophical horizons: A nontraditional philosophy reader* (pp. 159–171). Belmont CA: Wadsworth. (Original work published 1973)

Darrow, C. (1973). Excerpt from *The story of my life.* In P. Edwards & A. Pap (Eds.), *A modern introduction to philosophy,* 3rd ed., pp. 446–453. New York: Free Press (Original work published 1932)

Dean, T. (1999). Multicultural classrooms, monocultural teachers. In I. Shor & C. Pari (Eds.), *Critical literacy in action: Writing words, changing worlds* (pp. 87–102). Portsmouth NH: Boynton/Cook Heinemann. (Original work published 1986)

de Beauvoir, S. (1995). Excerpt from *The second sex.* In M. Hallman, *Expanding philosopical horizons: A nontraditional philosophy reader* (pp. 25–31). Belmont CA: Wadsworth. (Original work published 1949)

Delgado, R. (1989). Symposium: Legal storytelling. *Michigan Law Review, 87,* 2073.

Delgado, R. (1990). When a story is just a story: Does voice really matter? *Virginia Law Review, 76,* 95–111.

Delgado, R. (1995a). Legal storytelling: Storytelling for oppositionists and others: A plea for narrative. In R. Delgado (Ed.), *Critical race theory: The cutting edge,* pp. 64–74. Philadelphia: Temple University Press. (Original work published 1989)

Delgado, R. (Ed.) (1995b). *Critical race theory: The cutting edge.* Philadelphia: Temple University Press.

Delpit, L. (1995). *Other people's children: Cultural conflict in the classroom.* New York: The New Press.

Demetrion, G. (1997). Adult literacy and the American political culture. In D.R. Walling (Ed.), *Under construction: The role of the arts and humanities in postmodern schooling* (pp. 169–192). Bloomington, IN: Phi Delta Kappa Educational Foundation.

Demetrion, G. (2001). Reading Giroux through a Deweyan lens: Pushing utopia to the outer edge. *Educational Philosophy and Theory, 33.1* (pp. 57–76).

Dewey, J. (1934). *A common faith.* New Haven: Yale University Press.

Dewey, J. (1960). *How we think.* Rev. ed. Lexington: Heath. (Original work published 1933)

Dewey, J. (1962). *Reconstruction in philosophy.* Boston: Beacon. (Original work published 1920)

Dewey, J. (1963a). *Experience and education.* New York: Collier. (Original work published 1938)

Dewey, J. (1964a). Ethical principles underlying education. In R. Archambault (Ed.), *John Dewey on education* (pp. 108–138). Chicago: University of Chicago Press. (Original work published 1897)

Dewey, J. (1964b). The relation of theory to practice in education. In R. Archimbault (Ed.), *John Dewey on education* (pp. 313–338). Chicago: University of Chicago Press. (Original work published 1904)

Dewey, J. (1967). *Democracy and education.* New York: The Free Press. (Original work published 1916)

Dewey, J. (1976a). Nationalizing education. In J.A. Boydston (Ed.), *The collected works of John Dewey: The middle works, 1899–1924,* Vol. 10 (pp. 202–10). Carbondale: Southern Illinois University Press. (Original work published 1916)

Dewey, J. (1976b). The principle of nationality. In J.A. Boydston (Ed.), *The collected works of John Dewey: The middle works, 1899–1924,* Vol. 10 (pp. 285–91). Carbondale: Southern Illinois University Press. (Original work published 1916)

Dewey, J. (1983). Idealism and natural science. In J.A. Boydston (Ed.), *The collected works of John Dewey: The middle works, 1899–1924,* Vol. 13 (pp. 433–435). Carbondale: Southern Illinois University Press. (Original work published 1921)

Dewey, J. (1986a). A great American prophet. In J.A. Boydston (Ed.), *The collected works of John Dewey: The later works, 1925–1953,* Vol. 9 (pp. 102–106). Carbondale: Southern Illinois University Press. (Original work published 1934)

Dewey, J. (1986b). Education for a changing social order. In J.A. Boydston (Ed.), *The collected works of John Dewey: The later works, 1925–1953,* Vol. 9 (pp. 158–169). Carbondale, Southern Illinois University Press. (Original work published 1934)

Dewey, J. (1987). Authority and social change. In J.A. Boydston (Ed.) *The collected works of John Dewey: The later works, 1925–1953,* Vol. 11 (pp. 130–145). Carbondale: Southern Illinois University Press. (Original work published 1936)

Dewey, J. (1988a). *The public and its problems.* Athens, OH: Swallow. (Original work published 1927)

Dewey, J. (1988b). Sources of a science of education. In J.A. Boydston (Ed.), *The collected works of John Dewey: The later works, 1925–1953,* Vol. 5 (pp. 3–40). Carbondale: Southern Illinois University Press. (Original work published 1929)

Dewey, J. (1988c). *Individualism, old and new.* In J.A. Boydston (Ed.), *The collected works of John Dewey: The later works, 1925–1953,* Vol. 5 (pp. 41–123). Carbondale: Southern Illinois University Press. (Original work published 1930)

Dewey, J. (1988d). I believe. In J.A. Boydston (Ed.), *The collected works of John Dewey: The later works, 1925–1953,* Vol. 14 (pp. 91–97). Carbondale: Southern Illinois University Press. (Original work published 1939)

Dewey, J. (1989). *Experience and nature* (Rev. ed.). La Salle: Open Court. (Original work published 1925)

Dewey, J. (1990a). Attention. In J.A. Boydston (Ed.), *The collected works of John Dewey: The later works, 1925–1953.* Vol. 17 (pp. 269–283). Carbondale: Southern Illinois University Press. (Original work published 1902)

Dewey, J. (1990b). Construction and criticism. In J.A. Boydston (Ed.), *The collected works of John Dewey: The later works, 1925–1953.* Vol. 5 (pp. 127–143). Carbondale: Southern Illinois University Press. (Original work published 1930)

Dewey, J. (1990c). *The school and society.* In *The child and the curriculum. The school and society.* Intro. P. Jackson. Chicago: University of Chicago Press. (Original work published 1902)

Dewey, J. (1991). *Liberalism and social action.* In J.A. Boydston (Ed.), *The collected works of John Dewey: The later works, 1925–1953,* Vol. 11 (pp. 5–65). Carbondale: Southern Illinois University Press. (Original work published 1935)

Dewey, J. (1997a). Excerpt from *The child and the curriculum.* In S.M. Cahn (Ed.), *Classic and contemporary readings in the philosophy of education* (pp. 274–288). New York: McGraw-Hill. (Original work published 1902)

Dewey, J. (1997b). Excerpt from *Democracy and education.* In S.M. Cahn (Ed.), *Classic and contemporary readings in the philosophy of education* (pp. 288–324). New York: McGraw-Hill. (Original work published 1916)

Dewey, J. (1997c). Excerpt from *Experience and education.* In S.M. Cahn (Ed.), *Classic and contemporary readings in the philosophy of education* (pp. 225–363). New York: McGraw-Hill. (Original work published 1938).

Dewey, J. (1999). Letter to Horace Kallen, March 31, 1915. In L. Hickman (Ed.), *The correspondence of John Dewey, Vol. 1: 1871–1918* (CD-ROM, 03222). Charlottesville, VA: Intelex Corp.

Dewey, J., & Bentley, A.F. (1949). *Knowing and the known.* Boston: Beacon Press.

Draper, T. (1957). *The roots of American communism.* New York: Viking.

Dreiser, T. (1981). *Sister Carrie: The Pennsylvania edition.* Philadelphia: University of Pennsylvania Press.

Du Bois, W.E.B. (1973). Education and work. In H. Aptheker (Ed.), *The education of black people: Ten critiques, 1906–1960* (pp. 61–82). New York: Monthly Review Press. (Original work published 1930)

Durst, R. (1999). *Collision course: Conflict, negotiation, and learning in college composition.* Urbana: National Council of Teachers of English.

Dyer, R. (1997). *White.* New York: Routledge.

Eastman, M. (1959). *Great companions: Critical memoirs of some famous friends.* New York: Farrar, Straus and Cudahy.

Elbow, Peter. (1999). Inviting the mother tongue: Beyond "mistakes," "bad English," and "wrong language." *Journal of Advanced Composition, 19.3,* 359–88.

Fanon, F. (1995). Excerpt from *Wretched of the earth.* In M. Hallman (Ed.), *Expanding philosophical horizons: A nontraditional philosophy reader* (pp. 188–193.) Belmont, CA: Wadsworth. (Original work published 1965)

Feagin, J.R., Vera, H., & Imanim N. (1996). *The agony of education: Black students at White colleges and universities.* New York: Routledge.

Feinberg, W. (1998). *Common schools/uncommon identities.* New Haven: Yale University Press.

Feinberg, W., & Torres, C.A. (2001). Democracy and education: John Dewey and Paulo Freire. *Educational Practice and Theory, 23.1*, pp. 25–37.

Fine, M., Weis, L., & Powell, L.C. (1997). Communities of difference: A critical look at desegregated spaces created for and by youth. *Harvard Educational Review, 67.2*, 247–284.

Fishman, S.M., & McCarthy, L. (1995). Community in the expressivist classroom: Juggling liberal and communitarian visions. *College English, 57*, 62–81.

Fishman, S.M., & McCarthy, L. (1998). *John Dewey and the challenge of classroom practice.* New York: Teacher College Press and Urbana: National Council of Teachers of English.

Fishman, S.M., & McCarthy, L. (2000). *Unplayed tapes: A Personal history of collaborative teacher research.* Urbana: National Council of Teachers of English and New York: Teachers College Press.

Fordham, S. (1988). Racelessness as a factor in Black students' school success: Pragmatic strategy or pyrrhic victory? *Harvard Educational Review, 58.1*, 54–84.

Fordham, S. (1997). Those loud Black girls: (Black) women, silence, and gender "passing" in the academy. In M. Seller and L. Weis (Eds.), *Beyond black and white: New faces and voices in U.S. Schools,* (pp. 81–111). Albany: SUNY Press.

Fox, Tom. (1990). *The social uses of writing: Politics and pedagogy.* Norwood, NJ: Ablex.

Frankenberg, R. (1993). *The social construction of whiteness: White women, race matters.* Minneapolis: University of Minnesota Press.

Freire, P. (1973). Education as the practice of freedom. In P. Freire, *Education for critical consciousness* (pp. 1–84). New York: Continuum. (Original work published 1967)

Freire, P. (1976). Literacy and the possible dream. *Prospects, 6.1*, 68–71.

Freire, P. (1983). The importance of the act of reading. Trans. L. Slover. *Journal of Education, 165*, 5–11.

Freire, P. (1987). Letter to North-American teachers. Trans. C. Hunter. In I. Shor (Ed.), *Freire for the classroom: A sourcebook for liberatory teaching* (pp. 211–214). Portsmouth, NH: Boynton/Cook.

Freire, P. (1993). *Pedagogy of the city.* Trans. D. Macedo. New York: Continuum.

Freire, P. (1994). *Pedagogy of hope.* Trans. R. Barr. New York: Continuum.

Freire, P. (1996). *Letters to Cristina: Reflections on my life and work.* Trans. D. Macedo. New York: Routledge.

Freire, P. (1997). *Pedagogy of the oppressed.* Trans. M. Bergman Ramos. New York: Continuum. (Original work published 1970)

Freire, P. (1997a). Excerpt from *Pedagogy of the oppressed*. Trans. M. Bergman Ramos. In S.M. Cahn (Ed.), *Classic and contemporary readings in the philosophy of education* (pp. 460–470). (Original work published 1970)

Freire, P. (2000). *Cultural action for freedom*. Trans. L. Slover. Boston: Harvard Educational Review. (Original work published 1970)

Frieire, P., & Macedo, D. (1987). *Literacy: Reading the word and the world*. Westport, CT: Bergin and Garvey.

Gibbs, J.T. (1988). *Young, Black, and male in America: An endangered species*. New York: Auburn House.

Gilyard, K. (1991). *Voices of the self: A study of language competence*. Detroit: Wayne State University Press.

Gilyard, K. (1997). Cross-Talk: Toward transcultural writing classrooms. In C. Severino, J.C. Guerra, & J.E. Butler (Eds.), *Writing in multicultural settings* (pp. 325–332). New York: Modern Language Association.

Gilyard, K. (1999). *Race, rhetoric, and composition*. Portsmouth, NH: Heinemann.

Giroux, H.A. (1991). Postmodernism as border pedagogy: Redefining the boundaries of race and ethnicity. In Henry A. Giroux (Ed.), *Postmodernism, feminism, and cultural politics: Redrawing educational boundaries* (pp. 217–56). Albany, NY: State University of New York Press.

Giroux, H.A. (1992). *Border crossings: Cultural workers and the politics of education*. New York: Routledge.

Glass, R.D. (2001). On Paulo Freire's philosophy of praxis and the foundations of liberation education. *Educational Researcher, 30.2*, 15–26.

Glaser, B.G., & Strauss, A.L. (1967). *The discovery of grounded theory: Strategies for qualitative research*. New York: Aldine de Gruyter.

Gleason, B. (2000). Remediation phase-out at CUNY: The "equity versus excellence" controversy. *College Composition and Communication, 51*, 488–491.

Goldblatt, E. (1995). *Round my way: Authority and double-consciousness in three urban high school writers*. Pittsburgh: University of Pittsburgh Press.

Gonsalves, L.M. (2002). Making connections: Addressing the pitfalls of White faculty/Black male student communication. *College Composition and Communication, 53.3*, 435–465.

Gottlieb, R.S. (1992). *Marxism 1844–1990: Origins, betrayal, rebirth*. New York: Routledge.

Gramsci, A. (1971). *Selections from the prison notebooks*. Eds. Q. Hoare & G.N. Smith. New York: International Publishers.

Greenberg, K.L. (1993). The politics of basic writing. *The Journal of Basic Writing, 12.1*, 64–71.

Greenberg, K.L. (1997). A response to Ira Shor's "Our apartheid": Writing instruction and inequality. *Journal of Basic Writing, 16.2*, 90–94.

Grego, R., & Thompson, N. (1996). Repositioning remediation: Renegotiating composition's work in the academy. *College Composition and Communication, 47*, 62–84.

Grumet, M. (1988). *Bitter milk: Women and teaching.* Amherst: University of Massachusetts Press.

Guerra, J.C. (1997). The place of intercultural literacy in the writing classroom. In C. Severino, J.C. Guerra, & J.E. Butler (Eds.), *Writing in multicultural settings* (pp. 248–260). New York: Modern Language Association.

Habermas, J. (1972). *Knowledge and human interests.* Trans. J.J. Shapiro. Boston: Beacon Press.

Hadden, J.E. (2000). A charter to educate or a mandate to train: Conflicts between theory and practice. *Harvard Educational Review, 70.4*, 524–537.

Hallman, M. (1995). Introduction. In M. Hallman (Ed.), *Expanding philosophical horizons: A nontraditional philosophy reader* (pp. 1–6). Belmont CA: Wadsworth.

Hansen, D.T. (1995). *The call to teach.* New York: Teachers College Press.

Harrington, S., & Adler-Kassner, L. (1998). "The dilemma that still counts": Basic writing at a political crossroads. *Journal of Basic Writing, 17.2*, 3–24.

Harris, C. (1993). Whiteness as property. *Harvard Law Review, 106*, 1707–1791.

Heller, L.G. (1973). *The death of the American university: With special reference to the collapse of City College of New York.* New Rochelle, NY: Arlington House.

Hicks, E. (1981). Cultural Marxism: Nonsynchrony and feminist practice. In L. Sargent (Ed.), *Women and Revolution* (pp. 219–238). Boston: South End Press.

Higham, J. (1963). *Strangers in the land: Patterns of American nativism, 1860–1925.* New York: Atheneum

Hirvela, A. (1999). Teaching immigrant students in the college writing classroom. In M.H. Kells & V. Balester (Eds.), *Attending to the margins: Writing, researching, and teaching on the front lines* (pp. 150–164). Portsmouth: Boynton/Cook Heinemann.

Holland, D.C., & Eisenhart, M.A. (1988). Women's ways of going to school: Cultural reproduction of women's identities as workers. In L. Weis (Ed.), *Class, race, and gender in American education* (pp. 266–301). Albany, NY: State University of New York Press.

Holmes, J.H. (1973). Ten reasons for believing in immortality. In P. Edwards & A. Pap (Eds.), *A modern introduction to philosophy*, 3rd ed. (pp. 250–260). New York: Free Press. (Original work published 1929)

Hook, S. (1995). *John Dewey: An intellectual portrait.* Amherst, NY: Prometheus Books. (Original work published 1939)

hooks, b. (1989). *Talking back: Thinking feminist, thinking black.* Boston: South End Press.

hooks, b. (1995). Excerpt from *Ain't I a woman: Black women and feminism.* In M. Hallman (Ed.), *Expanding philosopical horizons: A nontraditional philosophy reader* (pp. 199–209). Belmont, CA: Wadsworth. (Original work published 1981)

Horner, B., & Lu, M-Z. (1999). *Representing the "other": Basic writers and the teaching of basic writing.* Urbana: National Council of Teachers of English.

Horwitz, M.J. (1992). *The transformation of American law, 1870–1960: The crisis of legal orthodoxy.* New York: Oxford University Press, 1992.

James, W. (1973). The dilemma of determinism. In P. Edwards & A. Pap (Eds.), *A modern introduction to philosophy*, 3rd ed. (pp. 34–46). New York: Free Press. (Original work published 1884)

Johns, A.M. (2001). ESL students and WAC programs: Varied populations and diverse needs. In S.M. McLeod, E. Miraglia, M. Soven, & C. Thaiss (Eds.), *WAC for the new millenium: Strategies for continuing writing-across-the- curriculum programs* (pp. 141–164). Urbana: National Council of Teachers English.

Johnson-Bailey, J., & Cervero, R.M. (1996). An analysis of the educational narratives of reentry black women. *Adult Education Quarterly, 46.3,* 142–157.

Kallen, H. (1924). *Culture and democracy in the United States.* New York: Boni & Liveright.

Karier, C. (1975). *Shaping the American educational state: 1900 to the present.* New York: Free Press.

Karier, C. (1986). *The individual, society, and education.* Urbana, IL: University of Illinois Press.

Katz, M. (1971). *Class, bureaucracy, and schools: The illusion of educational change in America.* New York: Praeger.

Katz, S.R. (1999). Teaching in tensions: Latino immigrant youth, their teachers, and the structures of schooling. *Teachers College Record, 100,* 809–840.

Kliebard, H.M. (1995). *The struggle for the American curriculum, 1893–1958.* New York: Routledge.

Kochman, T. (1981). *Black and White styles in conflict.* Chicago: University of Chicago Press.

Kozol, J. (1992). *Savage inequalities: Children in American's schools.* New York: Harper Collins.

Kutz, E. (1986). Between students' language and academic discourse: Interlanguage as middle ground. *College English, 48,* 385–396.

Kutz, E., Groden, S.Q., & Zamel, V. (1993). *The discovery of competence: Teaching and learning with diverse student writers.* Portsmouth, NH: Heinemann.

Laden, B.V., & Turner, C.S.V. (1995). Viewing community college students through the lenses of gender and color. In B.K. Townsend (Ed.), *Gender and power in the community college* (pp. 15–28). San Francisco: Jossey-Bass.

Ladson-Billings, G. (1994). *The dreamkeepers: Successful teachers of African American children.* San Francisco: Jossey-Bass.

Ladson-Billings, G. (1998). Just what is critical race theory and what's it doing in a nice field like education? *Qualitative Studies in Education, 11.1,* 7–24.

Ladson-Billings, G., & Tate, W.F. IV. (1995). Toward a critical race theory of education. *Teachers College Record, 97.1,* 47–68.

Landsman, J. (2001). *A White teacher talks about race.* Lanham, MD: Scarecrow Press.

Larson, R.L. (1991). Using portfolios in the assessment of writing in the academic disciplines. In P. Belanoff & M. Dickson (Eds.), *Portfolios: Process and product* (pp. 137–149). Portsmouth, NH: Boynton/Cook Heinemann.

Lazere, D. (1992). Back to basics: A force for oppression or liberation? *College English, 54,* 7–21.

Leki, I. (1990). Coaching from the margins: Issues in written response. In B. Kroll (Ed.), *Second language writing.* Cambridge: Cambridge University Press.

Leki, I. (1991). Preferences of ESL students for error correction in college-level writing classes. *Foreign Language Annals, 24.3,* 203–218.

Leki, I. (1992). *Understanding ESL writers: A guide for teachers.* Portsmouth, NY: Boynton/Cook Heinemann.

Leki, I. (1995). Good writing: I know it when I see it. In D. Belcher & G. Braine (Eds.), *Academic writing in a second language: Essays on research and pedagogy* (pp. 23–46). Norwood, NJ: Ablex.

Lewis, L.H. (Ed.). (1988). *Addressing the needs of returning women.* San Francisco: Jossey- Bass.

Lichtenstein, P.M. (1984). Some theoretical coordinates of radical liberalism. *American Journal of Economics and Sociology, 43.3,* 333–339.

Lincoln, Y.S. (1990). The making of a constructivist: A remembrance of transformations past. In E.G. Guba (Ed.), *The paradigm dialog* (pp. 67–87). Newbury Park, CA: Sage Publications.

Lincoln, Y.S., & Guba, E.G. (1985). *Naturalistic inquiry.* Beverly Hills: Sage Publications.

Locke, J. (1997). Excerpt from *Some thoughts concerning education.* In S.M. Cahn (Ed.), *Classic and contemporary readings in the philosophy of education* (pp. 144–61). New York: McGraw-Hill. (Original work published 1693)

Lu, M-Z. (1999a). Conflict and struggle: The enemies or preconditions of basic writing? In B. Horner & M-Z. Lu, *Representing the "other": Basic writers and the teaching of basic writing* (pp. 30–55). Urbana: National Council of Teachers of English. (Original work published 1992)

Lu, M-Z. (1999b). Professing multiculturalism: The politics of style in the contact zone. In B. Horner & M-Z. Lu, *Representing the "other": Basic writers and the teaching of basic writing* (pp. 166–190). Urbana: National Council of Teachers of English. (Original work published 1994)

Luttrell, W. (1989). Working-class women's ways of knowing: Effects of gender, race, and class. *Sociology of Education, 62,* 33–46.

Mackie, R. (1981). Contributions to the thought of Paulo Freire. In R. Mackie (Ed.), *Literacy and revolution: The pedagogy of Paulo Freire* (pp. 93–119). New York: Continuum. (Original work published 1980)

MacLean, M.S. & Mohr, M.M. (1999). *Teacher-researchers at work.* Berkeley: The National Writing Project.

Mahiri, J. (1998). *Shooting for excellence: African Americans and youth culture in new century schools.* Urbana: National Council of Teachers of English.

Marshall, I., & Ryden, W. (2000). Interrogating the Monologue: Making whiteness visible. *College Composition and Communication, 52.2,* 240–259.

Marx, K. (1967). *Capital: A critique of political economy.* Vol. 1. (Ed.) F. Engels. Trans. S. Moore & E. Aveling. New York: International Publishers. (Original work published 1867)

Marx, K. (1978). The German ideology. In R.C. Tucker (Ed.), *The Marx-Engels Reader* (pp. 146–200). New York: W.W. Norton. (Original work published 1932)

McCarthy, C. (1988). Rethinking liberal and radical perspectives on racial inequality in schooling: Making the case of nonsynchrony. *Harvard Educational Review, 58.2,* 265–280.

McCarthy, C. (1993). Beyond the poverty of theory in race relations: Nonsynchrony and social difference in education. In M. Fine & L. Weis (Eds.), *Beyond silenced voices: Class, race and gender in United States schools* (pp. 325–346). Albany: State University of New York Press.

McCrary, D. (2001). Womanist theology and its efficacy for the writing classroom. *College Composition and Communication, 52,* 521–552.

McLaren, P.L. (1994). Postmodernism and the death of politics: A Brazilian reprieve. In P.L. McLaren & C. Lankshear (Eds.) *Politics of Liberation: Paths from Freire* (pp. 193–215). New York: Routledge.

McLeod, S.H. (1997). *Notes on the heart: Affective issues in the writing classroom.* Carbondale: Southern Illinois University Press.

Miles, R. (1993). *Racism after "race relations".* New York: Routledge.

Miles, M.B., & Huberman, A.M. (1984). *Qualitative data analysis.* Beverly Hills: Sage Publications.

Mill, J.S. (1973). Of liberty and necessity. In P. Edwards & A. Pap (Eds.), *A modern introduction to philosophy,* 3rd ed. (pp. 52–58). New York: Free Press. (Original work published 1843)

Mura, D. (1988). Strangers in the village. In R. Simonson & S. Walker (Eds.), *The graywolf annual five: Multi-cultural literacy* (pp. 135–54). St. Paul, MN: Graywolf Press.

Mutnick, D. (1996). *Writing in an alien world: Basic writing and the struggle for equality in higher education.* Portsmouth, NH: Heinemann.

Mutnick, D. (2000). The strategic value of basic writing: An analysis of the current moment. *Journal of Basic Writing, 19.1,* 69–83.

Nelson, J. (1990). This was an easy assignment: Examining how students interpret academic writing tasks. *Research in the Teaching of English, 24,* 362–396.

Nieto, S. (1996). *Affirming diversity: The sociopolitical context of multicultural education,* 2nd ed. White Plains, NY: Longman.

Noddings, N. (1996). On community. *Educational Theory, 44,* 245–267.

Oakes, J. (1985). *Keeping track: How schools structure inequality.* New Haven: Yale University Press.

Ogbu, J.U. (1988). Class stratification, racial stratification, and schooling. In L. Weis (Ed.), *Class, race, and gender in American education* (pp. 163–82). Albany: State University of New York Press.

Omi, M., & Winant, H. (1994). *Racial formation in the United States: From the 1960s to the 1990s.* New York: Routledge.

Orner, M. (1992). Interrupting the calls for student voice in "liberatory" education: A feminist poststructuralist perspective. In C. Luke & J. Gore (Eds.), *Feminisms and critical pedagogy* (pp. 74–89). New York: Routledge.

Paley, W. (1973). The watch and the human eye. In P. Edwards & A. Pap (Eds.), *A modern introduction to philosophy*, 3rd ed. (pp. 419–434). New York: Free Press. (Original work published 1802)

Plato. (1993). *The last days of Socrates.* Trans. H. Tredennick & H. Tarrant. London: Penguin Books.

Plato (1997). *The republic.* Excerpt in S.M. Cahn (Ed.), *Classic and contemporary readings in the philosophy of education* (pp. 39–109). New York: McGraw-Hill.

Perl, S. (1980). A look at basic writers in the process of composing. In L.N. Kasden & D.R. Hoeber (Eds.), *Basic writing: Essays for teachers, researchers, and administrators* (pp. 13–32). Urbana: National Council of Teachers of English.

Phillips, D.L. (1993). *Looking backward: A critical appraisal of commmunitarian thought.* Princeton: Princeton University Press.

Pratt, M.L. (1987). Linguistic utopias. In N. Fabb, D. Attridge, A. Durant, & C. MacCabe (Eds.), *The linguistics of writing* (pp. 48–66). New York: Methuen.

Pratt, M.L. (1991). Arts of the contact zone. *Profession 91* (pp. 33–40). New York: Modern Language Association.

Prendergast, C. (1998). Race: The absent presence in composition studies. *College Composition and Communication, 50.1,* 36–53.

Ree, P. (1973). Determinism and the illusion of moral responsibility. In P. Edwards & A. Pap (Eds.), *A modern introduction to philosophy*, 3rd ed. (pp. 10–27). New York: Free Press. (Original work published 1885)

Reed, I. (1988). America: The multinational society. In R. Simonson & S. Walker (Eds), *The graywolf annual five: Multi-cultural literacy* (pp. 155–160). St. Paul: Graywolf Press.

Rodby, J. (1996). What's it worth and what's it for? Revisions to basic writing revisited. *College Composition and Communication, 47,* 107–111.

Rodriguez, R. (1982). *Hunger of memory: The education of Richard Rodriguez.* New York: Bantam.

Roediger, D.R. (1991). *The wages of whiteness: Race and the making of the American working class.* New York: Verso.

Roediger, D.R. (2002). *Colored white: Transcending the racial past.* Berkeley: University of California Press.

Rose, M. (1989). *Lives on the boundary: The struggles and achievements of America's underprepared.* New York: Penguin.

Royster, J.J., & Taylor, R.G. (1997). Constructing teacher identity in the basic writing classroom. *Journal of Basic Writing, 16.1,* 27–50.

Royster, J.J., & Williams, J.C. (1999). History in the spaces left: African American presence and narratives of composition studies. *College Composition and Communication, 50,* 563–584.

Russell, B. (1970). *Marriage and morals.* New York: Liveright Publishing Corporation. (Original work published 1929)

Russell, M.G. (1983). Black-eyed blues connections: From the inside out. In C. Bunch & S. Pollack (Eds.), *Learning our way: Essays in feminist education* (pp. 272–284). Trumansburg, NY: Crossing Press.

Sandel, M. (Ed.) (1984). *Liberalism and its critics.* New York: New York University Press.

Santos, T. (1988). Professors' reactions to the academic writing of non-native speaking students. *TESOL Quarterly, 22,* 69–90.

Schlegel, J.H. (1995). *American legal realism and empirical social science.* Chapel Hill: University of North Carolina Press.

Schlesinger, A., Jr. (1992). *The disuniting of America: Reflections on a multi- cultural society.* New York: Norton.

Schneidewind, N. (1985). Cooperatively structured learning: Implications for feminist pedagogy. *Journal of Thought, 20.3–4,* 74–87.

Shaughnessy, M. (1977). *Errors and expectations: A guide for the teacher of basic writing.* New York: Oxford University Press.

Shor, I. (1987). Monday morning fever: Critical literacy and the generative theme of "work." In I. Shor (Ed.), *Freire for the classroom: A sourcebook for liberatory teaching* (pp. 104–121). Portsmouth, NH: Boynton/Cook Heinemann.

Shor, I. (1992). *Empowering education: Critical teaching for social change.* Chicago: University of Chicago Press.

Shor, I. (1997). Our apartheid: Writing instruction and inequality. *Journal of Basic Writing, 16.1,* 91–104.

Shor, I. (1999). What is critical literacy? In I. Shor & C. Pari (Eds.), *Critical literacy in action: Writing words, changing worlds* (pp. 1–30). Portsmouth, NH: Boynton/Cook Heinemann.

Shor I., & Freire, P. (1987). *A pedagogy for liberation: Dialogues on transforming education.* Westport, CT: Bergin & Garvey.

Shrewsbury, C. (1993). What is feminist pedagogy? *Women's Studies Quarterly, 21.3–4,* 8–16.

Sleeter, C., & Grant, C. (1988). A rationale for integrating race, gender, and social class. In L. Weis (Ed.), *Class, race, and gender in American education* (pp. 144–160). Albany: SUNY Press.

Smith, J. (1997). Students' goals, gatekeeping, and some questions of ethics. *College English, 59,* 299–320.

Smitherman, G. (1977). *Talkin and testifyin: The language of Black America.* Detroit: Wayne State University Press.

Smitherman, G. (1999). CCCC's role in the struggle for language rights. *College Composition and Communication, 50*, 349–76.

Smitherman, G. (2000). "A new way of talkin'": Language, social change, and political theory. In G. Smitherman, *Talkin that talk: Language, culture, and education in African America.* New York: Routledge. (original work published 1989)

Soliday, M. (1996). From the margins to the mainstream: Reconceiving remediation. *College Composition and Communication, 47*, 85–100.

Soliday, M. (1999). Class dismissed. *College English, 61*, 731–741.

Spack, Ruth. (1997). The acquisition of academic literacy in a second language: A longitudinal case study. *Written Communication, 14*, 3–62.

Spradley, J. (1980). *Participant observation.* New York: Holt, Rinehart, and Winston.

Spring, J. (1996). *American education*, 7th ed. New York: McGraw Hill.

Starhawk. (1995). Witchcraft and women's culture. In M. Hallman (Ed.), *Expanding philosophical horizons: A nontraditional philosophy reader* (pp. 279–286). Belmont CA: Wadsworth. (Original work published 1979)

Stein, G. (1933). *The autobiography of Alice B. Toklas.* New York: Vintage.

Stenhouse, L. (1985). *Research as a basis for teaching: Readings from the work of Lawrence Stenhouse.* Eds. J. Ruddick & D. Hopkins. Portsmouth: Heinemann.

Stoldowski, S.S., & Grossman, P.L. (2000). Changing students, changing teaching. *Teachers College Record, 102.1*, 125–172.

Sternglass, M. (1993). Writing development as seen through longitudinal research: A case study exemplar. *Written Communication, 10.2*, 235–261.

Sternglass, M. (1997). *Time to know them: A longitudinal study of writing and learning at the college level.* Nahwah, NJ: Lawrence Erlbaum Associates.

Stygall, G. (1999). Unraveling at both ends: Anti-undergraduate education, anti-affirmative action, and basic writing at research schools. *Journal of Basic Writing, 18.2*, 4–22.

Suarez-Orozco, M.M. (2001). Globalization, immigration, and education: The research agenda. *Harvard Educational Review, 71.3*, 345–365.

Summers, R.S. (1982). *Instrumentalism and American legal theory.* Ithaca: Cornell University Press, 1982.

Swann v. Charlotte-Mecklenburg Board of Education. (1971). 402 U.S. 1.

Sylvester, P.S. (1994). Elementary school curricula and urban transformation. *Harvard Educational Review, 64.3*, 309–331.

Tarule, J.M. (1988). Voices of returning women: Ways of knowing. In L. Lewis (Ed.) *Addressing the needs of returning women* (pp. 19–33). San Francisco: Jossey-Bass.

Tatum, B.D. (1992). Talking about race, learning about racism: The application of racial identity development theory in the classroom. *Harvard Educational Review, 62.1*, 1–24.

Taylor, P.V. (1993). *The texts of Paulo Freire.* Buckingham: Open University Press.

Thompson, A. (1998). Not the color purple: Black feminist lessons for educational caring. *Harvard Educational Review, 68.4,* 522–554.

Torres, C.A. (1993). From the *Pedagogy of the Oppressed* to *A Luta Continua:* The political pedagogy of Paulo Freire. In P. McLaren & P. Leonard (Eds.), *Paulo Freire: A critical encounter* (pp. 119–145). New York: Routledge.

Traub, J. (1994). *City on a hill: Testing the American dream at City College.* New York: Addison Wesley.

Villanueva, V. (1993). *Bootstraps: From an American academic of color.* Urbana: National Council of Teachers of English.

Violas, P. (1973). The indoctrination debate. In C. Karier, P. Violas, & J. Spring (Eds.), *Roots of crisis: American education in the twentieth century.* Chicago: Rand McNally.

Walker, A. (1983). *In search of our mothers' gardens: Womanist prose.* New York: Harcourt Brace.

Weiler, K. (1994). Freire and a feminist pedagogy of difference. In P.L. McLaren & C. Lankshear (Eds.), *Politics of liberation: Paths from Freire* (pp. 12–40). New York: Routledge.

Weiler, K. (1996). Myths of Paulo Freire. *Educational Theory, 46.3,* 353–371.

Weis, L. (1985). *Between two worlds.* New York: Routledge.

Weis, L. (1992). Discordant voices in the urban community college. In L.S. Zwerling & H.B. London (Eds.), *First-generation students: Confronting the cultural issues* (pp. 13–28). San Francisco: Jossey-Bass.

West, C. (1993). *Race matters.* New York: Vintage.

Westbrook, R. (1991). *John Dewey and American democracy.* Ithaca: Cornell University Press.

Wiener, H.S. (1998). The attack on basic writing—and after. *Journal of Basic Writing, 17.1,* 96–103.

Williams, P. (1991). *The alchemy of race and rights: Diary of a law professor.* Cambridge: Harvard University Press.

Williams, R. (1976). *Keywords: A vocabulary of culture and society.* New York: Oxford University Press.

Williams, R. (1977). *Marxism and literature.* New York: Oxford University Press.

Wilson, W.J. (1996). *When work disappears: The world of the new urban poor.* New York: Knopf.

Yutang, L. (1995). Why I am a pagan. In M. Hallman (Ed.), *Expanding philosophical horizons: A nontraditional philosophy reader* (pp. 286–292). Belmont: Wadsworth. (Original work published 1937)

Zamel, V. (1995). Strangers in academia: The experience of faculty and ESL students across the curriculum. *College Composition and Communication, 46,* 506–521.

Zwerling, L.S., & London, H.B. (1992). *First-generation students: Confronting the cultural issues.* San Francisco: Jossey-Bass.

Index

Horwitz, M.J. 113

identity politics 174, 178, 179,
immigrants (involuntary and voluntary)
    9, 10, 11, 26, 32, 33, 34, 37, 65, 69,
    133, 134, 170, 171
instrumentalism of students 36, 37, 59,
    68, 69, 71, 72, 93, 132, 172, 176
intellectual inventory 27, 66, 88, 92, 168,
    175

James, W. 196
Johns, A.M. 30, 39
Johnson-Bailey, J., & Cervero, R.M. 78

Kallen, H. 171
Karier, C. 161, 163,
Katz, S.R. 114
Katz, M. 161
Kliebard, H.M. 1
Kochman, T. 78
Kozol, J. 135, 157, 160
Kutz, E., Groden, S.Q., & Zamel, V. 4, 31

Laden, B.V., & Turner, C.S.V. 78
Ladson-Billings, G. 12, 67, 76, 105, 109,
    110, 179
Ladson-Billings, G., & Tate, W.F. 69
Landsman, J. 95
Larson, R.L. 21
Lawrence, MA strike 163
Lazere, D. 6, 103
Leki, I. 3, 8, 18, 30, 49, 61, 103, 138
Lewis, L.H. 70
liberatory teaching 13, 22, 24, 62, 112,
    118, 121, 122, 140, 161
Lichtenstein, P.M. 90
likemindedness 59, 95, 109, 124, 132, 133,
    134, 136, 137, 162, 179
Lincoln, Y.S. 7,
Lincoln, Y.S., & Guba, E.G. 186
linguistic capital 71, 77, 82
Locke, J. 135, 157, 201
Lu, M-Z. 31, 61, 138
Luttrell, W. 69

MacLean, M.S. & Mohr, M.M. 6
Mahiri, J. 114
Marriage and Morals 38, 47, 193, 194
Marshall, I., & Ryden, W. 67
Marx, K. 72, 121, 158
Marxism 72, 90, 122
McCarthy, C. 88, 121
McCarthy, Lucille, background 9–12
McCrary, D. 78
McLaren, P.L. 127
McLeod, S.H. 17

Miles, M.B., & Huberman, A.M. 186
Miles, R 11, 67
Mill, J.S. 47, 196
moral growth 20, 23, 34, 44, 46, 78, 99,
    111, 114, 119, 171, 173, 189, 196
motivation, student 36–39, 51, 101, 172,
    176, 180
multiculturalism 60, 89, 170
Mura, D. 11, 203
Mutnick, D. 8, 40
mutual care (see care and caring)
Nelson, J. 17
Nieto, S. 18
Noddings, N. 183

Oakes, J. 135, 204
Ogbu, J.U. 11, 69, 134
Omi, M., & Winant, H. 76
organic intellectual 25, 63, 106, 160
organized intelligence 23, 119, 123, 125,
Orner, M. 184

Paley, W. 91, 192
Pedagogy of the Oppressed 13, 14, 140
Perl, S. 138
Phillips, D.L. 183
Plato 43, 45, 60, 94, 135, 157, 191, 192,
    201, 205
Pratt, M.L. 125, 183
Prendergast, C. 68
problem-posing 18, 50, 56, 122, 123, 133,
    137, 138, 146, 161, 162
progress, academic 111, 114, 173, 174,
    182,
proletariat 12, 14, 23, 26, 119, 120, 122,
    123, 125, 158, 165,
Pullman Strike 164, 165

race 9, 34, 62, 84–88, 96, 98, 99, 104, 105,
    108, 125, 133, 159, 160, 174, 175
racism 11, 25, 28, 37, 38, 46, 89, 90, 97,
    105, 127, 133, 173, 190, 198; institu-
    tional 26, 34, 62, 89, 97, 174, 199, 203,
    204; personal 29, 76, 174, 203
radicalism 12, 22, 170
Ree, P. 195, 196
Reed, I. 203
research, "basic" writing 5, 6, 17, 39, 63;
    education 4, 6, 7, 69, 78, 87, 95, 110,
    114, 135, 138; approach of this study
    2, 6–11, 60, 61, 137, 177, 185–188
resistance, student 15, 61, 69, 72, 112,
    151, 154, 161, 187
returning students 6, 65, 95, 96, 173, 176
Rodby, J. 17
Rodriguez, R. 63, 171
Roediger, D.R. 12, 68

About the Authors

STEPHEN M. FISHMAN teaches philosophy at the University of North Carolina Charlotte. Since attending his first writing-across-the-curriculum workshop in 1983, he has been studying student writing and learning in his classes. He is an alumnus of Camp Rising Sun, Rhinebeck, New York, an international scholarship camp founded in 1930 to promote world peace.

LUCILLE MCCARTHY teaches composition and literature at the University of Maryland Baltimore County. She is the coauthor of *Thinking and Writing in College* with Barbara Walvoord (1990) and *The Psychiatry of Handicapped Children and Adolescents* with Joan Gerring (1988).

Together, FISHMAN AND MCCARTHY have conducted a number of theory/practice studies of the classroom. These have appeared in *College English, Research in the Teaching of English, Written Communication,* and *College Composition and Communication.* In addition, Fishman and McCarthy have coauthored two books, *John Dewey and the Challenge of Classroom Practice* (1998) and *Unplayed Tapes: A Personal History of Collaborative Teacher Research* (2000).